ELEMENTARY PRINCIPAL'S

Portfolio of

MODEL SPEECHES

for

ALL OCCASIONS

P. SUSAN MAMCHAK

STEVEN R. MAMCHAK

PRENTICE HALL
Englewood Cliffs, New Jersey 07632

Library of Congress Cataloging-in-Publication Data

Mamchak, P. Susan, 1944–
  Elementary principal's portfolio of model speeches for all
occasions / P. Susan Mamchak and Steven R. Mamchak.
    p.   cm.
  ISBN 0-13-340449-8 (case)
  1. Public speaking.   I. Mamchak, Steven R.   II. Title.
PN4121.M3192   1996
  808.5`1—dc20   96-24960
                                                            CIP

Printed in the United States of America

10 9 8 7 6 5 4 3 2 1

ISBN 0-13-340449-8

**THE CENTER FOR APPLIED RESEARCH
IN EDUCATION**
West Nyack, NY 10994
A Simon & Schuster Company

On the World Wide Web at http://www.phdirect.com

Prentice Hall International (UK) Limited, *London*
Prentice Hall of Australia Pty. Limited, *Sydney*
Prentice Hall Canada, Inc., *Toronto*
Prentice Hall Hispanoamericana, S.A., *Mexico*
Prentice Hall of India Private Limited, *New Delhi*
Prentice Hall of Japan, Inc., *Tokyo*
Simon & Schuster Asia Pte. Ltd., *Singapore*
Editora Prentice Hall do Brasil, Ltda., *Rio de Janeiro*

INTRODUCTION
How This Book Will Help the Elementary Educator

Why are you reading this book? If you are an educator in today's elementary schools, then you are doing with this book the same thing a surgeon does when he or she examines scalpels and retractors, or a lawyer does when scanning a list of legal precedents, or what a carpenter does in laying out hammers and saws and screwdrivers; you are examining a useful and valuable tool of your trade—something you need in order to do your job in a thorough and efficient manner.

The day when an elementary educator sat in a classroom or office, performed the processes of administration and education in relative privacy, and operated *behind* those ivy-covered walls—that day is gone forever. Today's elementary educator is a highly visible, dynamic individual who not only handles the day-to-day operation of education within the elementary school but also serves as a front-line contact person with parents, politicians, the media, the general public, and especially the community in which the school exists and which the school is sworn to serve.

Today's involved elementary educator is only too aware of the demands that are placed on his or her physical energy, time, and ability to communicate—to communicate the essence of the modern elementary school to a world that continues to want more and more from the educational system.

Often, it seems never-ending. You must write a short article for your school's newsletter, the PTA wants a quotable comment for its publication; that guest speaker on Early Childhood Growth and Development will need an introduction from you this very night; tomorrow that civic group wants to hear from you about their community's elementary schools; don't forget that you are speaking at Mrs. Hobbs' retirement dinner on Friday; and, enjoy the weekend, because on Monday the press will arrive, and they will expect your statements as part of that article they are doing on the schools.

That is why you are reading this book. With all the demands on your time and talents, those tools that will help you perform your communications tasks in a viable, dynamic, and time-saving manner are an invaluable part of what you need to get the job done. *Elementary Principal's Portfolio of Model Speeches for All Occasions* is precisely one of those necessary tools that you will use to meet the demands of the challenging communications job that is yours as an elementary educator.

Are you meeting with a group of parents or community members for the first time? Perhaps you will use some of the material from SECTION ONE to "break the ice" and establish a rapport beneficial to all. That program on Drug Abuse at the school tonight may be "opened" and "closed" in a highly effective manner by using one of the speeches on that topic in SECTION THREE or SECTION FOUR. You will build substantial empathy with that community group by using one of the tailor-made speeches about elementary education in SECTION SEVEN, and you'll introduce the person about to retire in a memorable fashion with the material in SECTION TWO. Perhaps tomorrow you will use one of the special "Holiday Speeches" in SECTION SIX to give a presentation that will be understood by the children and thoroughly appreciated by the adults present as well. The uses of this book—this very special "tool"—are multiple, immediate, and invaluable.

Its uses go on and on. Look to SECTION FIVE for just the right commentary or inspirational invocation; touch the parents of your students in just the manner you wish by using one of the specially crafted speeches for parents in SECTION EIGHT; for moving eulogies and memorials, glowing testimonials, and even short and to-the-point graduation speeches, just look into SECTION TEN; and in a world where controversy is more "norm" than "exception," you'll want to refer to SECTION NINE, which handles some of the more troublesome problems besetting modern education and handles them with tact and understanding.

That's still not all. The materials in this book have the distinct advantage of being written *by* educators *for* educators. One glance at this material will convince you that these speeches come from people who are intimately familiar with today's educational scene. In a personable, dignified manner, bespeaking your position in both school and community, the entire panoply of elementary education is spread out before you in tested speeches and speech aids. You need change only a name or a situation in order to adapt them to your particular needs; to make them yours; to develop them into speeches that you will deliver with confidence to the edification of all who hear you.

SECTION ELEVEN and SECTION TWELVE add further to the value of *Elementary Principal's Portfolio of Model Speeches for All Occasions* by taking you step by step through the development, writing, and delivery of a powerful and memorable speech of your own, including insights into the successful handling of difficult speaking situations that have been gleaned from literally decades of effective, frontline public speaking experience in the field of education.

Whatever the communication need of the elementary educator may be, *Elementary Principal's Portfolio of Model Speeches for All Occasions* is the answer. Written and crafted specifically for the elementary educator, it is a source you will use time and again to meet your every public speaking need.

A carpenter without a hammer and saw would have a difficult time at best fulfilling his or her assigned task, as would a surgeon denied a scalpel, or a lawyer minus reference books. You will come to feel exactly the same way about this book. Once you have experienced the ease and facility with which you can adapt the material to your specific public speaking needs; once you begin to appreciate the appropriateness of the material to your position and needs as an elementary educator; once you have known the positive reaction and response of your audience in a myriad speaking and communication situations, you will recognize *Elementary Principal's Portfolio of Model Speeches for All Occasions* as the tool you need to state your case and that of today's elementary educational scene with precision and accuracy, to operate with skill and vision, and, as an educator, to build something truly fine for all those who will come after you.

This is a book for your desk—a book to be kept within arm's reach. It is a book that, as an elementary educator, you will use today and keep using; it is a book that will serve your communication and public speaking needs throughout many a tomorrow.

P. Susan Mamchak
Steven R. Mamchak

CONTENTS

Part One

Usable Material for Every Speaking Need

Section 1

"Hello Out There . . .": Icebreakers for All Occasions

Anyone who has ever spoken in public will tell you that you cannot merely stand up and "begin" your speech. The best material in the world, improperly presented, goes unheeded by the audience who refuses to pay attention—by the group whose mind is not on what you have to say.

You lead your audience into your speech, and the first thing you do toward achieving this goal is to establish contact. The analogy has been drawn that your speech is the open sea, but in order to arrive there, you have to make your way through a channel clogged with ice. Unless you break through that ice, your speech simply will not "sail."

In this section we will deal with "icebreakers," those commentaries, lines, and anecdotes that will help you establish rapport with your audience, set them at ease, and even get them well disposed to accept what you will have to say once your speech has been "launched."

Here's to happy sailing . . . *Bon Voyage*!

1

TOPIC: *First Time Before This Audience*

AUDIENCE: *Mainly for an Adult Audience Whom You Have Not Met Before*

Good evening, ladies and gentlemen. I'd like to thank the Master of Ceremonies (*or, Dr. Brown, Mrs. Jones, etc., as appropriate*) for that wonderful introduction. Now all I have to do . . . is live up to it!

This is my first time speaking with you people, and I wish I knew you folks a little better, because if I did, I'd offer to make you a bargain—if you promise not to believe the terrible things you've heard about me, I'll promise not to believe what the president of your group told me about you . . . !

I don't know about that bargain, but I will promise you that I will speak my mind to you; that I will speak it openly and with complete candor; that I will approach you with sincerity and with honesty; that I expect us to part as friends, though we meet now as strangers.

> *SPECIAL DATA: The time of this is less than a minute, but it does serve to show what an icebreaker does. Within the first sentences, you have, in a humorous manner, acknowledged the fact that you are somewhat anxious, asked that both they and you maintain an open mind, and turned serious enough to convince them of your sincerity and the importance of the speech that they are about to hear from you. This is no small task in so few words.*
>
> *This would also be appropriate if your speech were to be lengthy or detailed, as it gets you into the body of what you have to say in a relatively short time.*

2

TOPIC: *Speaker and Nervousness*

AUDIENCE: *Suitable for All Audiences*

Thank you, ladies and gentlemen, and good evening. I'm certainly looking forward to our first speaker this evening, whoever that might be . . . what's that . . . Oh, *I'm* the first speaker! Oh, yes, I keep forgetting!!!

You know, earlier this evening, your President (*or Ms. Smith, Dr. Greene, etc., as appropriate*) asked me if I was at all nervous about speaking before all of you tonight, and I just stood up tall, took a bite of my speech, shoved my apple pie into my jacket pocket (or bag) and answered, "All at not . . . er . . . Not all at . . . er . . . Not at all!"

Now, I would be lying to tell you that there is not a spot of apprehension in me, but I would also be deceiving you if I let you believe that I'm nervous because of you. Rather, I really want to do justice to my subject this evening; I want you to understand its importance—to see it as I see it—to feel it as I feel it. If you'll help me, we can begin.

SPECIAL DATA: If you have the ability to act this out with real feeling, this can get a nice laugh from the audience and get them settled quickly. Remember, if you are nervous, your audience will be, too, so it is your job to relax them. This does so in a humorous manner.

Note also that after a shared laugh, it gets down to business at once, and it goes a long way toward predisposing your audience to be favorable to the topic you will be discussing, identifying it with sincerity as an important issue and one well worthy of their consideration.

3

TOPIC: *Point of View*

AUDIENCE: *Mainly for Adults, Particularly Parents and Teachers*

I tell you quite frankly, point of view is something we don't consider enough when dealing with children. Certainly, they tend to see things quite differently from the way we see them, but that's not the half of it.

I remember a kindergarten child who was brought to me because he insisted on going home. He wasn't crying about it, he had simply informed his teacher that he didn't like the school and was going home. He was halfway down the school driveway before they reached him.

I tried to convince this lad that our school was a fine place to be. I took him out in the hall with me, and as we walked along with children passing on every side, I pointed out the cartoons on the walls and the display cases and the trophies and the smiling faces of the other students. Finally, I bent down and said, "Now, isn't this a very nice school and a good place to be?"

The kid looked up at me and said, "Mister (*Lady, Ma'am, etc.*), for all I know, this could be a real palace, but I tell you, it's hard to look at the school when all you can see are the kneecaps all around you!"

SPECIAL DATA: Time of anecdote, about a minute. This is a good story for an elementary school audience, and it can lead into a wide variety of speeches. One might follow with a speech about the proper view of a child's education or the need for improvement or curriculum changes, or even a school budget. If you keep the analogy going, it would be natural to conclude with the injunction to make certain that we keep our eyes on the school (our goal) and not on the kneecaps (our problems). This can be used effectively in any number of ways.

4

TOPIC: *Approaching the Problem*

AUDIENCE: *Suitable for All Adult Audiences*

Good evening, ladies and gentlemen.

The story is told of a small elementary school in an extremely rural district where the teacher, one day, became aware of a most disturbing odor beginning to infiltrate into the classroom. At first, she tried to simply ignore it, but all too soon it grew in intensity to the point where neither teacher nor students could help but notice.

"Teacher," said one small country-wise child, "I smelled that before. We got us a skunk in the cellar!"

The teacher evacuated the schoolhouse and immediately called the principal. As the children played and frolicked during this unexpected respite from the school day, the teacher and the principal discussed the situation.

"All we have to do is go down and shoo away the skunk," said the Principal. "It's not dangerous, but I can't do it. My suit would be ruined, and there are no facilities for me to shower afterwards."

"Don't look at me," remarked the teacher. "I'm not going to destroy a perfectly good outfit *and* get sick from the smell!"

Just then a first-grader came around the corner of the school house with a large paper clip on his nose, naked as a bird, and reeking of skunk.

"The skunk is gone, and I'm going to the swimming hole," he said. "The trouble with you city folks is that you just don't know how to approach the problem!"

> *SPECIAL DATA: Time of story, a little over a minute. The moral of this story is abundantly obvious. It is the approach to the problem that will determine our success. We are certain that you can see many ways in which an anecdote like this may be used to lead into a speech about a problem peculiar to your audience.*

5

TOPIC:	*Children's Perception of Adults*
AUDIENCE:	*Good for Adult Audiences—Teachers, Parents*

Mom and Dad both held down jobs outside the home, and one day they decided that it was time that Rachel, their six-year-old, had an appreciation for what Mommy and Daddy did to earn a living. Therefore, they decided they would each take the child to the job with them; the next day, Rachel spent the morning with her father on his job and the afternoon with her mother at her place of work.

Dad helped manage a company that installed swimming pools, and when several workers called in sick, he went to the job site, and Rachel watched him dig in the ground and carry off wheelbarrows full of sandy soil. "Good," he thought, "she'll see how hard I work!"

Mom worked for a travel agent, and it was one of those afternoons where everything went wrong. She felt as if the telephone had been permanently attached to her ear as she searched everywhere to confirm reservations and calm nervous customers. "Good," she thought, "Rachel will see how hard I work."

The next day in school, the teacher asked the child how she had enjoyed her day with her parents at work.

"It was OK, I guess, but I don't think they should call it work. Daddy played in a sandbox all morning, and all Mommy did was gossip on the phone for the whole afternoon!"

SPECIAL DATA: Time of story, about a minute. There are several points to be made with this, not the least of which is that children view things differently from the way adults do. It might also be used to ask for understanding of a particular job, task, or even the school in general. Of course, this could also be a plea to avoid misunderstanding between the home and the school by getting the facts straight from the beginning.

6

TOPIC:	*Quick Thinking in Tough Situation*
AUDIENCE:	*Suitable for All Audiences*

The principal (or 'I') had three students brought into her office.

"Yesterday afternoon," she said, "just after school let out, three students were running down the second floor hallway, and they almost knocked over the librarian. I am told that these three looked a lot like you."

She turned to the first and asked, "Was it you?"

The little boy gulped and perspiration stood out on his forehead as he lied, "No, Ma'am."

To the next child, the principal snapped, "And was it you?"

The little girl blushed deeply and also decided to avoid the truth as she whispered, "No, Ma'am."

Now the principal turned to the third child and continued, "And you, I want you to tell me the truth. Were you running down the second floor hall yesterday afternoon? The truth, now!"

"Ma'am," intoned the boy with arms spread wide to incorporate the other two, "with whom?"

SPECIAL DATA: Time of anecdote, less than a minute. Use this to talk about the need for quick thinking or being resourceful in a tough situation. You might also lead in to a discussion about the need for resourcefulness to solve the problems that face us in today's schools.

7

TOPIC:	*The Kindergarten Classroom*
AUDIENCE:	*All Adult Audiences, Especially Parents and Teachers*

I remember the first time I visited a kindergarten classroom as an adult. The thing that kept me in open-mouthed wonder was the fact that everything is labeled. In an attempt to get children familiar with the written word, everything in the class carries a label telling what it is. A chair bears the sign, "CHAIR"; the table carries the legend, "TABLE"; and even the wall has a sign proclaiming "WALL!"

Recently, I was walking past our kindergarten classroom, and I just felt like dropping in. There were all the signs, just as I remembered, and I went up to the teacher to compliment her. When she turned from what she was doing, I was taken aback by the fact that, taped to her forehead, was a sign that proclaimed her "TEACHER."

"Come now, Ms. Smith (*or, with permission, use the name of an actual kindergarten teacher in your school*)," I said, "surely the children know that you are the teacher; surely you don't have to remind them."

Ms. Smith looked at me with one raised eyebrow and said, "It's obviously been a long time since you were in a kindergarten classroom. This sign isn't to remind the children who I am; with all these bundles of pure energy in this one room, it's to remind me who is supposed to be in charge!"

> SPECIAL DATA: *Time of anecdote, about a minute. This might be used to lead into a talk on the difficulty of teaching on the elementary level, the need to remember that we must take charge of our children's education, or the necessity of giving children the direction they need. Certainly other uses will occur to you as well.*

8

TOPIC: *Parents and Children, I*

AUDIENCE: *Audience of Adults, Particularly Parents*

One winter day, the child was walking along with her father over a patch of particularly icy ground. The father stretched out his hand and told his daughter to take it as they crossed the area.

"No!" protested the child. "I'm a big girl now. I can walk by myself!"

They had not gone a foot before the child slipped and made a quick acquaintance with the ground. The father picked her up and again offered his hand.

"No!" repeated the child with equal vehemence. "I can walk by myself; I'm a big girl now!"

One yard later, and the previous scene repeated itself. This time, the child just lay on the cold ground and looked up at her father.

"You know, Daddy," she said, "I'm a big girl now, and I bet that if you just let your hand hang down by your side, I could reach it just fine!"

> SPECIAL DATA: *Time of story, around a minute. No matter what children may protest, they really need and want the guidance and protection of adults. You might use this to lead into a speech along those lines. It might also illustrate the need for children to develop independence, as long as they have a safe and secure base to return to for support and guidance.*

9

TOPIC: *Parents and Children, II*

AUDIENCE   *Audience of Adults, Particularly Parents*

"Hey, Mom!" yelled the little boy as he came home from school one afternoon, "they needed a class mother in school, so I said you'd do it!"

"Really," mother replied, "I think you should have asked me first."

"They also needed somebody to be an umpire at the class softball game," continued her son, "so I said I knew you'd be happy to do it!"

"Now just a minute . . ."

"Oh, yes, I also said you would make three cakes for the class party tomorrow!"

"Just a minute, Mister! Just what makes you think I'm going to do all these things you volunteered me for?"

"I just knew you would," answered the boy in wide-eyed innocence. "The teacher asked the same question you did, but I told her that anybody can be a mother, but you're my MOM and everybody knows that Moms can do anything!"

> *SPECIAL DATA: Time of anecdote, about a minute. Every elementary school has its share of dedicated mothers who unselfishly contribute their time and talents far beyond what might normally be expected. The above might be used successfully to introduce a speech given for volunteer workers. Of course, it is also illustrative of the fact that often children have a highly inflated idea of the time, energy, and capabilities of their parents.*

10

| TOPIC: | *Parents and Children, III* |
| AUDIENCE: | *Audience of Adults, Particularly Parents* |

Recently, I chanced to be on the boardwalk of a seaside resort, and as I momentarily rested on a bench, I became aware of a gray-haired man in his fifties who had a small child with him; I immediately judged the man to be a grandfather and his grandson to be around five or six.

I sat and watched as the little boy demanded an ice cream cone, which the older man bought for him at once. Next the child wanted a balloon, which the man also purchased for the lad. Then it was a stuffed animal—cotton candy—a multicolored beach hat . . . all of which was bought for the child by the grandfather just as soon as the little boy demanded them. Finally, I could take no more, and I felt I had to speak up.

"Sir," I said, "I really don't like to interfere, but do you know the harm you are doing by giving in to your grandchild's every whim? Why, in no time at all, he'll be totally spoiled!"

"Exactly!" the man answered with a grin, "And tonight when I leave him off with his mother and father, I'm going to look my son straight in the eye and say, 'Now, Mr. Smart Guy, you are going to learn what your mother and I went through when your grandfather took you out for a day!'"

> *SPECIAL DATA: Time of story, about a minute. We have used this several times, and it has never failed to get a laugh, particularly if there are senior citizens in the audience. This could be a lead-in to a speech about parental responsibility, nurturing, or even the nature of the school in the formative life of the child— likening the school to a grandpa or grandma who doesn't cater to the child's every whim, because it has the good of the total child in mind.*

11

TOPIC: *Making a Good First Impression*

AUDIENCE: *Suitable to All Adult Audiences*

After school one day, I drove over to the shopping center, and I was looking for a parking space in a very crowded area, when I noticed a young boy frantically waving—apparently at my car. I drove in his direction, and the lad ushered me into a parking spot he had been keeping free. I was going to give him a tip, but he was gone by the time I got out of the car.

I headed toward the store, and as I approached, there was the boy again, this time holding the door open for me. He disappeared again, only to reappear as I left the store, holding the door open once more.

"Now, wait a minute!" I shouted as I approached the child. "Do I know you? Have we met before?"

"I go to your school," the boy replied, "but I've only seen you in the halls."

"Well, perhaps we should get better acquainted?"

"We are," said the lad. "I'm gonna meet you in your office tomorrow morning, and I just wanted to make a good first impression before you heard the teacher's side of it!"

SPECIAL DATA: Time of story, about a minute. Good first impressions mean a great deal in any relationship. This story might illustrate that point, or you might use it with a group before whom you are speaking for the first time, suggesting that you hope, like the child in the story, that you and the audience will get to know each other in fact rather than by rumor.

12

TOPIC: *Getting Acquainted With Someone New*

AUDIENCE: *Suitable for Adult Audience*

I was looking out the window of my office recently, when I saw a child step onto the playground. I knew, because I had seen the child register just the day before, that he was new to the school, so I watched a while to see what would happen.

Very shortly, several boys his own age came running up. I couldn't hear what they were saying, but I could observe their actions.

One of the boys pushed the new child to the ground. The new kid got up and pushed the pusher to the ground. Another of the boys shoved the new kid; the new kid shoved back. Then everybody shoved everybody!

Just as I was about to call for the playground monitors, they stopped shoving, clapped each other on the back, and went off to play catch with a ball one of them produced from inside his jacket.

Now, the point of all this is that there are many ways to get acquainted with someone new, but I'd like you to understand that I am much too old to go through the pushing and shoving I just described, so if its all the same with you folks, I'll just say hello and shake hands with you later!

SPECIAL DATA: Time of remarks, less than a minute. Think of this as a quick way to introduce yourself and break the ice with a new audience—one you haven't spoken to before. It engenders a small smile and acknowledges the fact that this is a situation in which both you and the audience are getting acquainted.

13

TOPIC:	*Proper Communication Between Teacher and Child*
AUDIENCE:	*Suitable for Adult Audiences—Parents and Teachers*

The story is told that a class was taken out for recess by a brand-new teacher at the same time that a veteran teacher had her class on the field. The new teacher observed her class and noticed that one child was about to sit down against the wall of the school, and she looked further to observe the area where he intended to flop down.

"Charles!" she said, "several canines have obviously fouled your intended resting spot; kindly choose another!"

"Yeah!" said the child and kept heading for the spot.

"Charles!" the teacher said again, "let me reiterate my warning of the unsanitary conditions produced by a wandering canine. Please terminate your activities."

"OK, Ma'am. I'll just sit there and won't move!"

At that point the veteran teacher who had overheard all this, stepped up to Charles, whispered in his ear, and the boy made a sharp turn and headed for another part of the field.

"However did you communicate with the boy?" asked the new teacher. "I simply could not make him understand!"

"You'll learn," the veteran teacher smiled, "that communication isn't communication unless both sides understand. I just went up to him and whispered, 'Hey, Kid! Don't sit in the dog poo-poo!'"

SPECIAL DATA: Time of anecdote, a little over a minute. Let's make certain that we understand each other—that's the message of this story. It has special relevance to us as educators as a caution to speak realistically and plainly rather than in "educationese," as we are sometimes accused of doing. It might also be used when you have to address a difficult subject—letting the audience know that you will not mince words, but will plainly state your case.

14

TOPIC:	*Proper Communication Between School and Home*
AUDIENCE:	*Suitable for Adult Audience—Particularly Parents*

"Well, the least you can do is help me get the boxes out of the car," said the mother to the teacher, and she led the way to the curb where the family station wagon stood at the curb, its interior packed from floor to ceiling with white boxes tied with string.

"What's all this?" asked the teacher.

"You know perfectly well what this is," sighed the obviously harried parent. "It's the cookies you asked me to bake for the class. It took me almost a week and cost a fortune!"

"Just a moment, I never asked you to bake cookies for the class!"

"You certainly did! Last week, when I sent you two chocolate chip cookies I baked, didn't you give my daughter a message for me?"

"Yes, I told her to tell you, 'A thousand thanks for the two cookies you baked; they were really classy!'"

"Oh, no!" moaned the mother, "the message I got was, 'Thanks, really, for the two thousand cookies you're going to bake for the class!'"

> SPECIAL DATA: Time of anecdote, about a minute. The obvious moral here is to make certain that both the home and the school have their information straight. It is akin to the classic about the teacher who told the parents, "If you don't believe what your kids tell you about me; I won't believe what they tell me about you!" This could also lead in to a "let's understand each other" speech.

15

TOPIC: Proper Communication Between Teacher and Parent

AUDIENCE: Suitable for Adults—Parents and Teachers

The teacher was on the phone to the parent.

"Your child," said the teacher, "seems to have inculcated a maturity growth program which has alleviated a potentially traumatic personal crisis."

"What?" questioned the parent.

"I mean," the teacher explained, "that your offspring is beginning to exhibit a sensory control that is rather more indicative of the sociophysical patterns of students within his age bracket."

"What?" asked the parent.

"Look," stated the teacher, "your kid has stopped wetting his pants in class!"

"What great news," shouted the parent. "Why didn't you just say so?"

> SPECIAL DATA: Time of anecdote, less than a minute. This could be used effectively as part of a plea for communication between home and school. It is also an invitation to "speak plainly" and to make certain that we place our agenda squarely on the table. To quote the anecdote, "Why didn't you just say so?"

16

TOPIC: Proper Communication Between Parent and Child

AUDIENCE: Suitable for Adult Audiences, Especially Parents

The visiting couple were being given a tour of the house.

"Now this," said the husband, "is the children's playroom."

They were guided into a large room with various toys and wagons and colorful balls in evidence everywhere. What caught the attention of the visitors, however, was the wall that faced them as they entered the room.

"I beg your pardon," said one guest, "but I can't help but notice that the wall facing us is painted a bright yellow with an eight-by-ten foot black 'NO!' painted on it."

"Ah, yes," smiled the mother, "around here, we pride ourselves on our ability to communicate with our children!"

SPECIAL DATA: Time of anecdote, under a minute. This might be used effectively to emphasize that communication is necessary, and that it must be powerful and clear if it is to be effective, but that it need not be only negative, as in this story. Certainly, this could fit into any speech about either discipline or communication, especially between parent and child.

17

TOPIC:	*Importance of a Proper Attitude*
AUDIENCE:	*Suitable for Older Children and Adults*

The boy stood under a low-hanging branch of a tree on the playground and watched as four young toughs approached him menacingly.

"We're gonna beat you up!" snarled the leader of the gang.

"Ha!" laughed the solitary youngster, and with a scream, he jumped in the air, struck the limb of the tree with the heel of his hand—and the limb snapped in two and fell to the ground in a rustle of leaves and branches. The four would-be thugs stared in amazement, turned, and headed for a corner of the school behind which to hide.

After he watched them go, the boy retrieved the saw from behind the tree where he had hidden it and thought that he had better get it back before the custodian noticed it was gone. He paused for a moment, however, and looked in the direction the other four had taken.

"You know," he said out loud to himself, "that book was right—Attitude is *everything*!"

SPECIAL DATA: Time of story, less than a minute. Use this to convey the necessity of starting each process with a proper attitude; of knowing that faith and assurance can overcome almost any obstacle; of embracing the concept that we must believe we can win before we even have a chance.

18

TOPIC:	*The Difficulty of Parenting*
AUDIENCE:	*Suitable for All Adult Audiences, Especially Parents*

"Clean up your room!" Mother shouted for the tenth time, now with such an edge to her voice that little Paul was off to his room in a hurry.

Several hours passed, during which mother could hear frantic noises issuing from the vicinity of Paul's room. Finally, there was only silence, and Paul stood at the doorway.

"I did what you told me," he panted in exaggerated fatigue. "Can I go now?"

"First, I want to see your room!"

Paul and his mother climbed the stairs and Paul even opened the door for her. She stepped into a spotless room, with not a single toy or article of clothing anywhere to be seen on floor or bed or table top. It was in perfect order.

"I . . . I'm amazed," she gasped as she roamed around the place, "this is . . . this is . . ."

Then she opened the closet door and the accumulated playthings and soiled clothing and leavings of several weeks came tumbling out, knocking her to the floor.

Mother looked up from the nest of debris and exclaimed, "What's this?!?"

"Hey, Mom," said little Paul, "you said to clean up my room. I got it on tape, and you never said one thing about closets!"

SPECIAL DATA: *Time of anecdote, about a minute. This story might be illustrative of the need for preciseness of communications in effective parenting or the need for detailed guidance in the achievement of family goals. It is also good for a laugh, especially from parents.*

19

TOPIC: *The Difficulty of Working With Small Children*

AUDIENCE: *Suitable for Adult Audiences; Parents and Teachers*

It had been a particularly frustrating day for the teacher in the first-grade classroom; everything that could possibly go wrong had gone wrong, and at times otherwise normal and placid procedures had approached the brink of chaos.

Finally, the harried teacher threw up her hands and intoned to her class, "Why can't you act in a mature manner?"

Suddenly, the teacher felt a tug at her skirt and looked down to find one of her most active first-graders beckoning her to bend down.

The child came in close, cupped her hand and whispered in the teacher's ear.

"Mrs. Smith," she said, "I think it's only fair to remind you that we are only seven years old and won't be mature for many years. How come you didn't know that?"

SPECIAL DATA: *Time of anecdote, less than a minute. The last line here could become a lead-in to a speech on expectations in a classroom, or making certain that we understand with whom we are working and their limitations as well as their potentials. It might also be used for a discussion about whether we are asking our children to "grow up too fast" in today's fast-paced society.*

20

TOPIC: *Giving Sound Advice*

AUDIENCE: *Suitable for All Audiences*

I remember being in the hallway one day when I was approached by a fifth-grader.

"Ma'am," he said, "I've been looking all over for somebody who could understand me and take some time to give me some sound advice."

"Why, certainly," I answered, "this is what your teachers and I are all about. I'll tell you what, suppose I get you out of your class a little early, and we'll have lunch together in my office so we can talk about it. I promise, I'll try to give you the sound advice you seek. All right?"

"Wow! That would be great!" exclaimed the boy. "I must have asked five teachers, and they don't know anything about recording on laser disc for your CD. I'm sure glad you can finally tell me how to get the most sound out of that machine!"

SPECIAL DATA: This kind of "quick" icebreaker could be effectively used for any "informational" speech you might give. It shows, for instance, the need to define our terms and make certain that we are all speaking about the same thing. Also, you might use it to lead into remarks about the necessity of seeking solutions in the right places and with individuals qualified to help us.

21

TOPIC: *Learning to Work Together*

AUDIENCE: *Best With an Adult Audience*

We can learn things in the strangest places and under the most peculiar circumstances. I remember once, I had this fifth-grade girl before me for a serious disciplinary infraction.

"As I understand it," I told her, "when the teacher was helping another student, you shoved three or four erasers into the heating unit. Because of what you did, later on the smell was so bad, the class had to be taken out of the room, and now I am told that the room will have to be closed for two days while they fix the heating unit."

Now, I looked her straight in the eyes and said, "Well, has this taught you anything?"

"Oh, yes," she answered quickly. "It taught me that if I had organized the school and all the kids worked together, we could have shut down this place for a month!"

SPECIAL DATA: This short anecdote could be used to advantage in any situation in which the school and the parents or community are going to be working together. For instance, "Perhaps there is some truth in this child's statement, but instead of getting people to work together to shut down the school, let's vow to work together not only to keep it open but to make it the very best that it can be."

22

TOPIC: *Elementary Versus Secondary School*

AUDIENCE: *Upper Elementary Students; Adults*

Recently, a sophomore from the high school dropped by to visit with some of his former teachers. We stood in the main office for a moment while the boy told me about his experiences at the secondary school level.

"In the high school," he told me, "we have our own cafeteria that serves hamburgers; in the high school, we have our own lockers, and we change classes all day long; in the high school our gym even has a swimming pool in it!"

About that time, a second-grader from our school who had been visiting the Lost and Found in the main office could stand it no longer, and he slammed the door to the Lost and Found drawer and marched up to the visiting secondary scholar.

"Oh, yeah!" said the second-grader with intense school pride, "well, we got a six-foot tall Barney on our classroom wall! Let's see you beat that one!"

SPECIAL DATA: Here's one way in which speech material may be developed from this anecdote: Let the secondary school see to its needs, but at the elementary school level let us work continuously to meet the particular needs of our elementary students. Sometimes, we want them to grow up faster than they should, but let us always keep in mind that they are children, with the perspective and needs of children.

23

TOPIC: *Elementary Administrator's Viewpoint*

AUDIENCE: *Suitable for Adult Audiences*

As an elementary school administrator, there are times when I feel like the person who was walking past a construction area. There were several workers engaged in various activities, and the person asked three of them the same question, "What are you doing?"

The first worker replied flippantly, "I'm hauling bricks from one place to another and trying not to think about it!"

Said the second, "I'm earning a living the best way I can."

And the third answered, "I'm building a great hospital —- a place that will make tomorrow better!"

As an elementary administrator, I can really sympathize with the last worker's appraisal, because I realize only too well that here, in this school, we are not just moving children around from one grade to another; we are building for their future and building for our future as well. Here, we are aiming at nurturing the people who will make tomorrow better, and I am extremely proud to be a part of that.

SPECIAL DATA: Our inner perception of what we do has an immense influence on the type of job we will do. Understanding the importance of elementary edu-

cation and the administrator's part in it is a great step toward delivering any speech with passion and conviction. Let the audience know the positive and energizing path you tread.

24

TOPIC:	*Elementary Teacher's Viewpoint*
AUDIENCE:	*General Adult Audience*

We once had a teacher who was only four feet, one inch tall. She was a wonderful teacher, and her children loved her. Indeed, she had taught second grade for quite a number of years, and everyone enjoyed her wisdom and her obvious devotion to her students.

One day I said to her, "You know, with your teaching skill, you could have chosen virtually any grade in the school. Why did you choose second grade; what drew you there?"

"Isn't that obvious?" she answered. "You see how tall I am. Well, after some experimentation, I found that second grade was the one place where I could teach my students eye to eye! So that's where I stayed."

> *SPECIAL DATA: When that teacher first gave that answer, all of us laughed dutifully, but upon reflection, there's much more to her answer than a quip. We need teachers in elementary school who will see their students eye to eye, regardless of physical height. We need teachers who will try to understand and appreciate what it means to be an elementary student in today's world—who will identify with their students' needs. A good speech could be drawn along these lines.*

25

TOPIC:	*Elementary Student's Viewpoint*
AUDIENCE:	*Suitable for Any Audience*

I once had a child in my office to whom I had been talking about life and attitude—particularly his attitude in class and in the halls.

Finally I asked him to step over to my window.

"You know," I began, gesturing at the neatly mowed front lawn beyond the window, "it really comes down to your viewpoint. Some people see this school as a place that robs them of time from other things they'd rather be doing, but some see this as a place where they can learn and grow—a place where they are a part of something wonderful.

"Now," I ended, with my hand on his shoulder, "just look at our school out there, and tell me your viewpoint."

"OK," returned the lad, "but first, could you pick me up. I'm only three feet tall, and I'm having a devil of a time seeing beyond the window sill!"

SPECIAL DATA: This is a good anecdote for any speech about communications, particularly communications between the school and the home. Use it to show that different people will see the same thing in different ways, or to ask people to remember that what kids sometimes bring home from school is a product of their point of view. You might also use it to demonstrate that a child's point of view can differ greatly from that of the adults around her or him.

26

TOPIC:	*On the Playground*
AUDIENCE:	*Suitable for Adult Audiences*

The teacher arrived early for Playground Patrol, and she was glad she did. Before the first class had come tumbling out the door to the playground, she managed to catch a child who otherwise would have fallen down the stairs. Within the next five minutes, she had stopped two fights and tended to a scraped knee. Next she talked with a crying child and arbitrated a dispute over the legitimacy of a pitched ball.

Now she stood against the wall of the school, taking a breather, when a third-grade girl skipped by and stood for a moment regarding the teacher.

"Yes?" said the playground supervisor to the child, "May I help you?"

"Nope!" said the girl. "I was just thinking."

"Oh, thinking what?"

Answered the third-grader, "That you teachers sure got it easy. All you do is stand around all day and watch us play!"

SPECIAL DATA: As with the previous anecdote, this could be used for a speech on communication, but it could be used in a number of other ways as well. Perception of what is being done need not be a reflection of what is truly happening; or remember always to check out what you hear; or avoid rumors and check out the facts—all these suggest themselves.

27

TOPIC:	*Sports on the Elementary Level*
AUDIENCE:	*Good for Adult Audience of Parents*

The score was 26-0 when a distraught parent ran up to the coach.

"Coach!" exclaimed the parent, "It's 26 to 0 against us! For goodness sake, what are you doing?"

"Building character, of course," the coach answered, "building character!"

SPECIAL DATA: Was what the coach told the parent a "cop-out" or an essential truth of elementary education? We teach our children to win, but do we teach them how to deal with the troubles that life has a way of placing in our paths? Is our task only to instill knowledge, or are we to acknowledge the needs of growing personalities as well? This anecdote might be used effectively to introduce a speech on any of these topics.

28

TOPIC: *The Elementary School Nurse*

AUDIENCE: *Good for All Adult Audiences*

The second-grader silently entered the nurse's office and stood before her desk.

"A kid told me that this is a place where you give out Band-Aids," the child stated.

"Why, yes," smiled the nurse. "Why do you ask? Do you need a Band-Aid?"

"You bet!" exclaimed the second-grader. "The rhythm section can't keep time, the clarinet is flat, and the talent show is only two weeks from now. Our band can use all the aid it can get!"

SPECIAL DATA: We've used this to "prove" that the elementary school nurse is often misunderstood, as well as being a busy person with many tasks to perform. This could also lead into some comment about the versatility of the individual —- that the modern elementary school nurse does much more than just "pass out Band-Aids!"

29

TOPIC: *A Trip to the Principal's Office*

AUDIENCE: *Suitable for Adult Audiences*

"You have a young lady waiting in your office," my secretary told me. "Her teacher sent her down to have a little talk with you."

"Wow!" I murmured, "I have to be at a meeting ten minutes ago, and it will be at least an hour before I get a chance to talk to her."

"An hour!" came a voice from behind my open office door where the student had been waiting and obviously listening, "I can't wait for an hour! I have classwork to do! Besides, I don't know why my teacher wanted me to go to your office. It's nothing special; I've definitely seen better!"

SPECIAL DATA: This anecdote could be used to point out that the principal's office should not become just the place you go when you've misbehaved—that it should be open to students and parents and faculty and staff to improve relationships on all levels. It could be a prelude to an open invitation to parents and public to "drop in!"

30

TOPIC:	*Instilling Good Values*
AUDIENCE:	*Suitable for Adult Audiences*

Once, I dealt with a boy who had been caught shoplifting a hair dryer in a local store and was referred to the school rather than the police.

I sat in my office with the boy and his parents. The father wrung his hands and intoned, "Why, son? Why? Haven't your mother and I always instilled good values in you?"

"That's just it, Dad!" the boy explained. "That hair dryer was marked down from $34.95 to only $19.95, and you know that nobody in our family can resist a good sale!"

SPECIAL DATA: There are a number of possibilities with this one. For a speech on the budget: "Let's make certain that we don't establish false values; let's get full value; can we vote for a 'marked-down' budget?" In values training: "We must instill in our students a true sense of values; let's teach our students to recognize and cherish true value and not abuse it." To parents: "What you do at home will always have its influence upon children, even when they are very young."

31

TOPIC:	*How Other People View the Schools*
AUDIENCE:	*Good for Adult Audiences*

When I hear people talk about our schools, I am sometimes reminded of a town that had a very large town clock. At one town meeting, a citizen was sounding off about that particular landmark.

"The numbers are cracked and peeling," the citizen pronounced, "the tip of one of the hands is bent, and the clock face is dirty and streaked by rain! It's a mess!"

"Mister!" exclaimed the custodian of the clock who rose to speak next, "The reason you think it's so bad is that all you do is look at what's broke! Someday, you should come inside where I work, and see how well that darn clock really keeps time!"

SPECIAL DATA: The analogy here is obvious, but we have found this a good story to introduce the concept that as long as there are people standing outside the school, looking at "what's broke," they will never fully appreciate what our schools are doing in our community. Perhaps these people need to come into the school to see how well we "really keep time!"

32

TOPIC:	*Listening to What Children Say*
AUDIENCE:	*Good for Adult Audience*

I went past a classroom one day, and when I looked inside, there was a teacher (*NOTE: for a little humor, use the actual name of a teacher present with whom you have cleared it.*), talking and talking to a lone girl who sat in a student desk, nodding her head and grinning and looking intently at the teacher.

I popped in my head and remarked that I was sure the student would benefit from the extra help.

"Oh, this isn't extra help," the teacher said. "I just enjoy talking to her."

"One student?" I questioned.

"Yes! You see, this is Inez, and she just entered from South America. She doesn't speak a word of English, but she's the best listener I've ever had!"

> *SPECIAL DATA: There are times when children say more through their attitudes and the way in which they take in what we say than in any answer they may give on a written or oral test. Moreover, great eloquence of speech is no substitute for genuine concern. A speech along these lines might be suggested by this anecdote.*

33

TOPIC: *Learning About Money*

AUDIENCE: *Suitable for Adult Audiences*

The elementary class was learning about math and how to apply that knowledge to money. The teacher stood before one youngster and posed a problem.

"Suppose you had two dollars," the teacher stated. "Now, I come along and ask you to lend me fifty-five cents. How much would you have left?"

Without a second's hesitation, the youth replied, "Two bucks, 'cause I don't care if you are the teacher, I'm not givin' you a cent!"

> *SPECIAL DATA: You can use this introduction as an icebreaker for any speech in which money plays a part (fund raiser, budget, class project, etc.).*

34

TOPIC: *Five Lines With Which to Establish Rapport*

AUDIENCE: *Suitable for Any Adult Audience*

Half of what your children have told you about the school is true—but I'm not going to tell you which half!

* * * * * * *

I had a teacher once who told me that if I didn't settle down, I might never get out of school. I wonder how she knew?

* * * * * * *

Stick with me, ladies and gentlemen, and we'll reach Social Security together.

* * * * * * *

Did you hear? A group of scientists has been able to prove that there is life after the PTA!

* * * * * * *

I'm feeling very well tonight. In fact, this is the best I've felt since I was walking in the first-grade hall at dismissal time and someone shouted, "Free Puppies!"

> *SPECIAL DATA: The secret of establishing rapport with these lines is to make certain you fit the line to what the audience may be experiencing at that point. Take the last line, for instance. Suppose you are speaking after an activity where parents and children had to fit into tight quarters—a classroom or science room, perhaps—for a demonstration. Parents fully realize what it means to be jostled by a moving mass of children; that last line brings rapport, and a few laughs as well.*

35

TOPIC:	*Four Humorous Things to Say If You Make a Mistake*
AUDIENCE:	*Best Appreciated by an Adult Audience*

I suppose they call me an elementary educator because I've just demonstrated how to make a basic idiot out of myself.

* * * * * * *

Excuse me, but can one of you tell me where the rewind button is? I'd like to take that over!

* * * * * * *

Sorry about that! My tongue got in front of my eyetooth, and I couldn't see what I was saying.

* * * * * * *

A college education and four years of graduate school, and I'm still no better off than my mouth lets me be!

> *SPECIAL DATA: The only time an audience feels uncomfortable if you make a mistake is if you feel uncomfortable or embarrassed by it. If you forget a line, drop something, or even trip and stumble, it does not have to be a major catastrophe. Take it in stride and smile, perhaps using one of the lines above, amd you will find that the audience not only understands but is on your side; that is a definite advantage.*

IN CONCLUSION

Humor, appropriately used, can be one of your most effective public speaking tools. The audience that laughs with you is most often the audience that is for you, ready to listen to what you have to say, and well disposed to accept your ideas and comments. Keep in mind that a point well punctuated by humor is a point that will be remembered by any audience.

$\mathcal{S}$ection 2

"May I Present . . .": A Guide to Powerful Introductions

LET'S BEGIN

The absolutely first step in giving a good introduction is to get the proper information on the person you are introducing and make certain that it is accurate and up to date. You do *not* want to introduce someone as "Dr. Smith," only to find that she or he is only a doctoral candidate at the moment. That would be embarrassing for both you and the person introduced. Check your facts and clear those facts with the person just before the introduction if at all possible.

The following pages offer a number of introductions to adapt to your needs. Whatever you say, if you introduce a person in the way you would like to be introduced, you cannot go wrong.

36

TOPIC:	*Introducing Yourself*
AUDIENCE:	*Suitable for Most Adult Audiences: Parents, Teachers, Older Children*

Good morning, ladies and gentlemen, and thank you for coming.

Since I recognize several faces, I think I can safely assume that you recognize me as well. I see, however, a number of people with whom I am not familiar, and I'd like to say hello.

My name is _____ _____, and for several hours each day, I am permitted to be the principal of this building. What that means is often a matter of point of view.

To a first-grader, I am the person who often visits the classroom and asks about homework and sometimes joins in the playtime (That's my favorite!) and frequently participates in the cookies and milk as well.

To the teachers in this place, I am the one who checks their lesson plans every Friday afternoon, the one who holds meetings at least once a month that I hope and pray they will find useful and informative, and the one who is fiercely interested in helping this outstanding faculty be the best teachers they can be, so each and every one of their students gets the best those teachers can give.

To the school secretary, I am the apparently endless source of written materials, including reports, public relations, letters, handbooks and other things that must be typed, computed, reproduced, cleaned up, distributed, collected, and a lot of other things—all of which spell "WORK" in capital letters, three feet high.

To the custodial staff, I think I must often appear as a white-gloved army sergeant on inspection detail, or one whose frequent communications involve making sure that those microscopes get to the fifth grade and asking if that Language Arts book order ever came in!

To some, I am sure I am a heartless ogre (*ask one of the students who has had to be disciplined*) and to others, I am a wonderful and warm humanitarian (*ask the family of the child I have hugged and given a school award*) but mostly, I am just the person I am, and I try very hard to be the best principal I can be, working toward making this the best school for your children during these wonderful, troublesome, joyful, chaotic, and oh-so-important elementary years.

And now that I've introduced myself, and we know each other a bit better, let's get started with today's activities.

> *SPECIAL DATA: One way to introduce yourself effectively is to define yourself in terms of what you do, as in this case. We all know that a principal does a great deal more than is mentioned here, but this speech is being given to an audience at the start of an activity, so brevity is called for. Also, it is delivered with a sort of good-natured, tongue-in-cheek attitude, which is pleasing and acceptable to the audience while establishing just who you are.*

$$\boxed{\textbf{37}}$$

TOPIC: *Introducing a Guest Speaker for the Evening*

AUDIENCE: *Parents; Teachers; Adults*

Good evening, ladies and gentlemen, and thank you for attending this meeting. I think you are going to be very pleased that you made it tonight.

I say that because I know how important the subject of Early Childhood Growth and Development is to each and every one of you. Not only do you, as parents, have an interest in the subject, but you each have living, breathing subject matter at home who will, undoubtedly, be the recipients of what you learn during the course of this evening.

Many people claim to be experts on early childhood—after all, they lived through it, didn't they? Only a handful, however, have the background, the skill, the concern, and the proven record of success to qualify as true experts— people who truly understand, who have clear insights into the problems and frustrations of the subject, and who have the ability to communicate that care, concern, and knowledge to others, sharing with them the benefits gleaned from years of practical experience.

That is why I am so happy to introduce to you our guest speaker for this evening.

Dr. Helen Marsden Smith came into national prominence two years ago with the publication of her highly successful book, *The Miracle Years*. In this highly acclaimed study, Dr. Smith examined what she called, "the absolute miracle of growth and development that we call early childhood." Rapidly approaching record sales, this book has been warmly welcomed not only by the medical community, but by the general public as well, who have made it a best seller.

A graduate of Harcourt Medical School, Dr. Smith served an internship at the prestigious Kerndale Children's Hospital. Following that, she established her own very successful practice in pediatrics, specializing in early childhood medicine. Inspired by her work in her medical specialty, she then entered into extensive research in association with Halkmar Institute for Child Development. Over the years, her research, medical journal entries, magazine articles, and books for the general public have become widely accepted as a definitive word in the area of early childhood development and training.

These accomplishments alone are those on which an honored lifetime is established, but if you ask Dr. Smith, as I did earlier this evening, if there are any particular accomplishments she would like mentioned, she will tell you to be certain to mention that she is also the mother of Karen and Richard, in whom the wonder of love continues to grow and develop.

Here, then, is our guest speaker this evening—noted physician, renowned author, loving parent. And those, ladies and gentlemen, are the qualifications of a true expert.

Please join me in welcoming our guest, Dr. Helen Marsden Smith!

SPECIAL DATA: If the guest speaker for the program is an expert, then it is always fitting to enumerate the qualifications of that person for the area of expertise in which he or she is going to speak. An introduction like the one above would work well in that case. Should the guest speaker be someone with-

out such "formal" qualifications, then the contributions of that individual to the school or children or community should be stressed instead. Keep in mind that your purpose is to prepare the audience to be well disposed toward the guest speaker and what he or she has to offer. After you have introduced the guest, back away graciously from the podium and lead the audience in applause for the speaker.

38

TOPIC: *Introducing an Elementary School Teacher*

AUDIENCE: *First, Children, As in a School; Second, Adults—Parents and Colleagues*

Good afternoon, boys and girls. I'd like your attention right now, because I have something very important to tell you.

As you know, your teacher, Mrs. Harnanian, will be leaving at the holiday break to have a baby. When that happens, she will be staying home for the rest of the school year to take care of her new son or daughter. I know we will miss Mrs. Harnanian, but I also know that we are very happy for her, and we have a couple of happy surprises for her before she leaves, don't we?

With Mrs. Harnanian at home, however, we will need someone to take care of the class for the rest of the school year. Mrs. Harnanian and I have been looking for just the right person for that job, and we think we have found her.

Her name is Mrs. Martinez, and for the last year she has been at home taking care of her baby daughter. Before that, she taught for five years at River's End Elementary School, and one of those years, her students gave her a medal they had made, calling her their choice for "Teacher of the Year" at River's End.

Mrs. Harnanian and I know that you are going to like working with Mrs. Martinez, and we have told her that she will like working with you.

Let's give a great big welcome now to Mrs. Martinez!

* * * * * * *

Good evening ladies and gentlemen.

This evening, I have the distinct pleasure of introducing to you a true artist.

Now, every artist works in some medium. Some paint in oils and acrylics; some produce fine line drawings in pen and ink; still others sculpt shapes out of clay or carve them from blocks of the finest marble. Whatever they produce, their work is usually on display some place in order that we may view, appreciate, admire, understand.

That is why I take great pleasure in introducing Mr. Michael Spandor. Mr. Spandor has been an elementary school teacher of grades three and four in this township for the past twenty-seven years—the last five of them in this school, ever since the day it opened.

Let me tell you about his art. He does not paint on canvas with oils, but many a student's life and achievements have been colored by his care and concern; he produces no drawings with ink on paper, but he has imprinted love on his students and a fine design of honesty, integrity, and belief in their own abilities on many a confused third- or fourth-grade student; his statues are not of clay or stone, but his hands and his heart have helped to mold many a life, brush away many an errant tear, smooth many a rough and twisting path.

Mr. Spandor's work may never see the inside of an art gallery, but it is all around us, nonetheless. We see it in the altered lives and the academic success of the children who are fortunate enough to come under his wise and loving teaching.

Please join me in welcoming an outstanding elementary teacher, Mr. Michael Spandor!

SPECIAL DATA: The first introduction is to children, and is kept very straight-forward and simple. Note that never was it said that the new teacher would "take the place of" the one who was leaving. In the introduction to adults, an apt analogy is used to honor an obviously respected and loved elementary teacher. Had that teacher held a number of degrees or written magazine articles or had books published, that would have been added as well, probably before the analogy. As it stands, it is an introduction that really honors an exemplary teacher.

39

TOPIC: *Introducing an Elementary School Administrator*

AUDIENCE: *Adults; Parents; Teachers; Members of the Community*

Good evening, ladies and gentlemen. Welcome.

Tonight, I am going to introduce to you the principal of Dwight Road Elementary School, but before I do, perhaps it would be best to define our terms.

Exactly what is an elementary school principal? One definition I've heard is that an elementary school principal is a person who, when asked, "Do you have any children?" doesn't hesitate a moment, but answers immediately, "Oh, yes. I have 476 of them, and I'll have more once that new housing development opens up!"

Elementary school principals can describe their offices down to the last worn thread on the worn carpet on the worn floor. They know the office intimately, because they spend so much time there working in the pressure cooker that is today's educational scene. Indeed, it has been said that to become an elementary school principal is to become extremely well acquainted with the night janitorial staff!

An elementary principal is a study in availability. Whatever his or her schedule or however late she or he has to stay after everyone else has left, there is not a play in a classroom or auditorium that doesn't have the principal front row center; there is not a science fair or demonstration for parents for which she is not in the audience; there is not an argument or altercation between students that he does not have time to mediate; there is not a field day or class picnic that the principal is not a part of, whether judging the tug-of-war or cooking the hot dogs.

An elementary principal is a leader. He is the one on the sidelines shouting encouragement and often personally leading the cheers when everything is going well; she is the one who stands out front and accepts the responsibility and even the blame when things do not work as planned; he is the fighter before other principals and superintendents and the school board—and even the public—when it is a matter of getting something of value for his faculty, his children, his school; she is a tireless champion of justice and right who knows each child, appreciates each parent, respects each teacher, and deeply cares for the well-being and educational growth of every individual in her building.

Not every individual who bears the title matches up to the definition, but when that happens, when that elementary school principal is generally respected, appreciated, recognized, and sought after by educators, students, parents, and the community, then you have someone whom it is a distinct honor and privilege to introduce; then you have someone like the principal of Dwight Road Elementary School who is about to address us tonight.

Ladies and gentlemen, please join me in welcoming our speaker for this evening, Mrs. Rose Ostrainder.

> *SPECIAL DATA: Let's talk about honesty. The introduction you have just read is a very powerful, even heroic, tribute to a particular elementary school principal as well as an introduction. Certainly, it prepares the audience to be well disposed toward the speaker; therefore, consider this piece of advice: Don't say it unless you can mean it. This is true not only of this introduction, but of anything you say about another person in front of an audience. An audience is very quick to pick up on the fact that you may not be saying what you truly feel, and that would ruin your introduction and the speech to follow as well. If you can give the introduction above and mean it, that's fine; if not, stick to the speaker's honors, accomplishments, and academic credentials.*

40

TOPIC: *Introducing a Member of Central Administration*

AUDIENCE: *Adults: Parents; Teachers; Community Members*

Good evening, ladies and gentlemen. We have quite a night in store for us.

I can say that without hesitation, because I know all about our speaker, and I assure you that when it comes to ideas that are central to the educational scene, central to our understanding of existing programs, central to building our children into citizens ready for the next century, then our guest from Central Administration will certainly be the one to whom we will listen closely, for she is in a position to understand, to know, and to communicate to us.

As Assistant Superintendent of Schools, she has served with honor and distinction in the township for over seventeen years. In that time, as head of a vast number of committees, she has provided invaluable insight and direction in the formation of the curriculum of our schools and is largely responsible for the many fine programs that our elementary schools offer. In short, she has been and remains a very important factor in formulating and providing the very best for the children of this township.

At times, being a member of Central Administration can be a thankless job, since most citizens do not get a chance to see all the hard work and long hours that go into the excellence of their child's education. It is significant, therefore, that she has been the recipient of several awards from groups of citizens who have recognized her many, many contributions to the children of our community, and her continued work in their behalf.

I am privileged, therefore, to be able to introduce to you Assistant Superintendent of Schools, Dr. Shalla Rogers.

> *SPECIAL DATA: We have often found it to be true that the general public has a limited knowledge at best of what goes on in that mysterious place, "Central Administration." An introduction like this not only gently acknowledges that fact, but gives some insights into the contributions that a member of Central Administration may provide to the community, and should also predispose the audience to be receptive.*

41

TOPIC:	*Introducing a Superintendent of Schools*
AUDIENCE:	*Adults: Parents; Citizens; Educators*

Good evening, ladies and gentlemen.

It has been reported that when Harry Truman was President of the United States, he had a sign made for his desk. The sign read, "The buck stops here!"

Certainly, we are all familiar with the common expression "passing the buck." We know that it means to assign blame or responsibility to someone else. "It's not my fault; so-and-so didn't give me the right information . . ." or something of that type. The sign on President Truman's desk reminded him that all responsibility stopped at his desk. When something went wrong, it was he who took the heat.

Harry Truman was rightly praised for his courageous acceptance of the responsibilities of his office, and he set an example that would last long after he left office.

That is why I take pride in introducing our guest this evening. As Superintendent of Schools for this township for the past ten years, he is well aware of the weight of the "buck" that has frequently dropped on his desk. Throughout our building program, as well as in the throes of many budget crises, his voice has been the voice of reason and understanding, often in the midst of confusion and rising tempers. He has sought leadership to promote the philosophies in which he so deeply believed and then not shirked the responsibility of fighting for those beliefs in the face of formidable opposition. He has never pointed fingers or placed blame; he has accepted the responsibility of leadership and has never been reticent about standing up and shouting, "Follow me!" If something failed, he took the responsibility and forged ahead to do it better; if something succeeded, he praised the work of those who had stood by it while offering opponents an olive branch and an opportunity to join in the goal they both shared—the good of the children of this township.

I am very proud and happy to introduce to you the Superintendent of Schools of Rock Township, Dr. Harlan Stanton!

> *SPECIAL DATA: Unless there is a specific faction in the community who is opposed to him or her, the Superintendent always finds a good reception at speaking engagements. The introduction above was for a superintendent who*

had just gone through a rather heated conflict over budget cuts (we are certain you can sympathize). Since everyone in the audience knew about it, it was not ignored, but used to build the character of the Superintendent. If the Superintendent has done anything outstanding for the elementary schools that affects the children of your audience, be sure to mention that.

42

TOPIC: *Introducing a School Board Member*

AUDIENCE: *Mixed Adult Audience of Educators, Parents, Public*

Good evening ladies and gentlemen.

Our speaker this evening is a well-known and long-term member of (name the town or locality) Board of Education (or School Board). I have heard our guest ponder whether that fact is an asset or a detriment.

Certainly, when something goes wrong; when plans are not on schedule; when there is a mix-up that shortens tempers and frustrates those touched by our school system, a member of the School Board is a visible target at which to vent that frustration. Indeed, it is almost a "rite of passage" for a Board member to stand and "take the heat" from a citizen who may feel disenfranchised because some projected improvement did not materialize. Under this pressure—and more—our guest has stood firm, doing the job he has often said he felt was his mandate from those who placed him in his position.

Being a member of the School Board has its positive side as well, and our guest has often commented on the personal sense of accomplishment he has felt over the years in his work for the children of our township, Of course, those of us who have been here for a while know firsthand of the contributions of our speaker, including his fearless and forward-looking leadership in the building program that made this very school possible. Countless children have passed through our schools and enjoyed a number of benefits, of many of which they may not even be aware, thanks to the tireless, unheralded, and often misunderstood efforts of a man who has devoted his time selflessly and with amazing energy for the last twelve years.

I am, therefore, extremely pleased to recommend to your attention someone who understands our school system and speaks of it from experience rather than theory.

Ladies and gentlemen, may I introduce the president of (name of township) Board of Education, Mr. Harold B. Guiterman.

SPECIAL DATA: Members of the Board of Education or School Board often have a difficult time of it, since they are so visible to all points on the educational spectrum, and are often a focal point of frustration. It is good, therefore, to stress the real accomplishments of such a guest, particularly if the board member has been one for some time and established a good track record. For a new board member, you might want to stress the person's accomplishments outside the school system, or the person's great desire to serve the children of the township.

$$\boxed{\textbf{43}}$$

TOPIC:	*Introducing a Student Who Has Won an Award*
AUDIENCE:	*Children—Classmates and Schoolmates; Adults—Teachers and Parents*

Good afternoon, everybody, and welcome to the many parents I see in the audience.

You know, awards are wonderful things. In fact, I can't think of anyone who doesn't like to get an award. Whether it is a gleaming trophy with a small statue atop it, a plaque for the wall proclaiming the recipient in inch-high letters, or a simple paper expressing the sentiment, "Well done!"—whatever it may be, everyone enjoys receiving an award, and it has been my experience that they are often kept and cherished for many years to come, perhaps even for a lifetime.

We enjoy presenting these awards as well. All too often, we appreciate the efforts of others and are thankful for our association with them, only we do it in our minds and hearts, and we are silent about it to our friends, our classmates, and our community. In such a case, the person we really want to honor may be unaware of how thankful we really are for his or her efforts.

That is why I am so filled with happiness this afternoon to be able to present to you one of our very own—a student who has been and is a credit to her parents, her school, her community, and herself. This afternoon, she will receive an award that will recognize the academic, social, and personal effort she has put into this school year. This afternoon, we will be able to present her with something very real and tangible that will forever be a symbol of how we feel about having her as a part of our school. This afternoon, we will present an award while acknowledging a reward—our reward of knowing, working with, and having as a student or classmate someone who has the outstanding record of achievement and giving that our award recipient has.

Student body of Dwight Road Elementary School, faculty, ladies and gentlemen, please join me in recognizing one of our own—our classmate, our student, our neighbor, and the winner of this year's "Outstanding Student of the Year" Award—Tara Tamanski!

> *SPECIAL DATA: If the award you are presenting has a special name (named, let us say, after the founder of the town, etc.), then you might want to replace the phrase "an award" with the actual name of that particular honor. For example, "This afternoon, she will receive the highly coveted Arthur S. Fosterman Award for Student Humanitarian Achievement." If this is given as part of a graduation, adjust the remarks indicating time and who is present. Suit the speech to the particular occasion.*

44

TOPIC: *Introducing Someone About to Retire*

AUDIENCE: *Adults; Relatives; Friends; Colleagues—Retirement Dinner Audience*

As the final part of tonight's exercise, we get to hear from the person who has caused us to gather here this evening.

In a very famous Broadway musical, a group of chums sing a song that begins, "There's just a few more hours . . ." Of course, in that number from "My Fair Lady," they were speaking of one man's impending wedding and bemoaning the fact that they had ". . . just a few more hours" to celebrate comradeship with their pal before he left them for the estate of matrimony.

Our guest this evening is already an established citizen in that state, having recently celebrated his thirty-seventh wedding anniversary. Moreover, as in that musical, he is our "pal," a person we have come to know, a "comrade," if you will, in the day-to-day dramas we have acted out in the schools of this township. And again akin to that song, we have "just a few more hours" to work with him before he will retire, after thirty-eight years of service to the elementary schools and the elementary students of this township.

Others this evening have told you of his contributions, his dedication, his hard work, and his love for the elementary students of our school system. I can hardly add to that magnificent list of glowing achievements except, perhaps, to say that we are about to hear from our dear, dear friend as well, and that is a title we shall all honor in our hearts.

"There's just a few more hours . . ." the song went, and now, in the last of those hours, with a deep sense of thankfulness for the hours he has spent with us, and an even deeper hope for the happiness of the hours that may yet lie ahead for him, I am pleased to present to you our friend and our guest, Mr. Richard Fisher.

> SPECIAL DATA: *Retirement dinners usually feature a number of speeches, and they are quite often long, not to say overlong. Therefore, the shorter and more concise you can make both your retirement speech and your introductions at such an affair, the better off you will be and the more appreciative will be your audience. Let absolute sincerity be the key to what you say in your introduction, and you can't go wrong.*

45

TOPIC: *Introducing a Political Figure*

AUDIENCE: *Adults—Educators and Community Members*

Welcome, ladies and gentlemen, to what promises to be a very exciting and informative evening.

You know, despite the number of negative definitions of the word that have been promulgated on television and in other media, "politics" is not a dirty word. On the contrary, when defined in terms of our guest this evening, it can be an uplifting experience.

We must pause to reflect on the fact that were it not for politics and the people who work in political office (yes, they are called "politicians"), very little, if anything, would get done. In general, I speak of our roadways, and commerce, and social programs that are part and parcel of our lives. In particular, I speak of the educational process that citizens of the United States enjoy and the politicians who have labored many long hours to achieve legislation that will ensure the best in educational policy and programs for the children of our land. From my particular viewpoint, that means help for our elementary schools through recognition of their importance and through legislation that will maintain those standards they uphold right into the next century.

For that, we need political figures who are committed to education, who will work for the best in education, who have a vision of the future and a strong commitment to work with and for the children of today to prepare for an outstanding tomorrow.

Such a person is our guest this evening. I am very proud and happy to present to you a true "Friend of Education," a fighter for the right of all children to a quality education, and a "politician" in the very best and highest sense of the word.

Ladies and gentlemen, I give you our State Senator, the honorable Laura Bastone!

> *SPECIAL DATA: When introducing any political figure, it is well to check out in advance precisely the title by which that person is addressed and introduced. Toward that end, you will find that if you contact the staff of the visiting dignitary, they will gladly supply you with that information and may even provide additional information of a specific nature relative to your state or district that you may wish to include in your introduction. Introduce the political figure, shake hands, and then step back.*

46

TOPIC:	*Introducing a Well-Loved Individual*
AUDIENCE:	*A Group Already Well-Disposed Toward the Guest Speaker*

Welcome, ladies and gentlemen—a very good evening to you all.

I read a saying once that stated, "How long you've lived doesn't matter half as much as how much you've been loved." Now, a cynic might say that this is nothing more than the stuff of which a bumper sticker is made—a "cute" saying some grandma or grandpa might place on the back of the station wagon.

Well, that may be true for cynics, but not for us. For us, it is a golden truth, something to be cherished and applied in our lives. If it is, then the measure of a man or woman does not rest in the fact that she or he has reached some fabled age, for that is a matter of physiology; that person's worth to us is defined in terms of how much he or she is loved by the people with whom that person comes into contact day by day. Success is defined, not in terms of dollars in a bank, but in terms of the love of the children who run to meet you; the respect of adults; the warmth in the hearts of others when you greet them on the street. In short, success is measured in terms of the love that has been engendered in the hearts of the people around you.

I am about to introduce to you one of the most successful people it has ever been my joy and privilege to know. There are few people anywhere who have managed to win the love of children, adults, educators, and the community as he has. Indeed, his visit to our school is always an occasion for our children to gather 'round him to bask in the glow and the warmth this wonderful man brings with him.

Ladies and gentlemen, allow me to introduce to you a person who wears love as others wear a kingly robe—a true success and a beacon of light in this often dark and imperfect world.

Ladies and gentlemen, I give you Mr. Harold Oates.

> *SPECIAL DATA: One of the secrets of successfully adapting these speeches is to personalize them. The speech above is rather general; you can personalize it with the person's familiar name or mention of some particular incident for which the subject may be well known, or any other appropriate anecdotes. For someone as well loved as this speech indicates, you want to keep it warm and personal.*

47

TOPIC:	*Introducing a Parent*
AUDIENCE:	*Parents and Educators (at a PTA meeting, for example)*

What a pleasure it is for me to present our next speaker!

Allow me to introduce to you an extremely (and I do mean extremely) important person—just how important may, I believe, be defined by a story that I once heard. Please allow me to share it with you.

In that story, a flock of crows were planning a rebellion against a farmer on whose property they had gathered, and now they met in secret council to discuss their plans and develop a strategy for war.

"Let us band together and do away with the farmer," said one crow, "and when he is gone, we crows will have the corn field all to ourselves. Then, we can eat our fill, and there will be no one there to shoo us away!"

Just then, an older and a wiser crow stepped forward and, with a flutter of feathers, took his place to address the flock.

"My fellow crows," he began with authority in his voice, "I have lived on this farm and others for many years, and I would like to share with you one very important fact before you begin your great war of rebellion.

At that, the other crows drew near. The elder speaker leaned close to the assembly and continued, "Get rid of the farmer if you wish, but remember this—where there are no farmers, there is no corn!"

Please allow me to introduce to you an extremely important person—the parent of two children in our elementary school. She is a parent, and without her and people like her, there is not an educator in this room who would have a job, and the future of our community and of our world would be bleak and desolate indeed!

Ladies and gentlemen, please join me in welcoming Mrs. Judy Lopresti!

> *SPECIAL DATA: In all of these introductions, the name of the person being introduced is saved to the very end of the introduction. The impact on the audience is greater than if you begin by saying something like, "I'm going to introduce Mrs. Lopresti." Also, at the end of the introduction, allow your voice to rise to the end of the line so that your greatest emphasis in the sentence is on the person's name. It's good form, and it adds class.*

48

TOPIC: *Introducing a Very Involved Parent*

AUDIENCE: *Mixed Adult Audience of Parents, Teachers, School Officials*

Many years ago, I heard a statement that, by now, has achieved the status of a cliché. Nonetheless, it is a cliché whose truth has been tested and proven under a vast variety of conditions, over a number of years in public education. The cliché is this: If you want something done and done well, ask a busy person.

Now, I just said that the truth of that statement has been proven time after time, but, I dare say, never with such resounding clarity and truth as in the case of the very special person I am about to introduce.

Let me sum it up in one statement: "She is always there for us." Class mother? She is there. Publicity chairperson for our PTA? She is there. Fund raiser for student trips? She is there. Someone to lend a hand in the main office? She is there. Indeed, that may well be the keynote of her life of selfless giving: When it needs to be done, she is there . . . she is there . . . she is there.

Were we to seek an example of the "involved" parent, she would be the first to come to mind. She is not only involved with her children's education, but she has become a vital part of this school and the lives of all the children in it.

"If you want something done, ask a busy person." I will testify that I have never, never had an occasion where the school or I have sought her help that she has not responded affirmatively, and responded with her characteristic smile and an enthusiasm that has spread to all involved and gotten the job done.

Ladies and gentlemen, it is with great pleasure that I introduce to you Mrs. Jane Whyte!

> *SPECIAL DATA: Here, again, you must adapt these speeches to your individual situation. If you have some data as to specific projects or tasks that have been done by the subject, you should feel free to add this information, further personalizing your remarks. This is particularly effective if the audience is aware of some of the projects that the subject's assistance helped bring to fruition.*

49

TOPIC: *Introducing an "Expert" Speaker*

AUDIENCE: *Suitable for an Adult Audience*

Good evening, ladies and gentlemen.

By anyone's definition, our guest this evening is an "expert." Now, some comic soul once defined an expert as "somebody from out of town," and even by that definition, our speaker this evening would fit.

Holder of two doctorates in Elementary Education, she currently chairs the Education Department at Grandcliff University. Previously, she has served as consultant to our own State Department of Education, the State School Boards Association, and a host of prestigious committees on education and child development. The author of six learned volumes in the field, she also authored a book entitled *Reaching the Child Within*, which achieved national status as well as several weeks on the nonfiction best-seller list. A frequent guest on various "talk shows" on radio and TV, she is generally acknowledged as an expert in the field of elementary education, a subject, I need hardly add, that is very near and dear to the hearts of everyone here this evening.

So, if, indeed, an expert is "somebody from out of town," she certainly qualifies, but if an expert is someone who will help us better understand our roles as educators and parents, someone who will communicate to us essential truths and insights into ourselves and our children, someone who will enable us to better serve those who are so close to our hearts, and so vitally a part of our lives, then I take great pleasure in introducing someone who will serve us expertly—our speaker for this evening, a true "expert" in every, loving sense of the word.

Ladies and gentlemen, please join me in welcoming Dr. Ksenya Shepherd!

> SPECIAL DATA: *This all-purpose introduction helps to define the word "expert." Then, it is up to you to give a list of the speaker's accomplishments, positions, publications and the like. If the speaker has spoken to the group previously, it is a good tactic to mention that fact and remind the audience how much "we all got out of that."*

50

TOPIC: *Introducing the Faculty*

AUDIENCE: *Adults; PTA Meeting or "Back-to-School Night" Function*

Ladies and Gentlemen, I have a problem, and it is this: How do I introduce to you the people who are the essential part of the educational system of Dwight Road Elementary School—and do them the justice they deserve? That's my problem, and I don't know that I have a solution.

You see, it is they who conduct the education that takes place in this building, and they do it exceedingly well. I know that to be a fact, for as principal of this school, I have visited every classroom, sometimes invited and sometimes on the spur of the moment, and every single time, I have been deeply, deeply impressed with the level of education that is going on. Not only that, but even if I wore a blindfold, I could not help but also feel the care and concern that these people manifest on a daily basis—no, make that on a minute-by-minute basis—for their students, your sons and daughters. I am certain that they would call it "being professional" or "merely doing the job," but I will tell you that I have been there, and I have witnessed the care and the tenderness and the reaching out to the child who is hurt, and the guidance for the one who does not understand.

Perhaps, reluctant to put their feelings on public display, they would call it "professionalism," but there are others, myself included, who would tell you that the essential ingredient in their teaching is . . . love.

Therefore, allow me to introduce to you those exceptional people of whom I have spoken; those "essential entities" of your children's education; those with whom I am proud to be associated as an educator in this school.

Ladies and gentlemen, the faculty of Dwight Road Elementary School!

SPECIAL DATA: An introduction like this might be a prelude to asking the entire faculty to rise as you lead the applause for them. In this case, there are no individual introductions. If you want to introduce faculty members one by one, then do so before the final paragraph. Introduce each separately, asking the audience to hold applause until the very end. When the last person is introduced, gesture toward the group and make the final statement. Either way, this is a fine introduction of your outstanding faculty.

51

TOPIC: *Introducing the PTA Leadership*

AUDIENCE: *First PTA Meeting, PTA Banquet, or Similar Affair*

Someone once referred to this planet as "Spaceship Earth." The analogy is easy to follow. We are all here on this globe that is traveling through space at a fantastic speed, and we're all in this together, for not one of us has the ability to stop the world and get off.

Now, if I were to borrow that analogy and alter it just a bit, perhaps we could refer to this place as "Spaceship Dwight Road Elementary." Granted, we are not hurtling through space at thousands of mile per hour, even if it does sometimes feel that way, but we are most certainly all in this thing together, and as long as the good of our children is an integral part of that package, there is no one here who is eager to stop this spacecraft and get off.

In fact, it is just the opposite. We here at Dwight Road Elementary have been privileged to see a new "crew" sign on for the duties that every ten-month "space voyage" requires. These, of course, are our parents who selflessly give of time and talent to tend the "spacecraft," and give a great deal of aid and comfort to its complement of junior astronauts.

I speak of our PTA and the many contributions they make each year both to our physical plant and, very specially, to our students. In short, they make this spacecraft a good place to be, and they see to it that it zips along, running smoothly.

That is precisely why I take such great pleasure in introducing the PTA executive board to you this evening. These people, to uphold our analogy, are the navigators and captains and officers who make the ship function to its fullest capacity and lead us into those areas where we may find smooth sailing for all concerned.

First, I'd like to introduce . . .

SPECIAL DATA: At this point, introduce the PTA leadership one by one, perhaps saying a personal word or two about each one. Do this, however, only if you can do it genuinely, so that it sounds honest and spontaneous. As with the previous introduction, when you finish introducing the last individual, pause and say something like, "I give you the Executive Board of the Dwight Road Elementary PTA!" or whatever is appropriate to your situation. Then lead the applause.

52

TOPIC: *Introducing the Evening's Activities*

AUDIENCE: *Adult Audience for an Evening's School Program*

It is said that the person taking a bath who hears a noise, goes to investigate wearing only a towel, and steps into a surprise birthday party might properly remark, "If I had only known, I would have dressed for the occasion!"

Well, my function here this evening is to make sure you know—not to get dressed for a surprise party—but to be prepared for what's going to happen here tonight.

To begin, I want to tell you that a large number of people have worked long and hard and stayed after school to get this evening ready for you. I want to tell you that the demonstrations and presentations you will witness tonight are the result of learning and research and investigation and practice that is representative of the academic progress your children have made over the past months. I want to tell you that in many cases what you will be witnessing is a very important step in the mental and physical growth of your sons and daughters.

What I want to tell you is that we are all in store for something wonderful!

(*At this point, explain the evening's activities in chronological order.*)

Now, I hope that we are all "dressed for the occasion"—dressed in anticipation of the fine evening before us; dressed in appreciation of the efforts that have gone into its making; dressed in wonder at the miracle of learning and growth within the children whom we so dearly love.

So, what are we waiting for? We're all ready; let's go!

SPECIAL DATA: It has been our experience that you can have the best school program for parents that ever existed; it may be rehearsed and practiced and polished until it shines with the glow of professionalism, but if parents ask, what are we supposed to do next, or complain that they missed their child's presentation because they didn't know what room it had been switched to, then the final impression the parents take away will be a negative one. Every effort should be made to introduce the evening's activities in such a manner that they will be crystal clear to everyone. This might possibly include both a printed program and your reiterating the same information from the stage or dais. Your

smooth introduction to the evening can mean an evening that runs smoothly,
and one with which both those viewing and those presenting the program will
be well pleased.

53

TOPIC:	*Introducing an Elementary Educator*
AUDIENCE:	*Parents; Community Members; Fellow Educators*

Good evening, ladies and gentlemen. I am glad to see you all here this evening. I know we are going to have a wonderful time together, and we are going to learn a great deal along the way. So, let's get started.

To begin tonight's activities, I want to introduce to you a most peculiar individual. Now, I am sincere in saying that, and I trust that you will bear with me for a moment while I explain just what I mean when I make that statement.

You see, this is a person who limps into school with a wrenched back, a situation where every step brings with it a jolt of pain up her spine, and when asked why she is not home in bed, shrugs her shoulders and explains that she had promised her class that she would be there to help them through that standardized test, and she couldn't let them down, could she?

Who is this person? Well, she is someone who makes the rules, sets the rules, keeps the rules, and guides her students to the point in maturity where—we hope—they no longer need those rules.

. . . Someone who spends hours and hours seeking new and different methods for reaching that one, difficult student who can't seem to understand, and then forgets all those hours of work in the unspeakable joy that comes when the student looks up and she sees in his eyes that he knows, he has learned.

. . . Someone who soothes a hurt; settles disputes; referees games; dries a child's tears; joins in the child's laughter; turns tears into laughter; helps with homework; watches a child's mind explode in wonder; leads a class of young minds on many a journey of inner and outer discovery; and, when asked, calls it just another day's work.

. . . Someone who sympathizes, empathizes, puts on coats, takes off boots, cleans up spills, calms flaring tempers, settles conflicts before they begin, coaxes, cajoles, orders, guides, suggests, gently corrects, and enthusiastically applauds and encourages each and every student - - and all within the same school day.

. . . Someone who, in an often hard, cold, and indifferent world, does a remarkable thing—she cares and cares deeply for a group of other people's children whom she will often refer to as "my kids."

Ladies and gentlemen, this evening I wish to present to you that most peculiar individual, that wonder and marvel—an elementary school teacher—and one of the best of that magnificent breed.

Please join me in welcoming Ms. Harriet Callandro!

SPECIAL DATA: Certainly, few administrators will disagree that the heart of the
functioning elementary school is its faculty. Often, an elementary school teacher
will go far beyond what is required by any contract or the necessity of earning
a salary check. When this happens, you have a memorable teacher, one whom

the children are fortunate to have as a teacher. This teacher's reputation gets around; parents will fight to have their children placed in this teacher's class. This introduction was originally written for such a teacher, but it could, without specific references, easily be adapted as a tribute to "the elementary teacher" in general. If it is for a particular teacher with whom you are very familiar, you might want to add some specifics of which the audience is aware, such as a special activity the teacher directs every year.

54

TOPIC: *Introducing a Volunteer or Volunteer Staff*

AUDIENCE: *Adults; Parents, Teachers, People Whom the Volunteer(s) Served*

(NOTE: The following introduction is written to introduce a single individual. It is easily adapted for introduction of a group of volunteers by merely changing the number of certain words. For example, "this person" becomes "these people," and "he is a volunteer" becomes "they are volunteers.")

And now, I'd like to introduce to you someone very special.

This person I am about to introduce to you is a most extraordinary individual. You see, he is a volunteer. Yes, in today's world, which is so filled with a "what's-in-it-for-me" attitude, a "let-someone-else-do-it" philosophy, he stands as an individual who actually stepped forward and freely offered his services for the good of others; he is someone who has placed his most considerable talents at our disposal; he is someone upon whom we have come to depend; someone we think of as invaluable.

A volunteer is someone who works for long and frequently lonely hours, often unnoticed and very often unthanked. A volunteer is a person who labors diligently at the task and receives no payment, other than the knowledge of a job well done. A volunteer is an individual who sees the need, and, rather than do nothing but complain about it, steps forward and tackles the problem and grapples with it and sees it through. A volunteer is a giver—one who gives unselfishly that others may partake of the benefits brought about by his or her efforts. In short, a volunteer is a very special person—very special indeed.

The person I am about to introduce to you right now is one of these special people. He is a very special person; he quite aptly embodies all of the criteria I have just detailed. Around this place it is the consensus that everyone in Dwight Road Elementary School is blessed to have him here with us! Therefore, won't you please join me in acknowledging a volunteer and a true friend, Mr. Jonathan Henry.

SPECIAL DATA: The volunteers in any school are an essential part of that school's functioning. It is extremely appropriate, therefore, that they be recognized and shown that they are appreciated for what they do. This is not only good management; it is good sense. The introduction above recognizes the achievements of one volunteer. If you are introducing a number of volunteers, such as a committee, as a group, you can either refer to the group as a whole or mention each one's name individually at an appropriate place in the introduction.

IN CONCLUSION

Before the audience ever hears a single word from the person who will be delivering the speech or major address of the evening, they will hear from you. As the one who does the introduction, you should be aware of one very interesting fact: Your attitude toward the speaker will, to a very large degree, determine the degree of acceptance of that speaker by the audience. If you are pleased to have the speaker present, if you are enthusiastic about hearing what he or she has to say, if it is evident that you really look forward to the speech and speaker to follow—then your audience will as well. If your introduction promises something special to follow, and is delivered with energy and genuine enthusiasm, not only will your audience appreciate it, but the speaker most certainly will reap benefits as well.

$\mathcal{S}$ection 3

"And Away We Go. . .": The Dynamic Opening Speech

In the last section, we dealt with delivering a solid introduction for a speech or evening's activities. In this section, you are the speaker—the first speaker in an evening or program of speeches or activities. You are going to "kick off" the entire program. You are not the featured speaker, but will make the first address. You will serve virtually the same purpose as the first paragraphs in a novel or magazine article; you must capture the attention of the audience and get them involved in what's happening.

It's quite a task; it should impress you with the importance of the opening speech, but it should not make you apprehensive. A well-written, short and concise, enthusiastically delivered speech that sets the tone for what is to follow is certainly within your grasp.

The speeches here are geared for the openings of various activities. They are written in general terms, but you can adapt them to your specific needs; you can personalize them and make them relevant to your audience. With these speeches, you can get an evening "off the ground" in a dynamic and effective manner.

And away we go!

55

TOPIC: *Opening Speech for a PTA-Sponsored Activity*

AUDIENCE: *Parents, Teachers, Community Members*

Good evening, ladies and gentlemen, and welcome to what I believe is going to be an outstanding night of enjoyment and learning.

As you know, our program this evening is both brought to you and sponsored by our own Parent-Teacher Association. Down at the bottom of the last page of your program, you will notice a sentence in very small type that affirms that fact. Do you see it? It states simply, "Brought to you under the sponsorship of the Dwight Road Elementary School PTA."

You know, that is so small, out-of-the-way, and apparently insignificant that one might easily be excused for overlooking it or thinking that it is of minor consequence. To do that, however, would be to miss something very meaningful and very important.

What is the significance of that statement? Just that tonight's program is something that has been agreed upon by both the parents of the children of this school and the teachers of those children.

All too often, there are individuals who view education as a twelve-year war fought between the home and the school on the battleground of the growing child. "War stories" are told of parents threatening to sue individual teachers and the principal and the school, or of the teachers, argumentative and intransigent, insisting on usurping parental rights, and locked in fierce battle with the parents.

In such cases, one often comes up with the very disturbing image of a parent standing on one side of a child and the teacher standing on the other side, each holding onto an arm and pulling vigorously, while the distraught and unhappy child is in serious danger of splitting right down the middle. Oh, yes, this is a very threatening image indeed!

That is precisely why a sentence in very small type at the bottom of the last page of a program is so very important. You see, it stands as a very clear and fine symbol of the cooperation, the understanding, and the spirit of the home and the school working together—the spirit that has characterized the PTA of Dwight Road Elementary for many years and will, I am certain, continue to be their hallmark in the years to come.

Here, you most certainly will not see enmity, but a high sense of shared purpose—the shared goal of effectively and efficiently working together to advance the education and growth of the most important people in the equation—our children. You see, when that happens—when the school and the home meet as partners in such an important undertaking—then everyone benefits, especially those we care so much about, who occasioned our getting together in the first place.

That is why I asked you a moment ago to read that sentence, "Brought to you under the sponsorship of the Dwight Road Elementary School PTA," for that alone should tell you that we have a very special evening in store for us, an evening that will be enriching, enlivening, and, perhaps most important of all, something that will ultimately be of benefit to our children, to our homes, and to our community.

(*NOTE: At this point, if you wish, you might detail the components of the evening's program, or give any special information that your audience might need, depending on the nature of the program.*)

I'm certain that you are as eager as I am to continue with this evening's activities. I know they will be exciting; I know the program will be worthwhile; I know it will benefit me and enhance my relationship with the children of this school.

Remember that statement at the bottom of the last page of your programs for this evening; this activity is under the sponsorship of the Dwight Road Elementary School PTA—therefore, it can do no less!

SPECIAL DATA: This opening speech for a PTA-sponsored activity emphasizes the cooperation between the home and the school—cooperation that produces a school functioning fully for the good and the growth of the individual child. Especially today, this home-school cooperation is being stressed by virtually every educational group in the country. An activity agreed upon by both teachers and parents, therefore, is a good occasion to stress this cooperation, citing your school as the good example. Be enthusiastic, and keep in mind that the feeling you wish to convey is that of what the cooperation of your parents and teachers has accomplished and how proud you, personally, are of that fact.

56

TOPIC:	*Opening Speech for a Fund Raiser*
AUDIENCE:	*Mainly Adults With an Interest in Fund Raising*

I'd like to share with you a personal memory. Please bear with me; this won't take long.

When I was young, a few million years ago, as young as the children in this school, I remember several times when my desire to have something far exceeded my ability to pay for it. Perhaps it was a model airplane or a trip to the movies with my friend who lived down the block or a triple-decker ice cream cone. Whatever the object, the problem would often be that our pockets were empty, Mom or Dad had been tapped out as a source earlier in the week, and the desired goal seemed to be slipping further and further away.

It was at this point that Mom or Dad or some other adult would suggest that we do something absolutely unique for the money—earn it! So radical was this concept to our young minds that it took some time for all its implications to fully register. Well, after due consideration, plus the fact that our pockets were still empty and no cash had magically appeared in spite of our wishes, we decided to at least give it a try. Now, all we had to face was the task of figuring out the "how" of the situation.

Since it was summer, and the heat was sending shimmery waves off the pavement and throats were parched and dry, we came up with the brilliant idea of opening an orange drink stand. After congratulating ourselves for some time on our inventiveness, we took the next step in our plan and made the concession stand itself out of a folding table and some construction paper (after all, we had to print our names and the prices of our wares, didn't we?). That finished, we stepped back to admire our work and immediately had to address the next problem. If we were going to make money selling orange drink, and we were doing that because our present resources were nonexistent, then how were we ever going to afford to buy the oranges and paper cups and sugar and all the rest that goes with it? We staggered under the weight of the concept we had just learned—in this world, it takes money to make money!

Let us all understand that such a statement has nothing to do with greed; it is merely a declarative sentence, a statement of fact, the truth of which is attested to by virtually every person involved in business, and surely by everyone here this evening as well. Now, I must tell you that I honestly don't really recall how much we made from our orange drink stand or even if the project died right there on the spot, but I do remember learning that lesson and learning it quite, quite well—it takes money to make money.

Let me amend that statement, for we all know why we are here this evening: It takes money to give our children the extras we all want them to have.

This evening is specifically designed as a fund raiser for our school. In a very few moments, you are going to start enjoying our student "carnival," sponsored by our own PTA, and we hope you will start spending as well, for every penny that you do spend will go toward our own student enrichment fund, and that fund directly benefits your sons and daughters, as all of us know and appreciate well enough to have come here tonight to this very special fund-raising event.

(*NOTE: At this point you might detail several points of interest or any other facts the audience might need to know in order to participate fully.*)

As you surely know, it takes more than just money to give our students the best; it takes you. It takes you, ready to participate; ready to enjoy the efforts of our students—your sons and daughters; ready to give for a cause you know is good, a cause you know will directly aid our children, a cause that will take what you give and give it back to your children in so many, loving ways.

So, let's get started, and while you're at it, be sure you stop by the main office some time during the evening. You see, I have this small orange drink stand set up, and I'd just love to see you there!

Thank you, and let's go!

SPECIAL DATA: Time of speech, a few minutes. If you are giving the opening speech for any program., from an evening of speeches to the student carnival mentioned in this opener, you should remember that you are the start of the evening's program and not the program itself, so keep the opening speech short. Look at this one for example; it gives a short anecdote related to the purpose of the evening, reminds the audience of the purpose of the activity, and then directs them to start the activity. That is, basically, the pattern of most opening speeches. You may also, if you want, outline the activities or highlight certain parts of the program as indicated in the speech above. Follow these guideliness, be enthusiastic, and your opening speech will be a success.

57

TOPIC: *Opening Speech for a School Dinner*

AUDIENCE: *Teachers; Parents; Administrators; Community Members*

I know, I know—when you're here for a dinner, and you see somebody like me stand up and begin to talk, it is not unusual for someone to poke his or her neighbor and comment that they should have had a burger and fries before they came. That is why I am delighted to announce that I have a gift for you this evening, and the gift is this—I'm hungry, too, so I shall be brief.

In fact, that's what I'd like to talk about for a brief moment—food. I know that all you have to do is look at me to appreciate that I have a long acquaintance with that subject, perhaps too close. Nonetheless, let's examine that subject; who knows, perhaps I might be able to whet your appetites for what is to come.

What do you think of when you hear the word "food"? Perhaps, as would many, you see a parade of items pass before your eyes—a roast chicken, spaghetti and meatballs, a hot dog with mustard, a T-bone steak, a double chocolate fudge cake, and other goodies that set our mouths to watering.

That, however, is not the only kind of food there is, and we all know it. Our literature abounds with reference to nonmaterial sustenance. For instance, Shakespeare wrote, "If music be the food of love . . ." (*Twelfth Night*), the Bible tells us, "Man does not live by bread alone . . . (*Matthew 4:4*), and I remember a poem from my youth that was written, I believe, by that great author, Anonymous, which goes:

> If of all things you are bereft,
> And in your store there is but left
> Two loaves, sell one and with the dole
> Buy hyacinths to feed your soul.

If I were to condense all of that magnificent wisdom into a single sentence, a statement that experience proclaims as a truth for us all, perhaps it would be this: While our physical bodies need real food to live and grow, the human spirit is fed on nourishment that goes far beyond the material.

Tonight, we come together to partake of one kind of food and to celebrate the other. In a few moments, we will join in sharing a fine meal, which I am certain we'll all enjoy, and I know we will come away from this evening physically satisfied. If there were nothing else; if that were all this evening offered, that would be fine, and we would all be satisfied, but I assure you, that is not all we will share tonight.

This evening we will also celebrate the food for the mind and spirit that is offered to our students on a daily basis in this school. Tonight, we will make an effort to appreciate the food that will nourish our children's minds and growing, developing personalities; food not found on the shelves of supermarkets or butcher shops or convenience stores; food offered only in the gourmet store that is otherwise known as Dwight Road Elementary School; food for thought; food that is turned into intellectual muscle; food that has added growth and agility and stability to a realm far beyond the physical. We, as parents and educators, have played a part in this growth, and have seen the results in our students—in our sons and daughters.

Make no mistake about it, ladies and gentlemen, this dinner is most certainly an outstanding time of fellowship for us, and we may enjoy and even revel in it, but we shall also band together afterward to exchange new ideas, to share our insights, and to explore the miracle of growth that we are privileged to witness in our children— our children who are nourished in the home and intellectually fed in Dwight Road Elementary each and every day.

To "break bread together" has always been a sign of friendship and togetherness, so it is fitting that we have come together to share this meal. We each "break bread" with our individual families; now let us break bread with our extended families, the parents and teachers of the children of this school.

So, by all means, let us feed our bodies tonight on the excellent fare about to be presented to us, but, like that poem I quoted a moment ago, let us "feed our souls" as well on this fine speaker we are about to hear, the fine companionship we will share at the tables, and the tastiness of the ideas we will take in and digest.

I don't know about you, ladies and gentlemen, but, personally, I can't wait to get started! *Bon appetit!*

SPECIAL DATA: This speech is an example of a tried-and-true rhetorical device. A single analogy or theme such as "food" is established, and the rest of the speech addresses the activity in terms of that theme. For example, we once heard a speaker liken elementary education to getting a car ready for a long journey, with the "long journey" being the individual's journey through life. Here the subject matter the school teaches its students—intellectual "food" that builds the mind —is compared to food we eat, which builds the body. You may well have other analogies in mind; by all means, use them!

58

TOPIC: *Opening Speech for a Program of Awards*

AUDIENCE: *Parents; Students; Teachers; Those Involved in the Awards*

Good evening, Moms and Dads, teachers, brothers and sisters, and all members of the various families represented here tonight, and welcome to the Fifth Annual Dwight Road Elementary Student Achievement Awards Night.

What a delight—what an absolute delight—it is to be able to stand before you to start off an evening of this nature!

You know, part of my job as principal of this school is to deliver bad news. For instance, I tell a child who has badly misbehaved just what the consequences of his or her actions will be; I advise parents of the placement of their son or daughter which is less than they had hoped; I call up to say that John or Mary has not done well and will most likely be repeating the year; your son threw a rock at another child; your daughter ran in the halls and caused another student to be injured. And so it goes; there are days when it seems to me that the negative side is all I handle.

At those times, I often have to pause for a moment and remind myself of something that Abraham Lincoln once wrote. In a letter to his friend, Josiah Speed, Lincoln stated, "I can see how a man can walk with his eyes on the mud and claim that life is nothing but doom, but I cannot understand how someone can lift his head to the starry heavens above and not be filled with wonder and hope for tomorrow." I remind myself to stop focusing on the mud and start concentrating on the starry heavens, and believe me, there is so much here at Dwight Road Elementary to be positive about!

I think about the fine education going on in each classroom in this building, with teachers opening young minds to a world of knowledge and wonder, and students seeing, discovering, learning, growing. I think about the very active and giving parents of our students who have contributed so much already, and who continue to give to the benefit of each and every child in this school. I think of our students, from the youngest right on to the upper elementary students, and the way in which I am so very privileged to see them grow, not only in body, but in mind and spirit as well. It is then that I stop looking at the mud and begin to appreciate the wonder of the stars and the heavens and the beautiful world that lies around us.

And that brings us to the delightful task that I have to perform tonight. I said it was a delight for me, and I mean that. Tonight, we will be concentrating on what is right with our schools; tonight we will focus on students who are not only doing what they should as students, but are going far beyond even reasonable expectations of success; tonight we will highlight and spotlight children who so live their lives that they renew our faith in humanity. Yes, tonight we will not be looking at the earth below but at the stars above, and we will be both amazed and privileged to see just how brightly they do shine.

The individual students to whom we will present awards this evening are outstanding in every way. They are a credit to this school, reflecting the fine education they are receiving during this critical and formative period in their lives. They are a credit to you, their parents, for the school has long recognized that education is a partnership, and without the home, the process is only half complete. We see, by the values and accomplishments of tonight's recipients, that the home has been an active and vital educational partner for these children. Finally, they are a credit to themselves, for within each one of them is that spark of love and honor and achievement and dedication to the good of others that they, as young as some of them are, have fanned into the flame that allows them to shine forth as stars.

So, yes, I am delighted; I am overjoyed to be a part of this evening's awards program. Tonight is an evening of fulfillment, an evening of joy, an evening of reminding ourselves that in the eyes of our children we see a bright future.

Let me say it again—What a delight; what a delight, indeed!

Let's get started!

SPECIAL DATA: Be aware of the composition of your audience. Although the award recipients are all elementary students, we can assume that the audience is composed of those who are, in some fashion, proudly related to the children—moms, dads, uncles, aunts, grandparents—all with flash cameras and gigantic grins. Yes, the children are the focus of the evening, but you are speaking primarily to the adults, and you can use language appropriate to that audience.

59

TOPIC: *Opening Speech for a "Parenting" Program*

AUDIENCE: *Parents of the Children in the School*

Let me begin with a question that I fully intend to answer myself, "Is there anyone more significant in a child's life than his or her parent?"

Now, I know what answer you expect me to give, but you're wrong, for the answer I pose is, "Yes, there are often people in a child's life who are, even if only for a while, more significant than Mother or Father!"

Wow, what a concept! Do I mean to stand here and tell you that there are individuals in your child's life who have more influence over your son or daughter than you do? Is that what I'm daring to say? Quite frankly, yes, there most certainly are.

Let me begin by telling you about a survey I once read that was conducted among a number of parents of upper elementary school children. The question asked those parents was, "What do you believe is the major concern, the biggest worry, of your children?" Well, the parents thought about it, and they came up with answers such as "not being able to earn a living" and "the destruction of the environment," and even "nuclear war," along with several other items of a dire nature. Then they asked the kids the same question. The overwhelming response of the children—their single biggest concern—was that the other kids in school would not like them, and that they would not be a part of "the group."

Now, that is what we, as parents, are often up against. Certainly, we can have an effect upon our children within the home, but let us be quick to realize that we can't keep even the youngest children in the home indefinitely. Indeed, even the youngest child's world is expanding at a phenomenal rate. Parents make their children a part of the home, we here at school try to make them a part of the community, and the TV and other mass media aim to make them a part of the world. Once in that community, once in that world, our children face a hundred, a thousand, an untold number of influences—all trying to become, if not more significant, at least as significant, as you, dear parents of our students.

In some cases, these influences are positive and provide for individual growth and achievement. We speak here of such organizations as the Scouts and various youth groups or religious organizations—you know the ones. But there will be other influences as well—those that will vie for your children's minds and souls, and I believe you are all familiar with these. You can be assured, for instance, that drugs and the drug culture will assault your child. Yes, you can be certain that your son or your daughter, somewhere along the line, will be offered a red-carpet entry into the worst that society has to offer.

When this happens, what safeguards do your children have? Only what we, as parents, may have happened to instill in them. Only those principles and patterns of behavior and values that have come out of the home; those qualities that have been instilled over the years by parents; instilled by love and through love, and in love and in the hope of the best possible future for each child.

A program like the one in which we are about to participate is invaluable in these most troubled times. If we cannot be that formative influence on our children, there are others who are waiting to step in and fill the need. We are, therefore, here tonight on a voluntary basis to learn about parenting skills, because we deeply desire to give our children the best of which we are capable. Toward the attainment of that goal, we will hear from several experts in the field.

(*At this point you might want to briefly detail the main features of the evening's program, including the individuals who will be speaking, and their topics.*)

Tonight's program is well worth our attention, our consideration, and our application. I know we will all be listening carefully, because the subject is so important to us all. Certainly, we will be considering the information we are given in terms of exactly how we may use it to be even better parents to our children. We want to take the ideas from this evening and apply them—not in some laboratory—but in our own homes, to give our children the best head start they can have as they prepare to step out into the world.

I, personally, am eager to get started; that world won't stop for our children, and we can't afford to wait either.

SPECIAL DATA: Consider carefully how you address an audience of parents for a program on parenting. Above all, do not tell them they are there to become good parents—they are good parents, and that's why they're there to learn even more. If there are teachers present also, this would be a good time to talk about the partnership of the school and the home. However you approach it, emphasize the need for the program and the benefits of it to everyone in the audience.

60

TOPIC: *Opening Speech for a Student Activity or Presentation*

AUDIENCE: *Parents, Students, and Teachers*

Good evening, ladies and gentlemen, and welcome to (*here mention the name of the presentation for the evening*).

You know, there are occasions when I wonder just how many times I have attended some special activity that is held here at our school. I can't begin to guess, of course, but certainly there must have been hundreds of occasions when we, in school, have presented something in this school that we label as "special."

Some of these "specials" have been given by groups or individuals from outside the school. We have had dramatic groups, magicians, singers with and without guitars, clowns, and a host of others, and almost every single one has been of value to us. We have enjoyed and appreciated their efforts.

Some programs have involved education in one way or another, whether through panel discussions between parents and teachers, insights given to us by an expert in the field jointly agreed upon by our Parent-Teacher organization, and other offerings that have enlightened us, informed us, and very possibly left us better parents and educators in the process. Certainly, these programs have been of great value to us.

And then we come to programs like the one we are about to experience this evening. I will tell you, and I will tell you honestly, these are the programs that I admire the most, enjoy the most, look forward to the most. This evening we will have the honor, privilege, and enjoyment of watching our students, our sons and daughters, our classmates . . . perform for you.

Tonight's performance is something on which they have worked very hard. I know this for a fact, as I attended several of their rehearsals and saw firsthand the effort and the dedication that went into every part, into every minute of what you are about to see.

I know of a certainty that I am going to enjoy what I am about to see, and I know that you will enjoy it as well.

Before we begin, however, there are a few things that your classmates, our students, your children want you to know.

(*NOTE: At this point, detail any specific instructions [e.g., please keep silent during . . .; no flash pictures . . .; hold your applause until . . . ; please don't use Exit 6 . . . ; etc.] the audience might need before the activity begins.*)

We really need your cooperation in order to have everything go according to plan for our hard-working and talented students. I have no fear in that regard, since I have counted on your cooperation in the past and have never been disappointed.

Before we start, let me say again that of all the programs this school offers and has offered over the years, it is student programs like the one we are going to see tonight that inevitably give me the most pleasure and enjoyment. So often, we send our children off to school, and, because we have so much that affects us in our modern world and so many demands upon our time, we may not notice that these children are doing something wonderful, something absolutely miraculous—they're growing! They are growing physically, to be sure, but they are growing in mind and in spirit as well. Every single day, their minds are expanding; they are learning, and, as a result, they are changing; they are maturing; they are developing to the point where they can present something as unique and special as the program we are about to see.

Is it not something truly wonderful to see all the weeks and months of intense effort finally come to its fruition? Isn't it exciting to see the children we know and love functioning as part of a team—as part of a group effort? Isn't it rewarding to view the results of knowledge and talent and the nurturing of both the home and the school? Isn't it a joy to be able to applaud the efforts of these, our children, as they present something that, in the final analysis, they have done for you—just for you? In short, isn't it great?

With that, let me get back to my seat, get out of the way, and let the important part of this evening begin.

Ladies and gentlemen, it is with the greatest pleasure that I present to you (*name of the production*).

SPECIAL DATA: *Any presentation involving just the students of the school will bring in an audience, and the larger the student cast, the larger the audience, particularly at this age level. Parents and cameras abound, and a full-sized gym can be so packed there is "standing room only." No offense to you, of course, but what they came to see is their child on that stage, so make your opening speech short and complimentary, and lead right in to the feature they all came to see.*

$$\boxed{\textbf{61}}$$

TOPIC: *Opening Speech for a Substance Abuse Program*

AUDIENCE: *Adults; Parents and Educators; Possibly Other Community Members*

Good evening, ladies and gentlemen, and welcome to what may well be one of the most significant programs you will ever see.

There are few things in today's world that terrify us more—both as parents and as educators —than the subject of tonight's program, the abuse of drugs. During the Middle Ages, the Bubonic Plague, also known as the "Black Death," devastated Europe, killing up to 60 percent of the population. The people of the time were powerless to do anything about it.

Today, we must not be deceived into thinking that plagues are a thing of the past. Plagues just as powerful and just as devastating most certainly do exist today, and there is a particularly virulent, dirty, and destructive plague that is in the process of ravaging our nation even now, at this very moment.

I speak, of course, of the plague that currently infests our streets, infests our social institutions, infests even our homes and our schools with its evil and devastation, as surely as the rats and fleas carrying the Bubonic Plague infested medieval lives. I speak, of course, of Drug Abuse, the subject of our program this evening.

If we need any assurance that the illegal use of drugs is a problem, we need only look about us. At one time, athletes on professional teams were individuals held in esteem, people whom we held up as role models for our children to emulate. While there are still athletes who struggle to maintain that image, scandal after scandal concerning these people and their continued abuse of drugs breaks upon the American people as we collectively wonder where our heroes have gone. At one time we respected the people we chose to represent and guide us, but, today, stories of corruption and drugs used for bribery or as a lead-in to debauchery reach into areas we once thought were, like Shakespeare's classic portrayal of Caesar's wife, "above reproach." The family, American business, the media—all those areas that were, at one time in our past, thought of as inviolate, have been violated by the plague of drugs—brought low before our eyes due to the destructiveness of drugs and drug abuse.

In each of the areas I've mentioned, there are individuals who have never been a part of the drug scene, who have kept their morality in the presence of depravity. We can respect and admire these individuals, and we do honor them. Nevertheless, we cannot afford to ignore this plague of our society and our times.

Why a program on drug abuse here? Why do we need to schedule an evening to learn about drugs? Why here in our own elementary school? These children aren't teenagers or gang members or young burn-outs; they're just kids. Surely, these children are too young to be affected in any way by drugs. Well, my friends, if any of you believes that, then you need this program most of all.

I have heard of a recent survey that indicated that children as young as third grade have become addicted to drugs in school, and even children in first grade and kindergarten have been exposed to drugs. I was told by an expert in the field that any administrator who believes that there are no drugs in his or her school is wearing a blindfold of willful ignorance. Personally, I am saddened and sickened by such knowledge, but I cannot dispute its truth. Drugs are a universal problem, and they are everywhere!

More to the point, however, is the fact that, if we want to do more than recognize the problem and worry about it; if we want to take steps toward a possible solution or at least attack that fortress of evil and give our children a fighting chance to resist and conquer, then right here and right now is most certainly the time and the place to start the educational process. We must begin to forge the armor our children most certainly will need to wear when we send them through the doors of this school and our homes and out into the world. That is true of every school and every home in our entire nation.

A program like this is a start—a first step, with many steps to follow. I take your attendance here tonight as indicative of your willingness to be a part of the solution; you care enough to be able to recognize the problem and you are willing to put in your time and effort to find solutions.

It is your children who will benefit.

Let's get started.

> *SPECIAL DATA: At some point in your speech, you may want to introduce panel members, giving their credentials or areas of expertise. At the conclusion of this speech, introduce the first speaker or presentation of the program. Drug abuse is a most serious problem, and an opening speech for a program on it should be serious; avoid humor.*

62

TOPIC: *Opening Speech for a Program Introducing the School*

AUDIENCE: *Parents and Community Members*

Good evening, ladies and gentlemen, and welcome to the fifteenth annual Dwight Road Elementary Open House Night!

Let's face it, we all like to show off from time to time. Think of it—do you remember that famous "Easter Parade" so popularized in New York where, come that fine spring day, people would stroll down Fifth Avenue to show off their finery? I think I can even recall Fred Astaire singing about it in some movie!

Now, let's add the fact that we are all curious. Someone once wrote, "Curiosity killed the cat," and some wise guy added, "Yes, but satisfaction brought him back again!" We all have within us that curiosity about places, about people, about life itself.

Add together a desire to show off and a natural curiosity, and what do you have? You have this Dwight Road Elementary Open House Night!

By now, your children have been in school a little over a month. To many of you, this means a new grade and new teachers and new assignments, while others may be with us for the first time, so everything is first-time new. Whatever the case, we expect that you will be curious about our school and our staff. From your children, you most certainly have heard stories and tales, and you are eager to see for yourself just what part of it is true. Oh, yes, you're curious.

And we . . . well, we're ready to show off a bit. May we be forgiven for that? I hope so. I know that few things are as obnoxious as someone who pats himself on the back and states, "Look how good I am!" I would not want you to get that impression of Dwight Road Elementary. Oh, no.

I will tell you, however, that it is hard to stand here and pretend that we are "just another school," when inside I am bursting with pride for our school, for our faculty, for our students, and for the high-quality education, growth, and learning that goes on in this place each and every day! I tell you, it is truly hard to be modest when you are as good as we are!

I hear some of you giggle at that, and, of course, you are right. I openly admit that I am very prejudiced about this school. As its principal, I get to see it from the inside out every single day. I get to see the efforts of an outstanding faculty who go far beyond what is required of them to bring the finest in education to our children—our students. I get to see a staff working together to see to the needs of each individual child. I get to see the children grow; I get to see them come into this building happy to be here and filled with anticipation for the good things that are going to happen.

In short, I am privileged, because I get to see this school at its very best day in and day out; each and every day it is in session, I get to experience all of it. Of course I'm prejudiced; this place is wonderful!

Don't take my word for it. In a few moments you are going to be invited to take an inside tour of this school; you will be invited to enter into the very classrooms in which your children spend their school day; you will meet personally with your child's teacher, and that teacher will be explaining what's taking place in that classroom and the thorough and highly efficient way in which the education of your son and daughter is being conducted. So, please don't take my word for it—see for yourself!

(*NOTE: If there are any procedural matters the audience needs to know, such as time considerations, or special exhibits to be seen, or room changes that should be observed, deliver them at this point. You may also deliver the same information at the end of the speech, as you see fit.*)

Before you go, however, I would like to say just one more thing. Personally, I am overjoyed to have this opportunity to introduce you to Dwight Road Elementary School. What we do here is a matter of public record, but I believe that once you see our school for yourself, once you experience what and how your children are learning, once you meet the people who care for your children . . . I believe that once you have done that, you will be as enthusiastic about it as your children are—as the teachers are—as I am!

Let's get started.

SPECIAL DATA: At the end of this speech, direct the audience as to their next move, whether that is leaving by certain exits, going to prescribed rooms, or where to get a cup of coffee. These "Open House" programs, or "Back-to-School Nights," are very popular.

$$\boxed{\textbf{63}}$$

TOPIC: *Opening Speech for a "School Board Candidates" Night*

AUDIENCE: *Adults Only; People Interested in School Board Politics or Election*

Good evening, ladies and gentlemen, and welcome to Dwight Road Elementary School's Annual "Meet the Candidates" Night, an activity sponsored by the Dwight Road Parent-Teacher Association for the continuing education of the parents and educators of this school and our community. This is the seventh year we have had the honor of holding this invaluable presentation, and we are delighted to continue the tradition.

American literary giant Samuel Clemens, better known as Mark Twain, had some major difficulties with the school board in his home town. Indeed, several public arguments took place at school board meetings, with Mr. Twain often being the loudest and most vociferous one present. It was during this time that Clemens wrote a scathing letter to the press in which he included this remark: God created the idiot. He did this for practice. When He had perfected the art, He made the School Board!

Of course, all that was over a hundred years ago, in another time and in another world, and, certainly, while we may look back at that particular incident and smile and even give a chuckle of appreciation for Mark Twain's acid wit, we are well aware—well aware—that nothing could be further from the truth in today's society, in today's educational scene. Given the intricacies of today's school systems, it has become a non sequitur; it simply does not make sense; it does not follow at all.

The men and women you see on this stage tonight are all running for the School Board of this community. Over the course of this evening, they will each be addressing you, making known to you their philosophies as well as their individual visions for the future of the schools in our community.

Each one of these people is qualified for a position on the School Board. If that were not so, they would not be here this evening. They all have sufficient support within our community to have their names placed on the ballot for the School Board election. If that were not so, they would not be here this evening. Each of them is concerned enough with the schools of our township that he or she is willing to put in hours of personal time and effort toward the good of the children of the community. If that were not so, they would not be here this evening.

But they *are* here this evening. They sit here before you, ready to present themselves to your attention and your scrutiny. They are ready to answer your inquiries; they invite your questions. They are qualified to be here; they are willing to be here; they are here because they want to serve your children, and because they want to serve you.

(NOTE: Introduce the candidates at this point; the following suggestion may be helpful: Introduce them in alphabetical order, by last name, as this precludes any charge of favoritism. Before the evening begins, ask each candidate or campaign manager to finish this sentence: "I believe . . ." relative to the campaign. Keep the answers on index cards and use them in your introductions, for example, "Our next candidate is Dr. Margaret Bailey, who believes that we can have quality schools and quality teachers without an increase in property taxes if we only use sound fiscal management tech-

niques." You can also add pertinent personal notes about each candidate. Special instructions, such as holding applause until the end, can be given here as well.)

Before we allow these candidates to address you, I'd like you to keep in mind that all of these people here tonight have more than enough tasks occupying their time and talents without serving on the School Board. They are all currently engaged in ongoing businesses and careers, and these place significant and heavy demands on them. Now they seek positions on the School Board of this community—positions that will require many hours of their time and a considerable amount of their energy.

What they are asking for is a series of long and weary nights, missed dinners, demands for time taken away from family and friends, and forgetting the meaning of the word "relax"—or that such a word is even in the dictionary. Out of a strong desire to serve the children, theirs and yours, who attend the public schools of this township, they seek a task that will frequently be thankless and often misunderstood.

That alone is worthy of our respect and our attention. Let us give both to our guests as we hear from them tonight.

SPECIAL DATA: School Board elections can often be heated and rather agitated, especially if there are opposing factions in the audience. Your opening speech must be impartial, and as an administrator and certainly as host for the evening, you must be impartial. Honor your guests, assume the very best motives, speak of them only in positive terms, and ask your audience to show them the proper respect.

64

TOPIC: *Opening Speech for a Guidance Activity*

AUDIENCE: *Adults—Parents of Students in the School*

Good evening, ladies and gentlemen. Before we get to this evening's activity, I'd like to share with you an anecdote I heard.

A friend of mine who works in a middle school told me of an actual incident in which she was walking down the hall of the school and was approached by a young man who was literally quivering with anticipation.

"Please help me," the boy all but sobbed, "I need guidance!"

"Of course, son," said my friend taking a step closer and placing a hand on his shoulder, I'll help you. Just try to relax for a moment, and we'll go to the Guidance Office. I know someone there who will listen to everything you have to say."

"But I need guidance!" shouted the youngster as he continued to jump up and down. "I need guidance, and I need it now!"

"Son," said my friend, becoming concerned about the agitated student, "I don't think you understood what I just said."

"No, Ma'am," moaned the lad, you don't understand. I'm new to this school; today's my first day, and if somebody doesn't guide me to the Boys' Room in the next couple of minutes, we're all going to be in trouble!"

Let's face it, we all need guidance at one time or another. Sometimes we need the kind of guidance that boy needed (I know I could use guidance opening those wonderful "child-proof" caps on medicine bottles; by the time I get them open, I no longer have the headache); and sometimes we need guidance of a far more serious nature (this might well include everything from career guidance through help dealing with a life problem such as marriage, the loss of a job, the death of a loved one, and so on). We all—each and every one of us—need guidance at one time or another.

Nor is guidance by itself enough. A child who has taken up with bad companions—with a street gang, let us say—gets a great deal of guidance from his peers, yet that is hardly the type of guidance we, as parents and educators, want for our children. Guidance alone is not enough; it must be good guidance. Good guidance starts with accurate information. By that I mean that I don't have to be burned in order to advise a student not to place his hand on a hot stove, but I had better know both the student and the curriculum before I recommend that child for enrollment in any particular course. That is only good common sense.

That is why a guidance activity like the one this evening is of such value to our students and to you. As parents, you are quite understandably concerned about the future of your children, now that they have reached their final year at Dwight Road Elementary and will, in several quick-passing months, be entering the departmentalized setup of the middle school.

Tonight's activity can go a very long way toward lessening both parental concerns and student concerns about that transition. Not only will you understand the workings of the middle school when you leave here this evening, but you will also be familiar with your children's tentative schedules of classes for next September, including any of the electives with which they may possibly be involved.

To accomplish this challenging task, we have with us this evening several outstanding individuals who are very familiar, one might even say intimately familiar, with the process and more than willing to share their expertise with us. Please allow me to introduce them to you; I'd like you to get to know them well.

(NOTE: At this point, you can introduce the people on the panel, stressing their credentials for participation in the guidance activity. See SPECIAL DATA section.)

I, for one, am certain that, with these fine individuals speaking to us and seeing to our inquiries, every concern will be addressed; every misunderstanding will be cleared up; and every question will be answered. This guidance activity is important to us because it is so important to our children. With this fine panel and the willingness of our guests to share and explain, I know we will leave here with a sense of satisfaction and appreciation for having taken the time and having attended this most valuable evening.

So let's begin.

SPECIAL DATA: An introduction of a participant during your opening speech should be short, and it should identify the person as qualified to participate in the evening's activity. For example, say, "May I present Mr. Joseph Smith, a veteran educator and currently head of sixth-grade guidance in the guidance department of Harris Middle School." Remember that your enthusiasm when you introduce these people will also go a long way toward making the audience receptive to what is to follow.

65

TOPIC: *All-Purpose Opening Speech*

AUDIENCE: *Suitable for All Adult Audiences*

Good evening, ladies and gentlemen, and welcome to this evening's activity. (*NOTE: Name your activity here.*)

I welcome the opportunity to open this evening's events. I love an opening, whether it be the opening of a play, or the opening of a restaurant, or the opening of a supermarket. At openings, everything is fresh and new; everything is at its best; everything glows with anticipation.

Yes, I love openings, but the opening I enjoy most of all is the opening of a mind. I tell you that as an educator, I have been present when a child's mind opens and learning takes place. What a privilege that is! What an honor! The student pauses, looks up at you, and you see the light begin to shine forth behind his or her eyes, and you know—you know—that student understands! For me, there are few greater moments than this particular time of wonder—the opening of a mind.

This is why I am so enthusiastic about my position this evening. I am getting the opportunity to open up a program that will, in turn, open up our minds; how can I help but be enthusiastic?

Considering the nature of this program and the people in it, I think we all have a right to anticipate something very special. Allow me, please, to show you what I mean.

(*NOTE: At this point you might consider doing one of three things: First, you can introduce each speaker or participant in the program. Second, you can state their names and their function in the program [e.g., "Next, we have Mrs. Helen Constable, who will explain how the cafeteria serves our students."]. Third, you can simply talk about the program or presentation in general terms.*)

So you see what I mean. This is a program that will serve us well in opening our minds toward fuller understanding.

Let me make a general statement and see if you agree with it. The statement is this: If we weren't interested in what's going on here, we would be somewhere else. I know that sitting through something you can't stand is akin to having root canal work done with an ice pick, but I also know that this is not the case this evening—and that is half the battle. There is interest here this evening, and you are eager to discover it. That is wonderful, because this program is ready to satisfy that interest—to satisfy it completely and efficiently.

That is the other half of the battle. It has been said that this world is filled with answers just waiting for people to search them out. If you have come seeking answers, you will certainly find them here.

Our evening promises to be both informative and enjoyable, so let's get started.

SPECIAL DATA: It is up to you to adapt this "all-purpose" speech to your situation; in fact, that is the essence of getting the most out of all the speeches in this section, as well as in the book as a whole. Take these speeches and try them out. Personalize each one by specific references to your school and to people, places, and situations with which your audience is familiar.

IN CONCLUSION

The opening speech, as we have suggested many times in this section, will set the tone for the entire evening that will follow. Nothing determines that tone more than your attitude and enthusiasm as you deliver that speech. Give the speech in a half-hearted, ho-hum manner, and the members of your audience will step over one another on the way to the nearest exit. Give it in a genuine manner, where it is obvious that you are sincerely anticipating what is to follow, and the audience will catch that feeling of anticipation and look forward to the program as well.

Go through the speech several times before the program. Be enthusiastic, and you'll open a program that will be enjoyed by all.

Section 4

"Until Next Time . . .": Effective Closing Speeches

Every program, every panel discussion, every presentation will come to an end. When that happens, it is not like a movie in a theater, where the audience just gets up and leaves when the picture is over. If this program is taking place in your school, and you have been in charge of it by introducing the entire program (see Section Three), then once the program finishes, the audience looks to you for direction on what to do next.

Of course, you could just stand up and say, "It's over; go home!" That would get rid of the audience, but they would leave feeling that something was missing, and they would be right.

If we may paraphrase an old cliché about teaching, you have "told 'em what they were going to see"; you have "let them see it"; and now your final task is to "tell 'em what they've seen." Your introduction and opening speech have set up the audience to be well disposed to the program or presentation. Then came the program or the speeches themselves. Now the program is finished, and your task is to close the activity by recapping the evening, making sense out of it and applying it to real life, and ending the evening on a positive note. The speeches in this section meet those criteria.

$$\boxed{66}$$

TOPIC: *Closing Speech for a PTA-Sponsored Activity*

AUDIENCE: *Parents; Teachers; Community Members*

That brings to a close this evening's activity. *(NOTE: You can mention the name of the specific event here.)*

Much has been said here this evening that we will want to take with us—to ponder and consider what we have learned and the views that we have shared. I know I speak for all of us when I say that this evening has been informative and stimulating, and I, for one, am glad to have had the opportunity to be here and be a part of it.

I would be remiss, however, if I did not pause for a moment to acknowledge those people who have worked hard and long to bring us a program of such high caliber. Since you are aware that this activity is sponsored by the Dwight Road Elementary Parent-Teacher Association, you know that the people on the committee responsible for this evening are part of that august group. They would probably prefer it if I just stopped now and allowed them to melt silently into the night, but in all conscience, I cannot allow all that hard work and dedication to go unrecognized.

Therefore, I'm going to ask the following people to stand, and I'd like to ask you, ladies and gentlemen, to hold your applause until just a little later.

(NOTE: At this point, call upon each person, using that person's name and affiliation. For example, "Chistine Mullery, PTA member, mother of a third-grader and a fifth-grader here at Dwight Road," or "Patrick Benson, PTA member, and one of Dwight Road Elementary's fifth-grade teachers." Have each one stand.)

Ladies and gentlemen, standing before you are parents and teachers who united together and worked together—and often commiserated with each other—in order to bring you the fine program we have just seen. I believe they deserve our thanks and our recognition.

(NOTE: At this point, lead the applause. When the applause has died down, and all are seated, conclude the meeting.)

Again, on behalf of us all, may I say thank you for a job not only well done, but well appreciated!

Finally, ladies and gentlemen, let me end by asking if you realize just how significant is the achievement of these people you have just applauded. Certainly, the program we witnessed was of great merit to us as parents and as educators, and we applaud the sensitivity to our needs that brought such a pertinent and marvelous presentation here tonight, but it goes far deeper than that.

The people I have just introduced to you represent the work of parents and the work of teachers in a joint effort—an effort to bring us something that will ultimately benefit our children both in the home and in the school. As such, they are a living example of the value of cooperation between parents and educators.

One occasionally (or, perhaps more than occasionally) gets the impression from the news media that the two groups are nothing more than separate armed camps, ready to do battle. While the sensational sells papers and raises TV ratings, it does not describe the people I have just introduced. These people, who worked so hard together, these people you have just applauded—these people represent the reality here at Dwight Road Elementary. Parents deeply interested in the growth, development, and welfare of the children here have joined hands and hearts and minds and talents with teachers who are deeply interested in the growth, development, and welfare of the children here. In working together on this PTA-sponsored activity, they have produced something very special and wonderful.

Remember, tonight's activity was brought to you by our own Parent-Teacher Association—and that is no small accomplishment!

> *SPECIAL DATA: The closing speech for any activity is extremely important. Remember that when it is your turn to sum up or close a program. Keep up the enthusiasm; allow your voice and your entire body language to tell the audience that they witnessed a superb program—that it was really special. If you are excited and enthusiastic, your audience will be, too.*

67

TOPIC: *Closing Speech for a Fund Raiser*

AUDIENCE: *Adults—Parents, Community Members, Teachers*

Ladies and gentlemen, allow me to ask you a question: Do you somehow feel a bit lighter now than when you came? I know, I know, that's an old joke—probably asked by Columbus of Ferdinand and Isabella when he was getting his ships together for that special trip to the Indies.

It is time now for this fund raiser to close; time for us to shut up the exhibits; time, now that you have participated so generously, for you to be going on home; time now to leave this place to the mercies of the cleaning crew.

It is also time to express our thanks to those people, both groups and individuals, who did so much to make this evening such a success.

(NOTE: At this point you might want to introduce the people responsible either as a group or individually, depending upon your assessment of the situation and / or time constraints.)

Please join me in recognizing their efforts. (*Lead the applause.*)

You know, I really believe that the vast majority of people don't mind attending these fund raisers and parting with a little cash if they can see to it that they are getting value for their money. In all reality, nobody asks any more why we are holding an activity like this one; no one ever assumes that any activity, school club, or student organization does not need cash. After all, when was the last time you walked into a supermarket and they gave you that T-bone steak you were eyeing on the basis of your good looks, your intelligence, or the fact that you really are a nice person? Yes, we all realize that in today's world, we need the funds.

Rather, I think the problem comes in when we, the giving public, perceive that what we give is being misused; is not going to the people or cause for which it was originally intended; is being used for the gain of the few rather than the good of the many. When we see on TV that some fraud has been unearthed that has not only bilked contributors, but has actually harmed the very people that it claimed it would help—those who stirred our hearts in the first place—we begin to feel the resentment. That's when the anger starts to grow.

And that, ladies and gentlemen, is precisely why you should be overjoyed that your purses and wallets are lighter and that this evening has been the success that it has. Here, there is no uncertainty; here, there is no cover-up; here, the maxim applies—what you see is what you get. For this evening, 100 percent of the funds collected go to the cause for which we had this activity. That's a fact, and you are more than welcome to check it out!

When a crime is discovered and the police are called in, the first thing they look for is the motive for the crime. To do this, they try to answer the question, "Who profits from it?" Now, there has been no crime here this evening—far from it—but I believe that we are justified in asking the same question. After all has been cleared away and swept up; after boxes of materials have been stored away for next year; after the sponsors and volunteers have rested, the question remains, "Who profits from it?"

The answer is that we do. Certainly, we as parents and educators will be no richer tomorrow morning, but our children will be the ones to benefit from the proceeds of this evening's program; our children will profit from the funds that will now be available to bring them both the necessities of learning and those small and exciting extras that enhance education; our children will reap the rewards of our giving this evening.

And, when our children profit, so do we . . . so do we. Let me repeat that—when our children profit, so do we . . . most certainly, absolutely, without any doubt, 100 percent of the time . . . so do we!

It has been a wonderful evening, and, all humor aside for a moment, we really have all had an excellent and enjoyable time being parted from our money, an excellent time that has been made all the more wonderful and gratifying by the knowledge of where that money will be going and who will benefit from it.

That's a good feeling and a good note on which to wish us all a good night.

Thank you for coming; have a safe trip home!

> *SPECIAL DATA: A concluding or closing speech is your last chance at that particular audience. Therefore, anything you want them to know had better be said to them before they leave. Stress the honesty and integrity of the fund raiser, particularly if any others in your area have recently been in question. Remember that the final remarks an audience hears are generally those that are best remembered. Present them with enthusiasm, and frankness, and end the evening or program on an upbeat note.*

68

TOPIC: *Closing Speech for a School Dinner*

AUDIENCE: *Adults; Possibly Students, Community Members, Parents*

What a fine evening this has been, has it not? We have had fine food along with fine companionship and fine speeches, and now, it is a fine time for us to say, "Good night!"

As far as the food is concerned, would I be forgiven if I told you that I'm "fed up?" It was indeed innovative and delightful, and the only complaint I heard all evening long was that there were no third and fourth helpings. In fact, I think that complaint came from me!

If you are in agreement with me so far, then you will also want to join me in thanking the people who have spent a good part of their time recently in putting together this well-run affair tonight. Please hold your applause and allow me to introduce them to you.

(*NOTE: At this point, introduce the committee, or whoever was responsible, possibly asking each one to stand and be recognized. If the dinner was prepared and served by parents [we've been to a number of those], be sure to have the "crew" step out of the kitchen. Finally, lead the applause with something like the following remarks.*)

This evening, we have reaped the rewards of their hard work. Therefore, let's show them just how much we appreciate their efforts.

Now, as for the company, who could ask for better? Often in home and school situations, we hear about one another through our children, who many times exaggerate or imagine things. How wonderful, therefore, to be able to meet face to face as friends across the dinner table! Certainly, at our table, we laughed, shared, informed, and enlightened one another. Whatever we knew or thought we knew when we sat down has been positively altered by the reality of the outstanding companionship we have all been privileged to share tonight.

And the speeches . . . ah, yes, the speeches. We will remember them . . .

(*NOTE: If you know that you are going to be the closing speaker, an effective technique is to take some notes during the speeches on the essence of each one; during your conclusion, restate the message and link it to the speaker. For instance, "We will long remember Dr. Smith's insights into the value of true communication—nor will we forget Mrs. Hemming's hilarious recounting of a child's-eye view of kindergarten."*)

These were fine speeches indeed, and now, please let us join one final time in showing our speakers just how much we appreciate their efforts this evening. (*Lead the applause.*)

It is time for us to end this evening and take up our private lives again.

(*NOTE: If anyone remains who has contributed to the evening and not been recognized and thanked by this time, do it now. If all parties have been thanked, continue with the speech.*)

I have it on the very highest authority that after a few hours of darkness, the sun will rise tomorrow morning and life will continue on as before. What we shall have tomorrow, however, is the memory of tonight with all its insights and learning, its laughter and reflection, its introductions and reacquaintances. I am thankful that we set aside this time to be together and resolve that we most certainly will do it again, very soon. Thank you all for a wonderful evening. Good night!

SPECIAL DATA: One of your tasks in this kind of closing speech is to be the spokesperson for the assembly in thanking the people who have put on the dinner or program you have just collectively enjoyed. We cannot repeat it too many times—the key here is your enthusiasm. Even if the food has disagreed with you and what you want most in the world is to get home and take your shoes off and have a nice antacid pill, don't rush these "thank you's" and don't toss them off as if they were an afterthought. A properly delivered "thank you" at the end of an affair like this can reap rich rewards in good feelings and rapport.

$$\boxed{\textbf{69}}$$

TOPIC: *Closing Speech for a Program of Awards*

AUDIENCE: *Award Recipients, Parents, Relatives, Community Members*

Of course, I cannot speak for you, ladies and gentlemen, but I will speak for myself when I say that this has been a very exciting evening.

Please allow me to share with you a personal memory. Many years ago, when I was a child, I loved to go to the movies. Those were the days, back when Thomas Edison ran the projector, when movies still spoke civilly and without substituting gutter language for wit and calling it entertainment. Those were the days of the "double feature" and the newsreel . . . the newsreel being the TV news in the days when not everyone had a TV.

I remember one newsreel in particular in which there was a medal given to an athlete who stood on a raised platform. Perhaps it was an Olympic event, but I honestly cannot recall; in fact, I don't recall any of the particulars. What I do remember is the fact that, as they placed the medal around the athlete's neck, a tear rolled down his cheek and the camera cut away to his coach, and the coach was crying as well. That I remember.

I recall it, because it made such a deep impression on me. Suddenly, even as a child, I could empathize, I could feel what that athlete was feeling, that combination of gratitude and love and fulfillment and relief and pride and all those emotions rolled up into one gigantic emotional state that was almost beyond comprehension, and certainly beyond expression in mere words. Even though I was still a child, my own eyes filled with tears. And I knew something else besides; I knew what that coach was feeling. I knew that for him, all the hours of training and stress and decisions and arguments and apprehensions and pain were suddenly, in one grand, wonderful moment, erased from his memory and all of it, all that he had gone through was suddenly worthwhile, worth whatever it took in terms of human effort to get to that point.

And that, ladies and gentlemen, is rather how I felt this evening as I joined you in the privilege of watching these awards being presented to the students of this school—to your sons and daughters. I want you to know that I am filled with pride—pride in everyone who is a part of this program.

I speak now to you students who have won an award this evening. That you have the award is something very special, and these and similar awards have been kept for years by people just like you, to remind them of the occasion. I want you to remember that the awards you received are not gifts from us to you. Oh no; they are for your efforts, for the fine job that you have done in the many areas for which you received these honors. I also want you to know that these awards stand for how we feel about you. You see, you have made very special efforts, and we realize that. Not only do we realize your special efforts, but we feel that you are very special—very special indeed. No matter what the future brings, these awards, which now are yours, will always stand for that.

I speak now to the parents who are here this evening and the teachers and the coaches. This may be an elementary school, and the sports represented may not be at the level that you will find on your TV on a Sunday afternoon, and the science awarded may not be of the caliber for a Nobel Prize in Physics, and the writing may not impress a Pulitzer Prize committee . . . this may be an elementary school, and we may be small in size, in stature, and in comparison to the adult world, but we are gigantic when it comes to spirit. That spirit has been more than amply represented here tonight. The effort put in by each student is proportionally just as great, just as heroic, just as monumental as that of any counterpart in an older and bigger world. Your children are to be congratulated.

And you are to be congratulated as well. Yes, I'm talking about you. You see, whether it is outside on the playing field, in the structured atmosphere of the classroom, or within the love and comfort of the home, there is, for every award that has been presented here tonight, a very special someone who guided, a someone who helped, a someone who directed, and—most important—a someone who cared. In case you haven't realized by now, that's you, and I really wish we had an award we could present to each and every one of you as well.

In a way, perhaps we do, because if you will look at the students who have received the awards this evening, most certainly you will see your awards, too. They are truly our living awards. We get to see them each day, and you parents get to take them home.

Now, as we take our awards and make our way home, let us cherish this time as a very special evening to remember. It has been a good night—a very good night indeed!

> *SPECIAL DATA: Everybody loves awards. This includes getting awards and watching the people we love get awards. If the event is to honor a large number of children, you can rely on having it well attended. In closing such an evening or program, you will want to congratulate everyone who was part of the event, and to indicate how significant and meaningful these awards are. Finally, any closing speech on an awards program that includes praise for the parents as well as the students (as does this) is certain to be remembered and appreciated.*

70

TOPIC:	*Closing Speech for a "Parenting" Program*
AUDIENCE:	*Adults—Parents, Teachers, Concerned Community Members*

What a wonderful evening this has been! How we have laughed together and shared together, and I believe that everyone here will agree with me when I state that we learned together as well. Oh, yes, this has been a very special time indeed.

Now, as we approach the close of this special time, I think that it is altogether fitting and proper for me to recognize the people who were involved in bringing us this wonderful activity.

(*NOTE: Here you might introduce the organizers of the affair. You might also wish to recognize each of the speakers with a short comment or reference to his or her speech. See the second NOTE in Speech 68 for a description of that technique.*)

Ladies and gentlemen, will you please join me in acknowledging the efforts of these fine people in bringing us this program tonight. (*Lead the applause.*)

You know, our world is highly regulated, and depending upon what you desire, your path is fairly well prescribed. For instance, should you wish to be a teacher, you know that you face four years of college and that the final year involves doing practice teaching under an approved mentor. Then will come your first position and your teaching certification. That's simply the way it is, and you know that it is going to be that way from the time you first express your desire and plan to be a teacher to your high school or college counselor. That's it—that is what you must do in order to prepare to be a teacher.

Or, suppose that your desire is to be a doctor. Again, your schedule of preparation for that is prescribed, and you know what you will be going through. You are aware that you will go through college, then medical school, then an internship and a residency. You are aware of all that's needed—from the years of tireless effort required, right down to the names of the courses you must take in the college or university you will be attending. This is what you must do in order to prepare to be a doctor. It would be ridiculous to suggest that an individual feels like being a doctor, rents an office and puts out a sign, and is a doctor by virtue of those actions. No, there is a prescribed path.

The list goes on, limited by no means to the two professions I just mentioned. Whatever we might choose to be, there is a "road map," there is a "course of study," if you will, that tells us where to go and what to do—a very real aid in preparing us for the careers in which we wish to spend most of our adult lives, whether we want to be lawyers, auto mechanics, investment bankers, or plumbers. There are things to be learned, call them "foundational knowledge" or "tricks of the trade," in order to do the job efficiently and effectively. This is evidentially true of every task on earth, I believe, except one.

Parenthood comes upon us unawares. Now, I don't mean by that that we have no idea of how we became parents; certainly, we are well aware of the physiology of the process. I mean the eighteen-plus-year job that awaits us once the child is born. I mean the task of being parents. Most of us are good parents, and our childen are living examples of our care and love and concern; however, we didn't get the training we would have gotten to be pharmacists and secretaries, or electricians and salespersons. All of us have parenthood dropped upon us without any preparation or training, other than material we may have gleaned from books on the subject or the advice of our own parents, which, in many cases, worked for them in the past but not for us in the here and now.

That is why a program like the one in which we have been privileged to participate this evening is so special and so necessary. Allow me to pose a few questions for you to consider: Did you learn something tonight that you will put into practice in your home? Did you gain a special insight into a problem with which you have been dealing? Do you understand some behavior of your children that has previously puzzled you? Will what you have experienced tonight be of help to you in the days—in the years—to come? I know the answers I would give to these questions, and I am reasonably assured that they are your answers as well.

For that alone, this evening has been invaluable. As it was also insightful and entertaining, we can not only appreciate it; we can use it to help us through our tomorrows.

> *SPECIAL DATA: Let us give you one word of warning on all this: Under no circumstances do you suggest that a program like this is going to help them be better parents, or, as we once heard, "become the parents you should be." An audi-*

ence sitting there trying to figure out if you just insulted them and called them rotten parents is not an audience well disposed to accepting what has been said. A concluding speech like this, therefore, should be delivered in a very sincere manner, with a "we're-all-in-this-together" attitude.

71

TOPIC: *Closing Speech for a Student Activity or Presentation*

AUDIENCE: *Students and Parents*

I have one question for you: Wasn't that wonderful?

It would be so easy just to say that the evening is at an end and dismiss this gathering. It would be easy, because we are all eager to go to our children and see them and tell them what a fine job they have done, and how we appreciate their efforts and the time they have spent in bringing this activity to us.

As I am certain you will appreciate, however, they will be a while yet cleaning up and getting ready to meet you, and I am going to take those very few moments to say a few things that need saying.

First of all, activities like the one we have just witnessed do not just "happen." Rather, they are the result of organization, planning, and countless hours of hard and often frustrating work. Certainly, this is true for the students you have just seen, but it also applies with particular emphasis to the directors and other adults who have helped our children, as the popular expression goes, "be the best they can be."

Allow me to present them to you now.

(*NOTE: Mention all the adults who are a part of the student presentation. Be sure to name not only the teacher-director and other teachers who have participated, but all parents who have helped. You may even wish to say, for example, "Mrs. Jones is a class mother at our school," or make other similar comments. Also, make certain the director knows you are going to be making these introductions so that he or she will be available to be introduced following the presentation, rather than off somewhere, helping with cleanup. Plan ahead!*)

Let's show these fine people just how much we appreciate their outstanding efforts with our children and the massive amount of their personal time they have put in to make this evening a success. (*Lead the applause.*)

Before we go, let me ask you a question. What is it that we have seen tonight? Of course, there is the obvious answer; we have viewed a student presentation of James M. Barrie's "Peter Pan," (*insert the appropriate description of your student activity*), but we have seen much more than that. We have seen the end result of a great deal of hard work on the part of a great many students, teachers, parents, and all concerned, but we have seen much more than that. We have seen adorable children, clever costumes, and innovative dance, and we have heard some fine music both played and sung, but we have seen much more than that. However much we have been enthralled and entertained and had our hearts melted by what our children have done this evening, we have experienced much more than that.

Tonight we have been privileged to watch our children grow, to see them mature, to experience them as they take one more step toward becoming the fine people we know and pray they will be. The ones who danced—were they the same ones who, just last year, were tripping over the coffee table in the living room and occasionally banging into walls for no reason at all? The ones who sang so sweetly and charmingly, were they the same ones who, just last year, were screaming at a brother or sister at one-hundred-plus decibels? Those who spoke those lines and enthralled us with their acting skills, were they the same ones who, just last year, couldn't remember their home address or who sat blankly staring at the TV screen as if in a coma? These children who remembered lines, remembered rehearsal dates, memorized lyrics to songs, recalled intricate patterns of movement—tell me, were they the same ones who, just a year ago or perhaps only yesterday, had forgotten to take out the garbage for 37 days in a row? Yes, these are the same children—the same children with a difference.

You see, they are growing; each and every day brings them closer to maturity; each and every activity like this one teaches them more about life and adds more nurturing soil for the quick-growing tree. Each day spent with you and with us here at the school allows them to expand positively in mind and body and spirit.

What a privilege it has been for all of us—for you and for me —to be allowed to be a part of that process!

Thank you for coming. Good night!

SPECIAL DATA: Student presentations are almost always well attended. In fact, a safe general rule is: "The more children involved in the activity, the bigger the audience at the time of the presentation." The auditorium is likely to be overflowing with parents, grandparents, and relatives by the score. This is an excellent opportunity for you to promote a great deal of school-community good will and get that audience well disposed toward the school.

72

| TOPIC: | *Closing Speech for a Substance Abuse Program* |
| AUDIENCE: | *Parents and Community Members* |

Ladies and gentlemen, we have participated in something very special this evening. I have the sense of someone standing on the beach during a storm, who has just been struck by a huge wave. I feel overwhelmed, apprehensive, and frustrated by a personal inability to turn back the tide. After what we have just seen and heard, I believe that is a very apt analogy.

I want to thank our panel (*or our guest speaker*) for the wonderful job done on this very difficult problem (*turning toward the panel or speaker*). Your expertise is obvious, your presentation was riveting, and your commentary was so insightful as to provide us with ample food for thought for some time to come.

I applaud your efforts, and I know that the ladies and gentlemen of the audience wish to join me in thanking you for a most informative and helpful presentation. (*Turn back to the audience and lead them in applause for the panel or guest speaker.*)

(*NOTE: If you want to publicly recognize or thank any individual or people who were instrumental in the presentation, this is the place to do so.*)

You have given us so very much to think about—so much to consider. Some of what you have told us tonight, I would—quite frankly and speaking only for myself—I would rather not have heard; I would rather not have been aware of. I don't want to believe that second- and third-graders are hooked on drugs; I don't want to believe that there are kindergarteners and first-graders who are handicapped and disabled because they were born crack-addicted; I don't want to believe that there are individuals who will haunt a school yard or lurk on the way home carrying a selection of Hell in tiny packages to be passed out to our students—our children, our sons and daughters. No, everything in me that wants the best for our kids; that wants their childhood be a time of growth and laughter and learning and wonder . . . everything in me that loves those children does not want to hear of these horrors, of these living nightmares that surround and threaten the ones we care for so very much. No, I don't want to hear it at all, and I am certain that many of you will join me in that feeling.

And yet, because we do love our children, we cannot help but hear it. To close our eyes to the drug problem, however horrid and distasteful it may be, is to invite disaster. It is said that knowledge is power, and let us hope that is true. In the knowledge that we gained tonight from these speakers (*or this speaker*), there is the promise that at least we have some armor to don when we set out to fight the monster called *drug abuse*.

Not only are we aware of the problem, the extent of the problem, and the process by which that ominous specter, that omnivorous monster threatens to entrap our children, but because of that awareness, we know better how to approach the problem and, most important, how to talk with our children about it.

It may not be possible for us to stop drugs or to eliminate the drug culture or even make a dent in the general availability of drugs, but it is possible for us to affect our children in order that they may not only be aware of the dangers that face them, but may be armed with a knowledge and a resolve that will allow them to say NO—to turn away from the allure of drugs. That is possible; that is within our grasp, and that is the worth and value of a program like the one we have just witnessed here this evening.

There is a saying, "Ignorance is bliss," but only, to finish the quote, "when it is folly to be wise." With drugs, as we have learned this evening, it is the sheerest of follies to be ignorant about the problem, for that ignorance will do nothing more than allow the problem to proliferate. Rather, "Knowledge is bliss," because with that knowledge comes the resolve to do something about it. For the sake of our children, we will. That we promise and covenant—for the sake of our children, WE WILL!

We leave here tonight with just such knowledge and with just such heightened resolve. We have learned from what has been presented to us this evening, and that, added to the personal resolve of every parent and educator here tonight, will be to the ultimate benefit of those we so deeply love—our children.

This program is over now, and I wish you a good evening, but—more important—with what we have learned and our devotion to the good of our children, I wish you a better tomorrow.

SPECIAL DATA: There are very few people who do not appreciate the fact that drugs and drug abuse are a social horror; recognition is constantly growing that drugs present a problem everywhere, from those "mean streets" of the city right on down, sadly and unfortunately, to the halls of the elementary school. Knowledge of the subject is essential, but once that is established, what counts is action. The closing speech above is a gentle reminder of that fact, and a rea-

sonable call to action. If time permits, you can add an explanation of the programs your school offers, and invite parent participation.

73

TOPIC: *Closing Speech for a Program Introducing the School*

AUDIENCE: *Adults—PTA Members; Community Members*

You know, I am certain—I mean, I am positive that I just heard one of our fathers over here say to his wife, "Oh, no! Don't tell me we have to listen to this guy again before we can get to the coffee and doughnuts!"

Well, I have some bad news and some good news for you, sir. The bad news is yes, you do have to listen to me one more time, but the good news is that I shall be very brief, and the doughnuts are well worth waiting for!

Part of the reason I am addressing you again is that this evening has come to an end, and I really don't want you to leave without, in some way, recapping the evening—summing up our experience together tonight.

(*NOTE: At this point, if the evening has involved a program of some sort in which certain parents, teachers, administrators, etc., participated and presented materials, it would be proper to thank them and acknowledge their efforts. If it was the sort of activity where parents visited rooms on their own and listened to the teachers tell about their classes, then you might want to thank the faculty in general for their cooperation and participation. Suit your acknowledgment to the occasion, then lead the applause.*)

Now you have seen the school and had an opportunity to listen to the teachers talk about their classes (*a subject on which they can grow quite eloquent*) and to meet with all of us in the Main Office. Now you have had a chance to see the physical plant where your children spend a very large part of the day, along with meeting and getting to know the people who are in charge of their education during that time. In short, you have been introduced to Dwight Road Elementary School, and we have, together, taken the first step toward truly knowing each other—perhaps the first step toward becoming friends.

There is an old story I once heard about an evil prince who wanted to discredit a wise man whom the people loved. The evil prince thought up a plan to do this in which he would disguise himself as a peasant and go to the marketplace where the wise man taught. In his hand the prince would hold a dove. When the time came, the prince would ask the wise man one question: "Tell me, wise man," the Prince would ask, "this dove which I hold in my hand, is it alive or is it dead?"

Now, this was a trick question, because however the wise man answered, he would be wrong. If he said the dove was dead, the prince would open his hand and let the bird fly away; but if the wise man said the dove was alive, the prince would crush the bird in his hand and let it fall dead to the ground. Either way, it would appear that the wise man was wrong and could not even tell the difference between a bird that was alive and one that was dead.

The next day came, and the evil prince took the dove with which he intended to trap the wise man and went to take his place among the crowd in the marketplace.

With the dove in his hand, he faced the crowd and the old man. "Tell me, wise man," he shouted in a loud voice, "is this bird alive or dead?"

The crowd hushed, and all attention was drawn to the scene as the wise man turned and confronted the prince.

"That which you hold in your hand," the wise man said as he sighed gently, ". . . why, it is . . . what you make of it."

I said a moment ago that tonight we have taken the first step toward knowing each other and possibly ending up as friends. We stand with that bit of knowledge, that starting point of a relationship, in our hands, and while we are very far from being evil princes or even good princes for that matter, we hear the same response and know that the words are for us: "It is what we make of it!"

Let us end this evening on an optimistic note. Let us believe that this night is the start of a relationship between the home and the school that will, like a brilliant dove, take flight and mount the sky on silver wings. Make no mistake about it, it is within our power to achieve that goal. "It is what we make of it!"

We are so glad you came; we are so glad you've gotten to know our school; we are overjoyed that we have started on the path of becoming friends. Good night!

> *SPECIAL DATA: These events are always well attended; parents are curious, and their children have spoken of nothing else for a month. You want the parents to leave with a feeling that they are welcome and that you consider them a part of the school; you want to establish a working rapport that will serve well in all future endeavors together. Make this speech upbeat and stress the abiding partnership of the home and school; tell parents what a fine and upstanding school their children are attending*

74

TOPIC: *Closing Speech for a "School Board Candidates" Night*

AUDIENCE: *Adults—Parents, Teachers, Community Members*

If elections are a democratic process, then the process is for everyone—for those who agree and for those who disagree; for those who are for "our side," whatever that may be, and for those who are against; for those who make us nod in agreement and for those who cause us to shake our heads in disbelief. The opinions of all sides must be heard, and the minority opinion must be respected as much as that of the majority. What's more, this must take place in an atmosphere where all may express those opinions free from threat of reprisal.

We have had an excellent opportunity to witness democracy in action this evening. I am certain, ladies and gentlemen, that you will wish to join me in thanking the people who have made this evening possible.

(NOTE: At this point, introduce the people who worked on arranging the evening, and lead the audience in a round of well-deserved applause for their efforts.)

I ask you, what would a "Meet the School Board Candidates" Night be if it were not for the participation of the School Board candidates themselves? If we may agree on anything, certainly it is that their time is precious. Recognizing that fact, we cannot help but be grateful that they would take the time and make the effort to join us here this evening in order that we may all be better informed for the upcoming election.

I, for one, wish to thank them for their desire to serve and for their presence here this evening.

(*NOTE: You can use the "I believe" statements suggested in Speech 63, Opening Speech for a "School Board Candidates" Night, to sum up the stands of the candidates and to recap the evening as well.*)

Ladies and gentlemen, these are our candidates for the School Board of our community. Please join me now in showing them our appreciation for their presence this evening. (*Lead the applause.*)

On a personal note, I'd like to thank you, ladies and gentlemen of the audience. The rightness or wrongness of it aside for a moment, occasions such as school board elections can get, let us say, "rather heated." Perhaps this is only natural because these elections have so much to do with the people whom we love the most—our children. Events like tonight's "Meet the Candidates Night" have the potential for becoming overcharged emotionally, and I have been present when those emotions have boiled over. The reason doesn't matter, for both sides believed that they were in the right. The end result was that all sides ended up saying things they did not really mean, and that they would gladly have retracted later. When "later" came, however, they were no longer able to do so, much to their sorrow.

Therefore, I congratulate and thank you, ladies and gentlemen, for your conduct here this evening. In true democratic fashion, you listened to all sides, even those with which you did not agree. When it came time for questions, yours were insightful, probing, to the point, and most informative, leading us to an examination of the facts and the issues rather than personalities, and I know that I learned a great deal from them; I'm sure we all did.

Our thanks to the candidates who presented their positions so well, and to all those who worked so hard to make this night possible.

Good night, and don't forget to vote!

SPECIAL DATA: In some "Meet the Candidates" programs, everything runs smoothly, but there are others in which knock-down-drag-out arguments occur that can "blow the roof off the place." On at least one known occasion, an irate citizen had to be removed physically by a local police official. If an audience has remained civilized in the face of political debate, they are to be congratulated. Thank everyone equally; don't make judgments.

75

TOPIC: *Closing Speech for a Guidance Activity*

AUDIENCE: *Mixed Audience: Parents and Probably Students*

Ladies and gentlemen, as we conclude this evening—and a wonderful evening it has been—let us pause just a moment longer and show our appreciation to several individuals, some of whom you have seen and some who have worked behind the scenes. They have all made this a very worthwhile and fulfilling evening.

(*NOTE: At this point, introduce the organizers or implementers of the program as well as recognizing any special efforts. You may wish to check out some of the techniques for acknowledgment and showing appreciation that have been mentioned earlier in this section.*)

Now let's hear it for their efforts on our behalf! (*Lead the applause.*)

Tonight has been an outstanding example of the value of a Guidance mechanism in our schools. I believe that as we end this evening, we are better informed and more confident about what is to come for our children when they enter the middle school than we were at the start of tonight's program. I will add to that one other valuable quality as well—we are far less apprehensive about that future, because with knowledge comes a light for the darkness; knowledge conquers uncertainty every single time.

Some of us might like to conceive of ourselves as "self-made" individuals; people who "did it alone"; people who did it "our way," who neither asked for nor had a need of guidance. Most of us, however, know just how untrue and unrealistic a picture that presents. From an older brother or sister teaching us the proper way to ride a bicycle, to our Mom or Dad coming down hard on us for a wrong we have committed, to the kids on the block with their unspoken rules on how to belong to the group, to school and that one "special" teacher who helped us to understand in a very special way, to that inspiring person who took the time to get us interested in our life's work, to the many along the way who taught informally and gave suggestions and aided us, sometimes pushing and sometimes gently leading in the right direction—all, all of these people have played a part in shaping us as the individuals we are today. All have become a part of us; all of them have offered guidance in one way or another.

That need, the need for guidance in our lives, continues even now, in our adult lives. We may seek that guidance now from a spouse, a business partner, a member of the clergy, a special consultant, or just a friend, but we still need and still seek out some form of guidance.

What was true for us and is true for us, is true for our children as well. They have the same need for direction that we do—the same need to be guided from time to time. Certainly, you, as parents, provide that guidance at home, and we in the schools try to do our part to guide our students in the paths they should take. I have seen the school rise to the occasion, both formally and informally.

Tonight, some very knowledgeable individuals have given you real guidelines that your children will be using as they leave this elementary school for the middle school. That knowledge is invaluable and will help you as well as your children in determining the direction of their future education and, I hope, making the path smooth—or at least getting rid of all the major rocks in the road. I speak of those formal guidance activities, but I would speak of another kind of guidance as well.

Perhaps here in the elementary school, we need guidance services even more than the secondary schools and colleges. Here, during the most formative yeas of a child's life, we may not need knowledge of the entrance requirements of the Ivy League universities, but each and every student has need of guidance through these difficult passages of childhood that have been too often romanticized and, in reality, not so accurately remembered for their confusion and frustration and tears.

I have seen teachers with their arms around a student's shoulders, calming the fears of that student, gently explaining, expertly allowing the student to discover those truths that will stand him well in life, that will offer a light for her path. Combine these dedicated people right here in our school with the professionals like those who spoke tonight, and add the parents who seek to know for the good of their children, and you have a combination that will truly guide each and every child today to find the best tomorrow.

That's a most comforting thought, and a good way to end our evening.

> *SPECIAL DATA: With increasing publicity about the necessity of a good education if one wants to have a fighting chance in the highly competitive world of the future, activities related to educational guidance are well attended, even on the elementary school level. The closing speech above aims at assuring your audience that the guidance offered at your school is outstanding—something from which their children will benefit greatly. Such assurance goes a long way toward establishing a school-community rapport that makes a functioning school even better.*

76

TOPIC: *All-Purpose Closing Speech*

AUDIENCE: *Suitable for Virtually Any Audience*

When I was a child, and it came time for my brother, my sister, and me to stop our play for the day and head on upstairs for bathing and bed, there was a brief and inevitable ritual that was observed in our home, and observed with, as I seem to recall, all the regularity of all rituals everywhere.

When the day had ended and bedtime came, my mother would come into the room, or perhaps rise and stand before us, but get our attention in one way or another. Then, taking that one good deep breath that serves as the basis of every good message of merit, she would proceed to make her pronouncement.

"Well," she would say, "all good things must come to an end."

That was it. There was no other profundity, no deep-meaning and significant phrase to follow that struck at the root of metaphysical reality. No, there was just that little cliché; one small, worn-out, ultrasimplistic cliché. "All good things must come to an end!"

What meaning it had for us! The day, our day, was done. Good day or bad, it was over, and now it was time to rest, to dream, and to get ready for the new day that would, with absolute certainty, be there when we awoke.

I share that memory with you this evening, ladies and gentlemen, because I feel that it has a good deal of relevance for all of us who have attended this program tonight. I see so many parallels. We may not be at play tonight, but I feel that I can say with a high degree of certainty that everyone here has enjoyed the program just presented.

(*NOTE: You can name the particular activity or program you have just seen; for example, "Everyone here has enjoyed our seminar on Creative Parenting." You can also personalize your anecdote about all good things coming to an end.*)

Now, however, it's time to remember, "All good things must come to an end." As Yogi Berra was wont to remark, "It's *dejá vu* all over again!"

Let us, however, pause a moment and consider that this analogy is really only half true. Yes, this evening, the fine program we have been privileged to witness, has come to an end. That is true, but unlike children, we are not going off to bed and leaving our interests behind. What we have learned tonight, what we have seen tonight, what has stirred us tonight as parents and as educators will stay with us as we make our way home. It will be in our conversations as we prepare for rest and, who knows, it may be (to paraphrase Shakespeare) "such stuff as dreams are made of." When tomorrow does come, when we open our eyes on a new day, these concepts will still be with us.

This has been a very special night. Yes, all good things must come to an end, but what has been taught and shared and learned here will not end with a night's sleep; it will continue to be with us for that new day—enlightening and enriching us.

Thank you for coming and good night!

SPECIAL DATA: You can adapt the All-Purpose Closing Speech to the particulars of your situation, altering the anecdote as needed. May it serve you well.

IN CONCLUSION

In show business there is a maxim, we are told, that says, "Always leave them laughing." Well, we are certainly not in show business, but if, for a moment, we may adapt that maxim, perhaps our maxim should be, "Always leave them thinking." Let your closing speech convince your audience not only that they have had a good time, but that they have participated in something good and worthwhile as well.

Section 5

"A Few Good Words . . .": Invocations, Convocations, and Commentaries

We would need a pretty large calculator to add up the number of times we have been asked, apparently on the spur of the moment, to "say a few words" about some situation or program or activity that was taking place. These requests seem to fall into three categories, which constitute the title of this section: Invocations, Convocations, and Commentaries.

An "invocation" consists of words that give some special meaning or flavor to an event. In another time, it might have been called a "blessing" or a "benediction."

A "convocation" is literally a "calling together." These words tell the assembled group that they have done well to assemble for the cause at hand. It's a "welcome and let's get started" speech.

A "commentary" implies more than a sentence and less than a full speech. A commentary may be required of you by the situation itself, or the people in charge may ask you to comment, or the media may be clamoring to have a commentary from you.

Over the next several pages, you will find examples of all three types of "good words." We are certain that you will find something to meet your needs.

77

TOPIC:	*All-Purpose Invocation*
AUDIENCE:	*Suitable for All Adult Audiences*

It is a good and wonderful thing when a group of people as different and diverse as we are here today join together with one accord to meet our common needs. I believe there are few who would disagree with that.

(*NOTE: You can detail the specific program or project that has brought you all together at this point, but be brief!*)

A diverse group of people also indicates a diversity of beliefs. Those beliefs have meaning and relevance within each individual heart, and I know that in our hearts we now seek that relevance for the task that lies before us.

Each of us seeks personal strength, for we know that we have a job to do if we want to accomplish our goals. Each of us seeks guidance in order that what we do and learn and say and act upon will be what is needed for what we wish to accomplish. Each of us seeks direction, for certainly we have come ready to give of ourselves for what lies before us, and each of us seeks the best way in which to help. All of these things, yes, all of these things, we would certainly agree upon and ask as we begin this endeavor.

We would, I think, ask one thing more; I believe we would ask that as we come together, we do so in such a manner that we will celebrate our diversity while we strive to unite in our common cause. May we become one cause, one group, and one pair of hands that will work together in order to form something that lasts—something that lasts for our sakes and for the sake of our children.

> *SPECIAL DATA: Let's talk for a moment about God. There was a time when such an invocation as this one would have automatically invoked "God's blessings" on the people. Currently, it is probably better to avoid such a direct reference, remembering that your purpose is not to stir controversy. Remember also that your personal faith is yours, but in the public schools of America, as one century winds down and another struggles to be born, a heightened awareness of legalities suggests that an invocation like the one above is less likely to be controversial.*

78

TOPIC:	*Invocation for a Sporting Event*
AUDIENCE:	*Mainly Parents and Older Elementary Students*

In a few moments we will start a contest between teams, but before we do, let us pause for a little while and remember that these teams are not impersonal; they are made up of individuals, of students from our own school, of your children and ours.

It is fully appropriate, therefore, that our thoughts turn inward for a while and that we find in our hearts a common desire for these children as they come upon this field to play, as they engage in the shared activity of sport.

And, if our hearts would speak, what would they say?

Let them play well. May this activity strengthen their growing bodies, and may they grow in the glow of health, with each step a step toward a life of happiness and the overall joy that such health may bring.

Let them play fairly. May they learn those values of honesty and fair play that so many others have found in sports, and may that fair play become a part of them as they grow and mature into the citizens of tomorrow. May they learn the value of sportsmanship without falling prey to its vanities. May they look back on their participation with just pride and without regret.

Let them play safely. May they play free from injury. May the enthusiasm of their youth be guided and protected in such a way that their joy may be undiminished by any pain or trouble. May they be as joyful at the end of this activity as they are now at its start.

These things, together, I believe we would ask, for we wish no harm to any player, while we wish enjoyment and growth and health to all who play.

These are our children, and we keep them in our hearts.

Now, let's enjoy the game.

SPECIAL DATA: While elementary sports may not approach the status of National or American League teams, sports on any level do evoke an interest, especially from parents. This type of invocation is appropriate for any game, as it expresses concerns that all parents have. Be sincere and keep it from the heart, and you can't go too far wrong.

79

TOPIC: *Invocation for a Patriotic Assembly*

AUDIENCE: *Adults—Parents, Educators, Community Members*

Sir Walter Scott's words, "Breathes there the man with soul so dead,/who never to himself has said,/"This is my own, my native land!" offer inspiration to us all.

Before we begin this evening's activities, I think it's altogether fitting and proper to pause for a moment and allow each one of us, in his or her own heart, to contemplate the country we honor tonight, the country where we are free to gather together—each of us different, yet each of us the same.

A popular song, written years ago but still heard extensively throughout our land begins with these words: "God bless America, land that I love." Whatever our individual beliefs, whatever each of us cherishes within the sanctity of his or her own heart, however we individually choose to give birth to those feelings, there is surely within each of us a desire that our land, our country, the place where we choose to raise our children, be "blessed."

May we continue under the benefits of a democracy. May we continue to grow in mutual understanding of each other and mutual respect for individual rights as provided in our Constitution. May we continue to teach our children the values of honesty and dedication and commitment that have made our country what it is. May we grow ever closer to each other in order that our diversity may come to bind us together in love and understanding as "one nation, under God, indivisible." May "God bless America, land that I love."

Let this, then, be the desire of our hearts as we enjoy the program that we are about to see. We all love our country, and now it is time to celebrate that feeling.

SPECIAL DATA: Don't let anyone tell you that patriotism is an old-fashioned idea that is on its way out. Quite the contrary, there is something about our flag flying against a sky of blue with our national anthem playing that will bring tears to the eyes of the strongest of us. Never try to be clever or humorous during a speech of a patriotic nature; keep it straightforward and rely on love of country and pride in our nation to guide you.

80

TOPIC: *Invocation for a Conference or Learning Activity*

AUDIENCE: *Adults—Teachers and Educators*

To gather together with people who are congenial is always rewarding; to gather together for an activity like the one we are engaging in tonight is not only rewarding but also gratifying in some very special ways.

We are here to learn. We ask that our minds be opened that what is presented to us may be to our edification, and that we may use the knowledge we receive to grow and become even more aware.

We are here to understand. We ask that our hearts may unite and that with knowledge may come appreciation for the depth and feeling that it conveys; that we may see beneath the surface with new eyes.

We are here to appreciate. We ask that along with the knowledge, and the understanding that it brings, may come a deeper appreciation for all that is involved in it, for all the work and discernment and effort that are part and parcel of what we shall come to know, and that through that appreciation may come a resolve to cherish the knowledge.

We who are here tonight ask that the fervor of our anticipation be matched by the vigor and enthusiasm of those who will be addressing us. We ask that our hopes for this evening may not just be met, but may be surpassed in every way. We ask that we may look back on this evening as a time of growth and a valuable addition to our lives.

We are here to learn; we are here to understand; we are here to appreciate. May all these goals be met.

We are here; let's begin.

SPECIAL DATA: This speech is appropriate for a regular conference or workshop, but can also be used for such special learning activities as creative parenting, substance abuse, or other programs.

81

TOPIC: *Getting Together to Win*

AUDIENCE: *Suitable to Most Adults or Older Children*

Tonight we have come together in this place for a very special reason.

Tonight we have come together to win.

Now, I realize that there are those who might well ask, "Isn't that a rather bland statement? Doesn't it rather beg the question? After all, no group ever comes together to lose. Every group wants to win."

Of course, there is truth in that, but I still contend that it takes a special group of people with a special motivation and a singular dedication to be the ones who, with single-minded devotion, know that they have come together to win. There are groups who have come together with less than these qualities—groups that have tried and have fallen short of their goals in spite of their desire. There are groups that, with the desire, never get started because they are too busy concentrating on flaws and weaknesses in themselves and others. I've known many such groups.

A group of people who have come together to win, however, is different. From the start, there is a concentration on the task ahead; from the start there is a focus on shared strengths rather than individual weaknesses; from the start, there is a common resolve that nothing shall keep them from the goal they struggle to attain; from the start there is an anticipation of success so strong you can feel it in the very atmosphere of the place where they are gathered; from the start there is a knowledge of victory acquired through experience.

Pause a moment now and allow your senses to appreciate that feeling, because it is present here tonight. It is not flattery to appreciate reality; it is not appeasement to recognize dedication; it is not deceit to acknowledge the feeling and the direction and the fervor of those of us who are here, ready to begin.

Tonight we have come together in this place for a very special reason.

Tonight we have come together—to win!

SPECIAL DATA: There are occasions when what is really needed is a "pep talk." Don't underestimate its power; the pep talk is no longer relegated to the locker room at half time. A good pep talk can inspire listeners to resolve and dedication and accomplishment of their goals. If you believe in what you can do, sincerely believe it, your belief will be conveyed to your audience.

82

TOPIC: *Getting Together to Build Something Positive*

AUDIENCE: *Aimed at Parents, but Suitable for Most Adults*

Take a look at the TV or read the headlines of a local or big city newspaper, if you dare, and you will read of atrocities that take place on our doorsteps that make the carnage of war look like so much child's play by comparison.

I tell you that it is easy to tear things down; it is easy to disparage; it is easy to destroy.

If there is a party in a classroom, and that classroom needs to be decorated for the occasion, it will take an entire class of willing hands and several teachers with inexhaustible patience; it will take them almost all day to get balloons blown up and strung and hung and crepe paper twisted and bannered across the room and colorful ribbon cascading from light fixtures. Yes, it will take all day.

Now, when that party is over, all those decorations have to come down. There is an endless supply of volunteers for this activity, and, believe me, three or four children, intensely devoted to the activity, can strip the classroom bare of decoration in two minutes flat. Yes, it is an easy thing, sometimes absurdly easy, to demolish, to destroy, to pull down.

If that is the case, then we are not here this evening to have an easy time of it, for our purpose—the very reason we get together like this—is not the easy job of tearing down, but the difficult, frequently exhausting, often frustrating task of building something lasting, something real, something positive. Certainly, we all know the work involved; certainly we are all aware of the need; and, certainly, our coming together as one body indicates that we all have the dedication to work toward our shared goal

(*NOTE: You can add the specific reason for your gathering here, e.g., passing the current school budget, building a new media center, and so forth.*)

Of course, this will take work and time and intensity of effort, but we are all convinced of the worth of building something positive or we wouldn't be here tonight.

We have come together, not to pull down, but to build up.

What are we waiting for? Let's get started.

SPECIAL DATA: Of course, we never get together to build something negative, but it is still a good idea to tell people from time to time that what they are doing is good and proper and the right thing. We all need stroking, and if you can do it and mean it in your heart, then you are going to establish a rapport that will take you through almost any crisis. That rapport is something positive—very positive, indeed.

83

TOPIC:	*Getting Together to Fight for a Cause*
AUDIENCE:	*Those People Who Would Come Together to Fight for a Cause*

There are certain truths in life, and here are some of them . . .

No one ever mowed the front lawn by thinking about it on the living room couch; no one ever built a bridge by daydreaming about how much to charge as a toll if it ever got completed; no one ever painted a picture or chiseled a statue or composed a symphony by sending a contribution to the National Endowment for the Arts; and—most certainly—no one ever won a cause, however worthwhile, without fighting for it.

There is an old cliché that we have all heard: "If it's worth having, it is worth working for." Certainly, the wisdom of that speaks for itself, and I cannot add to its truth. I would, however, amend it slightly.

Allow me to rework it to say, "If it's worth having, it is worth fighting for." Indeed, there are few things of value and worth in this world for which we do not have to fight, either to attain or to maintain; that has meant everything from the taking up of arms in the defense of our country to the struggle to attain worthwhile programs and curriculums in our schools. Whatever the case may be, it has involved a group of people, convinced of the importance of the struggle and ready to enter that struggle, to engage the opposition and to fight until that goal—that worthwhile and important goal—was finally attained, until the mission was accomplished.

Make no mistake about it, that is why we have gathered here this evening. We are convinced of the worth of that for which we strive. . .

(*NOTE: Here you can name the specific goal for which you have all gathered and will work together, such as "the worth of passing the school budget," etc.*)

. . . and we are convinced of our need to fight for it in the days to come.

Of course, we realize that it will not be easy; of course we realize that there will be opposition; of course we realize that we will have to fight for our cause, but that is precisely why we have banded together in unity.

Because we believe, we can do no less.

SPECIAL DATA: In a motivational speech, you must convince your audience that you believe in their cause just as much as they do. Remember, a leader never leads by saying, "Go that way." A leader leads by saying, "Follow me!" Keep your enthusiasm level high, be sincere, and add any gestures that seem appropriate. To make it more personal, pick out various individuals in the audience and say a few lines of the speech to each one. A personal, one-on-one appeal will serve you well.

84

TOPIC:	*Getting Together to Start a New Year*
AUDIENCE:	*Teachers and Staff*

Welcome back!

Well, here we are . . . again.

Now wait a minute, wait a minute. Are you sure you're supposed to be here? I mean, surely it was only a week ago, two weeks at the very most, that I was standing before you, congratulating you on another outstanding school year, and wishing you a safe and happy summer. What happened to the time?

Now, I am certain that many of us feel that way. We hardly started the summer hiatus, and here it is over and done; here we are sitting and listening; and here is the school year straining at its leash, so to speak, and all ready to pounce upon us once more, demanding our full time and certainly commanding our attention.

And that is why we have come together. We are here to coalesce from individuals at a beach or a mountain lake or a second job or however you spent your summer, into a solid, functioning entity known as the faculty of this school. Ladies and gentlemen, the new year is about to start and we have come together to start it.

Something within me believes that this gathering today is more, much more, than a contractual obligation. I have been privileged to be present at the start of many a new school year, and always, along with the smiling complaints and the good-natured joking, there is a very serious undertone of preparation for the year ahead, of a positive appreciation for what will come, of a readiness to do what will be needed, and of an eagerness to get started.

Perhaps the summer was too short, but that summer lies behind us now and we have gathered together to start a new year. We know we can handle it; we know we will get through it; we know that we will help our students from the first day to the last—with plenty of tears and laughter along the way - - for that is what we have done, and done with pride, in every new year we have faced.

Here we are again.

Let's get to it!

> *SPECIAL DATA: However much teachers (and sometimes administrators) may complain about the summer's being too short, they really are happy when the school year begins. Here, that fact is acknowledged and the welcome and the challenge made quite clear. Whatever "welcome back" speech you give, make certain that you are sincere, and tell your faculty how happy you are to have them back. Praise given genuinely and from the heart is always well received.*

85

TOPIC: *Getting Together to Support Our Children*

AUDIENCE: *Best Suited to Parents of the Students in the School*

It has been said that a parent is a person with a bulging wallet—bulging with photographs of his or her child. In fact, I heard an old joke that describes parents as people who watch a five-year-old carve his initials into their brand new mahogany coffee table with a screwdriver and remark, "Isn't that wonderful! He can write his own name!"

As that anecdote may drive home, there is quite a difference between support and indulgence. What's more, most parents I know will laugh at that story because they have experienced the natural desire to indulge their children in all sorts of things and have had to temper that feeling with a higher law, if you will, of support—of undergirding their children with values and a code for living that will help to carry them through their lives.

Indulgence is easy; support often requires tears and resolve and sleepless nights. Indulgence says, "Go ahead! Do what you want!" Support states, "This is the way; go ahead and try; I'm here to help if you fall."

Indulgence is easy; support requires effort.

We have come together tonight to support our children, with every implication of that word, and it will not be easy. Indeed, doing what is best for a child in order to provide a support that will last is an endeavor that cannot be taken lightly, that may not be entered into half-heartedly, that must be taken without the allowable possibility of ever turning back.

Indulgence is easy; support requires effort.

And yet, with love comes the responsibility to supply that effort for our children, and the very presence of so many here tonight is ample and convincing testimony that we here assembled have come together without reservation to provide that support.

Therefore, although they may not know nor perhaps even appreciate the depth of that commitment now, let us join in actively supporting our children in the present, so that we may present a bright and glowing future to them all.

> *SPECIAL DATA: On what occasion might the commentary above be used? Any time you have a gathering of parents to do something toward furthering their children's education, you can add these comments to a speech you are giving, or use it alone. Appropriate occasions might include forming an intramural sports program, scheduling for the middle school, parent-teacher conferences, or a meeting of parent volunteers, to name just a few. Every parent wants to support his or her child; it is your job to provide direction.*

86

TOPIC:	*Getting Together to Improve/Develop/Enhance our School/ Curriculum*
AUDIENCE:	*Adults—Volunteers, a Committee, or a PTA Group*

We have come together this evening to make a good thing even better. Let me explain what that means.

I had a friend once who was an artist. He painted in oils and produced what I, at least, considered true works of art.

Many times I was present when he would finish a canvas. He would take it off his working easel and place it on a shelf, facing outward. I asked him once if that was to allow the painting to dry, and his answer was that that was partially true. He also placed it on the shelf in order to look at it, examine it, study it in the days ahead, and determine if any changes were needed, if any detail might be added to somehow enhance the scene, if he had missed something along the way.

Indeed, there were times when he would take down the painting and begin to stroke its surface with brush and paint. When he was finished, I would look and there would be a new shadow that added just the right depth or a new shade of a color that gave a face new life, or a bird in the sky that perfected the balance of the entire piece. He had studied an already fine picture and had made changes that added to its beauty, that made it even more beautiful and special than it had been before.

In a very real sense, we are that artist, and we have come together to do what my artist friend did. We are going to study an already outstanding canvas to see if any changes are needed—to make it even more special and helpful and vital and alive in serving the needs of the children of this school.

We have not come together to destroy, but to create—to take a good thing and make it even better.

There is work before us.

Let's get started.

SPECIAL DATA: Anyone who has been in education for a reasonable period of time realizes that change is an inevitable part of the process. Nothing stays the same, because the world refuses to stop and remain the same for any given length of time. Society is constantly changing and the school is part and parcel of society, so it must change as well, or become outmoded and useless. If you're involved in education, then you also realize that there is often a fair amount of resistance to that change from all points—from faculty to parents to the community at large. This is a good speech, therefore, at the start of any process that will change a situation—the curriculum, a policy of the school, or some outside change that will alter the functioning of the school.

87

TOPIC:	*Commentary on a Losing Sports Season*
AUDIENCE:	*Adults; Possibly the Local Media*

It is part of my job to answer questions. I realize that, and I most certainly will not avoid that responsibility. Before I do get down to answers, however, there are some questions that I would like to ask. If you'll bear with me, I think that within their answers you will find my own as well.

I have three questions: Did they enjoy it? Did they learn from it? Did they grow? If the answer to those three questions is "yes," then I could care less what figures on a piece of paper say, because they don't tell the whole story; they lie. Indeed, it was the famed Prime Minister of England, Benjamin Disraeli who remarked, "There are three kinds of falsehoods: Lies, damned lies, and statistics."

No, statistics don't tell the whole story. They can't, because they are cold and impersonal, leaving out the essential humanity; in fact, when dealing with sports here on the elementary level, they don't even begin to approximate what really happened.

Of course we want to win. Who doesn't want to win? But we also have to remember that we are, after all, an elementary school—not the New York Yankees or the Dallas Cowboys—a fact that, perhaps, we do not reflect on often enough. With those teams, the goal of the game is to win. With them, winning means money and success is measured in financial terms. With us and the children (and note the word is 'children' and not hard-play, multi-injured, commercial-making professional athletes)—with us and the children, the goal of the game is to change the player. With us, winning means the growth of the individual player, and for us, success is measured in terms of such individual variables as the growth of honor and sportsmanship and team effort. All of these things statistics simply do not—simply cannot measure.

Rather, our statistics are the living children who have participated so well over this past year; the children whom we have seen grow, not only in physical ability but in spirit and maturity. These are the children who are with us each day, these are our living statistics of which we may be justly proud.

These statistics say we have won.

And, ladies and gentlemen, these statistics don't lie.

SPECIAL DATA: Granted, at the elementary level you do not have the emphasis on sports that you would in the high school. There, a winning or losing season can inspire everything from a town parade to threats of lost jobs. Nevertheless, if you have ever been involved with Little League or Pop Warner, you know that there are parents and community members who take sports, even sports on the elementary level, very seriously, very seriously indeed. This speech gets at some basic thruths about the subject and helps to put it all into perspective.

88

TOPIC:	*Commentary on a Winning Sports Season*
AUDIENCE:	*Adults; Possibly the Local Media*

How good it is to be able to gather together this evening to give honor where it is due and to recognize the effort of those who have contributed so much to the enjoyment and growth and development of our children.

I don't know how I can say anything tonight that can hope to compete with the lovely record we have all come to know. We have had a season of winning; that is a fact, and it is a fact of which we may all be justly proud.

Certainly, thanks are in order.

(Note: At this point, you can thank those who helped. If you are going to err, let it be on the side of completeness; try not to leave anyone out.)

Allow me to be the first to lead the applause for your selfless devotion and your hours of toil in behalf of our kids. *(Lead the applause.)*

And now, I'll tell you a secret. You see, although we are not an Ivy League school or a professional team—although we are, in the final analysis, an elementary school—that doesn't make winning any less sweet. It does, however, help to put that winning into perspective.

We have won, you see, in more ways than one. Certainly, we have won on the scoreboard and on paper, but we have also won in the growth and maturity and spirit evidenced by our children on the playing field and off. Through sports and the role modeling of people like you, not only have teams won, but individuals have grown, children have learned, bodies and minds have started to mature. They have come to know the physiology of play and the honor and code of behavior as well. They have played, and they have grown, and that has been very good for everyone involved.

The words *honor* and *truth* and *sportsmanship* may be worn out and tired in some quarters, but here they are the watchwords of the growth that has taken place in our children this year.

Look at them; look at your children.

Yes, we have had a winning season, and we are all winners for it.

SPECIAL DATA: Let's face it—everybody likes to win. Even though this is elementary school, winning is still fine and good, and your parents and community can get behind an elementary sports event just as firmly as those in the sec-

ondary school. Note how this speech identifies everyone as a winner. That's a good concept to stress; everyone has been part of the effort it took to win, and everyone takes a part of the victory as well.

89

TOPIC:	*Commentary on Student Achievement*
AUDIENCE:	*Students and Parents—An Evening Awards Ceremony*

This evening, we are going to talk about the achievements of a very special group of individuals, your children. We are going to show you what they have done; we are going to recognize their efforts; we are going to give credit where credit is due, and it is going to be a very enjoyable night for everyone here.

The following is a common experience, shared, I would think, by the vast majority of parents: Your son or daughter is in first grade, and he or she comes home one bright afternoon and presents you with a sheet of paper. You open it, and there is a vivid display of crayon or watercolor that jumps out at you in a panoply of reds and blues and yellows. Before you can say, "What's this?" your child volunteers, "It's a picture of us when we went on the picnic! See—that's Spot and that's Mikey."

Now, I ask you, what do you do? Do you stand there and deliver a lesson on the correct use of linear perspective in art? Do you suggest that the sun is usually yellow rather than green? Is this what you do?   Do you launch into a comparison of your child's technique and the brush stroke of a Rembrandt? Of course not! What you do is say, "It's wonderful!" and you mean it! Then, all at once, you're hugging your child and pinning the artistic masterpiece to the refrigerator with an assortment of odd-shaped magnets.

Why? Simply because that first drawing, as emotionally charged as it may have been, also represented a step forward for your child. It was an accomplishment, an achievement that included hard work, attention, application of knowledge—an achievement that carried with it the promise of even more to come. It did not matter what others might think about it; it was your child's achievement.

We are not here this evening to show you crayon drawings or watercolors of a purple sun playing on a magenta landscape, but we are here to celebrate the concept behind it. We are here to recognize the achievements of our students, our classmates, our sons and daughters. Like those drawings we mentioned, these achievements are the result of hard work, knowledge, and the focused efforts of these students. These achievements contain the essential effort they have put into learning and the essential promise of the limitless vista of achievement before them. They are the prelude for what is to come.

Come, let us join in celebration of what our children have done.

SPECIAL DATA: No child does it alone. A child who achieves does so with the help of many people—from the teacher in the classroom, to mother or father, to grandparents, to that "special someone" who encourages and acts as "coach" in the process. We give the honor to the children for their work, but it is well to remember that the parents have been there all along, and they are bursting with pride and eager to "get to it!" Therefore, make this speech short and to the point.

90

TOPIC:	*Commentary on Teacher Performance and Achievement*
AUDIENCE:	*Adults: Educators, Parents, Those Who Would Honor a Special Teacher*

We have many teachers in our lifetime, and all of them have their special place in our lives and in our hearts. Every so often, however, there steps forward one teacher who is special, who so imprints himself or herself on our minds and hearts that we cannot forget, that we relegate to a very special place in our hearts to be honored and cherished as long as we live. Each of us, I feel, has that special person who was a teacher . . . and more.

It was the nineteenth century philosopher and educator, Henry Adams, who remarked, "A teacher affects eternity; he can never tell where his influence stops."

That is as true today as when it was first written almost a century ago. Some years ago, I took an informed survey of educators, asking what, if anything, proved to be the deciding factor in their choosing to go into teaching. In more than eighty percent of the responses, it was claimed that one of the most important influences in their career choice was this —the influence of a teacher. Not just any teacher, mind you, but that special teacher—the one who took the time to be interested; the one who made the subject come alive and dance from the pages of the textbook; the one who inspired to such a degree that you knew it was possible for you.

Were I to ask all of you that same question, I dare say many of you would mention a teacher, even if that teacher was your mother or brother or scoutmaster or church youth group leader.

Certainly, teachers are hired to do their job, and they have a contract and are paid for their efforts; that is a matter of public record. Beyond that, however, come the intangibles—that performance or achievement that is not written in words, that cannot be codified or written into an individual job description. Beyond that, there are teachers who work virtually from instinct, who work from the heart, who cannot help but teach wherever they go, because they have the heart of a teacher and can do no less.

We recognize such a teacher this evening—one whose performance is based on love and truth and honor. This teacher's achievement is the achievement of the human spirit that carries others with it toward a goal they never considered themselves capable of attaining—providing the incentive that makes the impossible commonplace.

This is teaching at its best.

SPECIAL DATA: An outstanding teacher's dedication and expertise are evident in any school, and word gets around the school and the community. Sentiment grows, and the community is more than happy to honor such teachers. Be sincere in your praise of your outstanding teacher, and your audience will respond in kind.

91

TOPIC:　　　　*Commentary on the School Year*

AUDIENCE:　　*Teachers—Final Gathering of the School Year*

Well, here we are. I think it was only last week that I was welcoming you back from the summer hiatus and telling you about the school year that lay before us. Now the year has come to an end, and here we are.

There are some times when the best, the absolute best, that may be said about them is the fact that they are finished—to be entered into the realm of the soon forgotten. I've had times like that, and so have you. Experiences in every human life try us to such an extent that we simply cannot wait for them to be over. Well, look around you, ladies and gentlemen; I promise you that this is not one of those times.

This school year comes to an end, but from what I have seen and heard and been a part of, it ends because the time has come for it to end, and it will continue to live in our memories as one of the better, more productive, more energizing years that we have shared together. I hear that comment everywhere, for our students have told me that; our parents have told me that; and you have told me that. I will add to that my personal witness; it has been a good year, it has been a very good year indeed.

The story is told of the aged man who was asked if he had had a good day. Supposedly, his eyes sparkled, and he answered that at his age, any day you get through is a good day. Well, not only have we "gotten through," but I suggest to you that we have gotten through in style. If I began to detail now all the accomplishments that this past year has brought for us, for our school, and, most important, for our students, then I would be here much longer than your tolerance for me would permit.

Therefore, let this year be placed in its honored niche in our memories. Let us not forget it, but use it as a foundation on which to build—as a stepping stone, if possible, to an even better and more productive year to come.

Thank you; thank you all.

It has been most wonderful sharing this time with you.

SPECIAL DATA: There is something special and magical about the end of a school year. Everyone in the school has striven to get to this point; all activity throughout the year has been aimed at this moment; there have been jokes and moanings and complaints about time dragging on, and now, suddenly, it's over. It's almost anticlimactic, and, secretly, there is a bit of sorrow in that, for we've never known a good teacher who hasn't liked to come to school and looked forward to next year and what it may bring. Right now, however, you have all accomplished something wonderful, heroic and monumental, and everyone needs to hear that truth; it affects closure on the year in a very positive way.

92

TOPIC: *Commentary on Parental Involvement*

AUDIENCE: *PTA Meeting; Mainly Parents*

I'm thankful for many things in my life, and this evening, with your permission, I would like to tell you about one that you may not guess. I have always been thankful for parental involvement. After all, if you parents hadn't gotten involved in the first place, we would have no students here for you to become involved with now, would we?

Well, perhaps that was a feeble attempt at humor —very feeble— but I will tell you what is not feeble around this school; I will tell you of something very strong; I will tell you of one of the things that make this school a fine place for growing children with growing minds to be. I'm going to tell you about something very special and very precious to us here at Dwight Road Elementary. I speak of the voluntary involvement of our parents.

(*NOTE: At this point, you can thank parents who have become involved in the school. If the group is small enough, thank each one. If the group is too large, thank the leaders, or have all the volunteers stand and lead applause for them. Suit the method to your individual circumstances.*)

Let's hear it for these "involved" parents!

I would be remiss if I did not point out that virtually all parents are involved in their children's education, from checking homework to conducting trips to the library to acquiring a seashell at 12:15 A.M. for a science project due the next morning. Believe me, we well know of this parental involvement and we are well aware of its worth and merit. We thank you.

And for the people I recognized, I want you to know that your involvement, your efforts in our behalf and the behalf of the children of this school are deeply felt, and like that pebble tossed in a pond, your involvement sends out rings and rings of ripples that will touch each and every child and educator in this place.

Parental involvement—I'm its biggest fan.

Could you tell?

SPECIAL DATA: *Parents can be the school's greatest asset. Concerned parents have raised money for classroom equipment or books, handled enrichment programs, and been champions of the individual school at board meetings and in budget elections. Certainly, every school wants and needs parental involvement, but it must be positive parental involvement, for negative parental involvement eats up your time and leaves nothing but frustration in its wake. If you can get the parents on the school's side early in the year and elicit that type of involvement from the beginning, you will have a wonderful school year. Speeches like the one above will help to get you that involvement.*

93

TOPIC: *Commentary on the School/Curriculum*

AUDIENCE: *Mixed Audience—Parents, Educators, Community Members*

You know, this is a good place to be.

I have always considered this school a happy place. Of course I've had a few off days (who hasn't) and we all have those days when we are certain that the rain clouds will never go away, but for the most part, there have been precious few days when I have not walked into this building and found it a happy place to be—a place where I felt safe, a place that gave to me as I gave to it, a place where I was happy.

I think about that sometimes, and as I meditate, I find that there is a hope within me; a hope that everyone in this place shares my feeling. Oh, of course, I realize that in any place where more than two people share the same space, there will also be disagreement; I realize that there will be those who, for whatever reason, would be anywhere else but here. Nevertheless, I continue to hope that this place, and the teaching we offer here; provides an atmosphere where everyone will feel that safety and warmth; that everyone will feel something special upon arriving; that for all, this will be a happy place to be.

If a school is meeting the needs of its students, and by projection, the needs of the community it serves, then it will be a place where the individual is nurtured and satisfied with knowledge and encouraged to try out that knowledge—to experiment and grow. When that happens, when the school is a nurturing and nourishing place, it becomes a place where a person can come to find needs met, individuality accommodated, and growth—both mental and physical—encouraged. Such a place as that will, indeed, be a happy place to be.

I want to feel that this school is that happy place. I want to feel that we are meeting needs, that we are serving our community, that we are satisfying our students.

This is a good place for us all.

This is a happy place for us all.

This is a nourishing place for us all.

This is our school, and we are proud of it.

SPECIAL DATA: This speech is basically a motivational speech about the school itself, suggesting very clearly the positive environment for learning that it creates. You can easily convert it into a speech about a particular curriculm, since a curriculum, if a child is to succeed, must also be a friendly place where he or she is safe to explore.

94

TOPIC: *Commentary on a Positive Approach to Elementary Education*

AUDIENCE: *Any Audience*

As far as our students are concerned, there are three questions about this place that need to be answered.

Are we? Oh, yes, most certainly, we are!

Can we? Of course, we can!

Will we? That's why we're here!

Do you come here from the safety and the warmth of home, a little scared and a lot unsure, wrapped up in a blanket of Teddy bears and bedtime stories—stepping into a place of tile walls and glaring lights and who-knows-what at every turn? And do you, worst of all, have to let go of Mommy's hand and watch her disappear behind a yellow bus? Then come to us, for we have spent a lifetime trying to understand. Yes, we can dry those tears and we can even coax a laugh and we give hugs where there is only pain. Oh, yes, most certainly we are here for you. Of course we can help. That's why we're here.

Are you hungry, child? Did you see that butterfly, and sit and wonder how it flies, or have you ever wondered at the blueness of the sky, or climbed a mountain in wonder, or gazed at the clouds? Are you hungry, child, to know these things and more? Do you want to eat up the world and take it in? We can feed that hunger, child; we'll teach you things that satisfy and make you hunger all at once and altogether. Yes, we're here to feed you. Of course we can, and we'll watch as your mind grows strong and straight. It's waiting for you here; that's what we do.

Do you wonder at the ways in which you grow? Has the thought crept in unbidden that there are things you might like to do that will enfold a lifetime? We are here; we will share your dreams and help them to become reality. We understand what is happening to you, and we know that sometimes it's not easy. We've had those dreams as well, magnificent dreams that hold within them the promise of reality and the truth of tomorrow, and yes, we can, and yes, we will. Didn't you know? That's why we're here.

We are engaged in education—elementary and basic and primal to the needs of all the children who will come here, wide-eyed, filled with hope and wonder, hungry to know and to try and to reach and to grow!

Are we? We are! Can we? Of course! Will we?

Absolutely! That's why we're here!

SPECIAL DATA: In the right hands, a commentary or speech like this is a real winner, even eliciting a great deal of spirit of the "stand up and cheer" variety, but it has to be delivered sincerely by someone who is normally enthusiastic and able to act as a motivator. If you are like this, that's fine. If you are not, then leave it to someone else rather than deliver it in a half-hearted manner and have it fall flat. (That's good advice, incidentally, for every speech in this book.)

IN CONCLUSION

Most of the speeches in this section are complete in themselves and may be used just the way they are. They may also be used as parts of longer speeches, wherever you feel they may apply. Generally, with invocations, convocations, and commentaries, the situations in which they are used more or less dictate that they are to be kept short. A group of parents eager to see their children get awards will begin to tire of an introductory speaker very quickly. Remember, an audience that tires of you will not be well disposed to listen to what you have to say. Keep them short and keep them enthusiastic and genuine, and you will have no trouble at all.

$\mathcal{S}$ection 6

"At This Happy Time . . .": Holiday Speeches Throughout
the School Year

Everybody likes special days and holidays. For some children, the holidays mean getting out of school, and that is all there is to it. While that is understandable in children, it is a state that needs to be attended to, because holidays are held to honor certain individuals and occasions, and many of these are a distinct part of our heritage as Americans. It is good and fitting, therefore, that children learn about them and understand the true meaning behind them.

In this section you will find speeches for those holidays that occur throughout the school year.* They may be given in a schoolwide assembly if desired; or, with some minor changes, they can be made into articles for a school or PTA newsletter or publication; or, with appropriate adaptations, they may be given before groups of adults, since it is possible that you may be asked to address a specialized group on a holiday occasion, particularly one of a patriotic nature.

Enjoy the holidays!

---

* Consequently, the speeches in this section are geared primarily for delivery to student audiences.

99

$$\boxed{95}$$

TOPIC:	*Labor Day and the Start of the New School Year*
AUDIENCE:	*Students and Teachers—A School Assembly*

Well, here we are at the beginning of another school year. I can guess how happy you are to be putting the summer behind you and finally getting back to school where you really and truly want to be.

(NOTE: Pause for student reaction; you can milk this situation if you want to have some fun with your students.)

However you feel, here we are, and a new school year is about to start. It is all but certain that, within a very few days, a very short time, you will be back into the day-to-day operations of this place, and it may even feel as if you never left. I promise you that there are friends for you to meet, trips to be taken, games to be played, and much, much, much to be learned. What's more, it's all waiting for you . . . if . . .

If . . .

If . . .

That's a big word, "if." Let me tell you about it.

Does anyone know what holiday took place just last Monday? (*NOTE: You may wish to pause for a reply from your audience.*) That's right, it was called "Labor Day." Now, I am certain that many of you celebrated that holiday, and what's more, I am certain that you celebrated it in a great number of ways.

Perhaps some of you went to the beach (*or the mountains, or the park, etc.*). How many did that? That many? Very good, you may put those hands down. Now, let's see how many went on a picnic or had a big barbeque and party in your own back yard or maybe went to the home of a friend or relative? Oh, quite a few, I see. Well, I hope you enjoyed yourselves. Thank you; you may lower those hands.

You see, many people celebrated Labor Day in some special way. Now, it is true that many people think of this holiday as marking the end of the summer season. To still others, like you, perhaps, it is the end of the summer break and the start of school. These are not, however, the true meaning of "Labor Day."

When it started, Labor Day was a day to be celebrated on the first Monday in September of each year, and its purpose was to honor the working people of America. That's right, it was a special holiday to honor people who work, people like your mothers and fathers, for it is people like your parents who have built this country. What they do—the work that they do, whether at home or in an office or in a factory or in a store—whatever they do and wherever they may do it—this work goes to build up our country and make us great.

Now, here's the "if" I told you about. If this country of ours sets aside a special day, a holiday, in order to honor work, then America must think that work is something special, and we, as a nation, do think that. It was through work that the people who founded this country made it a special place to be; it is through work that your parents provide a home for you and try to give you some of the good things of life; and it is through work that you play your part—or didn't you know that you are a part of the workers of America?

Right now, your "job" is to go to school, and your "work" is to learn. Your teachers work at helping you, but it is you who must do the job. It is you who must study and do homework and learn. You older students have been doing that for some years now, and you can tell the younger students, in truth, that all the work you do here is rewarded and that it brings changes in you as you grow.

So, the nation sets aside one special day to honor the working people of our nation. But here at Dwight Road Elementary, you'll find that every day is Labor Day, for we do honor and reward and care about the valuable work you do here in your classes. Yes, it is expected that you will work as a part of your education, but I can promise you that we, your teachers, will be working right alongside of you to make your work enjoyable and something that will help you to learn and help you to grow in a good and positive manner.

There will come a time—perhaps not tomorrow or next week, but believe me, there will come a time—when you will come to celebrate the results of the "labor" that you have done right here in this school.

One Labor Day is done, but another is about to begin.

Welcome to the new school year!

> *SPECIAL DATA: The beginning of a new school year seems, inevitably, to be a time for speeches. You are "expected" to give a motivational speech, a pep talk, a "let's get started" address that gets them all off their summer and onto their feet. Something like this fills that need. It has enough in it to appeal to any adults present, yet it is a direct challenge to students, along with a rationale for their application and study. Even if your school started before the Labor Day holiday, in mid-August let us say, you can still use this speech by changing a line to something like, "Do you know what holiday will be coming up in about a week?"*

96

TOPIC:	*Columbus Day and the Spirit of Discovery*
AUDIENCE:	*Suitable for Student or Adult Audience*

You know, I can only guess at what courage it must have taken for people like Christopher Columbus and his crew to have set out in search of the new lands they thought awaited them somewhere across the vast and lonely sea.

No one had ever gone before them, and while they knew, in theory, that the world was round, there was still that quality of the unknown facing them. When they set foot on those ships and their sails filled with the breeze and they began to move the ships outward, outward, outward—away from the land they knew and into the uncertain, into the unknown—there must have been a moment when their hearts skipped a beat, when their minds rebelled, asking, "What are you doing here?" when everything rational and sane within them wanted nothing more than to turn back—to return to the safety of home port.

But they didn't turn back, did they? They pressed on; they went beyond the place where others had been before; they entered new and uncharted territory and they kept pressing on in spite of danger and hardship . . . and they reached their goal.

It is difficult for us to imagine what Columbus and his crew must have gone through. Today, we have TV sets that bring the world into our own living rooms. We watch and see ocean liners cross the Atlantic from, let's say, New York to Spain in a matter of days rather than months, and aircraft take us in luxury from one country to another, across thousands of miles of open sea in a matter of hours. We read of this, watch it on our TV sets, and we may even experience something like it personally in our lives, and because we do, certain things like distance lose their wonder and there is no "unknown" left any more for us to sail into. It's hard for us to realize the terror, and the courage that it must have taken these people to overcome that terror and to launch out in order to discover new worlds.

Perhaps it will take space, the "final frontier," to borrow a phrase, for us to have once more that spirit of setting out to discover—to go forward into the unknown and make it known, to make it ours.

> *SPECIAL DATA: If this speech is related to a school activity, you can continue along the track that each student is a "Columbus," in the sense that each has the task of discovering the knowledge and learning that the school has to offer. This speech can also be used to begin a schoolwide activity or project along the lines of "exploring the possibilities." Of course, it can be used as it is—just to acknowledge the day.*

97

TOPIC:	*Election Day and the Democratic Process*
AUDIENCE:	*Suitable for a School Audience*

Tomorrow is a special day—a very special day. Many people have worked very hard to have a day like tomorrow; some have fought to have it; some have even given up their lives to have it. Tomorrow is a very special day. Tomorrow is Election Day.

Now, I fully realize that to some of you, all Election Day means is . . . a day off from school. (*NOTE: If applicable, change to "a day when some people we don't know set up strange-looking machines in our library [or cafeteria, etc.] and people come in and out of the building all day."*) But that's not all there is to it. Oh, no, there is a far greater story to be told.

Election Day is the day when we elect the people who will be our leaders and our lawmakers for some time to come. This means that people like your mothers and fathers will come to a place, perhaps a place like this school, and they will vote for the person they think will do the best job. At the end of the day, when everybody who wants to vote has been given a chance to do so, certain people will add up how many votes each person running, each candidate, received. This is added to other votes that are coming in from all over. Finally, when all the votes from all the voting places have been recorded and added up, the person with the most votes, the person whom most of the people want, is declared the winner and will be given the job of being the people's representative for the time to come.

That's what tomorrow, Election Day, is all about, and all the steps I just told you about are a part of what is known as the "democratic process." It is that process that has helped to keep America free.

Now, I wonder if you realize that there are places in this world where there is no such thing as Election Day; where there are no elections; where people do not get a chance to pick the people who will be their leaders. It isn't very nice in those places, because the leaders can do anything they want, and the people who live there have no choice but to obey or face some very bad times.

Here, in America, we do have a say in our government. Through the democratic process, we have Election Day, when we choose our leaders, and, if we don't like what they do, we can say so by not voting for them or by any number of legal and effective methods of getting them out of office. This is all part of that democratic process; it's what keeps us safe, keeps us strong, and keeps us free.

So, you see, tomorrow is much more than a day off (*or "a day when many people will come to our school to vote"*). Tomorrow will be a day when we will all celebrate how good it is to live here in our country and have the privilege of being part of the democratic process.

(*NOTE: If this is to lead into a patriotic or informative program, or a class presentation, introduce it at this point and step back to allow the program to continue. Otherwise, the conclusion follows.*)

Finally, let me ask just who is part of this democratic process we have talked so much about, and that we shall see in action tomorrow? Well, your mothers and fathers are part of it, and your teachers are, and I am, and most of the adults in our town are. And, you might be surprised to learn, so are you. That's right, you. You see, right now you are part of the process of learning about it by going to school. Later, when you have grown older, which will be quicker than you think, you will vote for those running for office, and because you have studied and learned, because you have been taught and can understand, you will be able to make the choices that will be good for you and good for our country as well.

And that is democracy at its best!

SPECIAL DATA: Every school assembly is a learning situation. Certainly, with a speech like this, the students are learning. This was originally part of an assembly program on democracy, and it worked well. It is sometimes difficult for children to understand the complexities of the government, and this speech attempts to teach them something about it in a simple and straightforward manner. We should not overlook Election Day in our yearlong list of holiday celebrations.

98

TOPIC:	*Veterans Day and the Price of Freedom*
AUDIENCE:	*Suitable for Student Audience*

Veterans Day is a time that is, and should be, very special in the hearts of all Americans, because on that day, we pause to remember those who have fought to make America great and to keep America free. For some, perhaps for many in this audience, that will mean a parent or a close relative, and even grandparents may have served in some war that you now only read about in your textbooks.

That's what our veterans fought for—for you, their sons and daughters, to learn of war from a book in school rather than having to experience it firsthand on an actual battlefield. They don't want their children to have to fight as they did.

They have come to know how bad war is, and they fought so that it might not be part of your lives.

Every single one of them who fought for their country did so at a price—at a very great price. All of them paid the price of having to leave their homes and families and loved ones, to travel to places they did not know and be exposed to hazard and illness and death. That's a price they paid in common. Some were wounded and some lost a part of themselves, an arm or a leg, and they all carry their scars to the present day. Some of them paid the most precious price of all; they died, they gave their lives in places far from their homes so that those homes might be free. Yes, all of them paid a price, a mighty price, to defend the land of their families, the land that they cherished, the land that they loved.

Oh yes, there is a price to freedom, and on this Veterans Day, we honor those who have given much, who have paid the price, who have served that we might live in the glow of that freedom that was so special to them. On this special day we honor these veterans, and we honor them publicly—just as many of us continue to honor them within the privacy of our hearts each and every day of the year.

What's more, we are aware of a responsibility that this honor places on each of us who are part of this great country—the responsibility to see to it that their sacrifices, their heartfelt, selfless sacrifices, might not be in vain.

For us in the schools, that means teaching in such a way that they are never forgotten. We must teach what they did and gave for their country to the children who will follow, so that those children may fully understand and appreciate the opportunities they have. In the classroom and through programs like this one, we in the schools will continue to teach about the dedication with which these, our veterans, have given in the past to preserve the future.

That is not the only responsibility, however. There is another one, and it is one that falls on you. These people fought and died so that you might have the chance to grow and learn. It is your responsibility to grow and learn, to study and do well, to learn in school and prepare for your lives to come, that what they fought to provide for you may, indeed, be yours to pass on, one day, to your children.

Therefore, let Veterans Day be much more than a day off from school; let it be a day when you set aside some special time to think about our veterans, and let each of us in his or her own unique and special way, honor them within our thoughts, our words, our hearts, and our prayers.

It's altogether fitting and proper to honor those whose lives—and deaths, in some cases—have so honored us. Remember them. They did it for you.

SPECIAL DATA: If your speech is to introduce an assembly program, consider inviting some local veterans to speak for a few moments. Your local Veterans Association would be happy to supply people to speak or even give a presentation for such an activity as a Veterans Day assembly. With appropriate changes, this speech might also be given to a veterans group or other community group.

99

TOPIC: *Thanksgiving and Looking Ahead*

AUDIENCE: *Suitable for a School Audience*

Thanksgiving is a day designed for looking backward; Thanksgiving is a day designed for looking ahead. On this special day, we look back over the year that has passed and we pause as we get together, we pause to review what we have done and been a part of, and to give thanks for all that we have—for the blessings that we have enjoyed.

As I look back, I am thankful for so many things that are a part of my memories and my life. I am thankful for you. Yes, I am thankful for each and every one of you —those who do well and those who need a little help; those who behave well and those who need to be shown how to behave. I'm thankful for your smiles when you see me in the halls, and the way that some of you will go out of your way to come and say hello. I'm thankful for the fine job you do as students in this school; you make me proud of you in so many ways.

I am thankful for your teachers. I love coming into your classrooms and being there as your teachers lead you in exercises designed to build up your minds. I'm thankful that each one of your teachers is deeply interested in you and works toward teaching you all those things you need to know and want to know. I'm thankful for the way they all get together to cooperate for your benefit and to make this place the very special place of learning and growth that it most certainly is.

I am thankful to your parents. I love the way in which they give so freely of their time and talents, of themselves, for the good of this school. I'm thankful for they way they are always there when we need them—from a party in a classroom to our annual school fair, they volunteer; they see the need; they meet the need. They give this school the very best that they have to give, and I am more than thankful for it.

I am thankful for this school. Yes, I am thankful for Dwight Road Elementary. I love this place, because it is a good place to be, a place where you, our students, can come to explore and wonder and learn and grow and, yes, be happy. Truly, this is a good place to be, and I am thankful for it.

Thanksgiving is also a time for looking ahead. As we gather to give thanks for the blessings of the past, our minds and hearts cannot help but project to the year ahead of us. I am thankful that, over the next year, I will have the pleasure of watching you and working with you and growing with you. I am thankful that, over this next year as well as the years to come, I will have the pleasure of seeing your knowledge and skills increase as you grow in maturity.

I think of your teachers and the staff of this school, and I am thankful that, over the coming year, I will be dealing with such a fine group of professional educators who work so diligently to teach you and keep this school running smoothly. I look forward to the joy of working with them.

I think of your parents, and I am most thankful that we will continue to have a relationship over this next year that will allow us to grow even closer together. I am thankful that not a problem will arise, or a situation exist, or a need present itself that cannot be handled—and handled effectively—through the cooperation of the school and the home.

I think of this school, and I am thankful that this place, which is already a place that welcomes students and makes room for growth and encourages learning on all levels, will become even better, even more proficient in meeting the needs of its students. I am thankful that this school will continue to stand as an important part of our community. I am thankful that this school will always be a good place to be—a place that cares for the students it welcomes each day, a place where education is honored and the student nurtured.

Whether we look backward or ahead, let us be thankful for the many blessings we have received, and truly appreciative of the opportunities that lie before us. That's Thanksgiving!

> *SPECIAL DATA: Thanksgiving is the ideal time to remind ourselves and our students of the blessings we all share. The positive attitude of this speech sets an appropriate tone for the Thanksgiving holiday.*

100

TOPIC:	*Christmas and Hanukkah—and a World of Light*
AUDIENCE:	*Suitable for a School Audience*

Do I have to tell you what time of year it is? I don't think so. Outside, the days are growing shorter and shorter and the cold, penetrating breezes when we leave home in the morning make us glad for a warm coat. Inside, decorations are on doors and in classrooms, and there seems to be a very special feeling in the air—a feeling that something great is coming our way, just around the corner. Some of us, myself included, can hardly wait. We don't have to be told; we know what time of year it is!

Very soon, most of you here today will celebrate one of two very special holidays—holidays that will mean such wonderful things as families getting together (perhaps with some family members coming from long distances), lights and candles, special foods and special treats that everyone will enjoy, gifts and presents to make our hearts glad, and the retelling of special stories of events that will touch our spirits in very special ways.

I speak, of course, of the celebrations of Christmas and Hanukkah.

If you ask your classmates about these holidays, they will tell you of the many traditions that have developed in their own homes. In many homes there are trees with colorful ornaments and flashing lights; in many others there are candles that will burn and glow throughout the holiday time. Presents are being wrapped, and all of us wonder what delights lie in store for us when finally they are opened. It is a time when love just shines from every window; it is a winter wonderland of love and light, light and love—light that helps us see and love that helps us understand.

Hanukkah, the Festival of Lights, celebrates a miracle in which a lamp kept burning long after it should have gone out—a miracle that brought with it the gift of light. Christmas, the Feast of Love, celebrates love; it speaks of a birth long ago that continues to influence much of the world and spread a message of love.

A feast and a festival; love and light; insight and vision. Suddenly, there is a world of light, a world ablaze with the light of love.

Whatever the holiday you celebrate, the light of Hanukkah or the love of Christmas, I wish you the very best of holidays.

If only the world, every day of the year, were alive with light and love to the extent that it is now, at this very special time of the year, how wonderful it would be. If all darkness were suddenly banished along with hatred and prejudice and anger and pain, what a wonderful gift would be ours. If love ruled and light shone from each of us, touching everyone with whom we came into contact, then every day would have the special feeling, the inner glow that we all experience at this wonderful time of year.

A world of light; a world of love.

Now that's something worth having.

May they be yours now, and throughout this coming year.

SPECIAL DATA: In this speech, you have mentioned the two holidays, but not gone into detail about them. You are the best judge of the environment of your school and your community, but this speech should serve you well. In some areas of our country, Kwanza is also celebrated as one of the December holidays. If it is appropriate in your school, you can adapt the speech to include it.

101

TOPIC:	*Martin Luther King Day and the Struggle for the Prize*
AUDIENCE:	*Suitable for Any Audience*

I wonder if any of us here today have every had to really struggle for something we knew was right—the proper and good and right thing to do. I wonder how many of us have ever had to struggle and strive in the face of opposition just to attain something that was rightfully ours to begin with. How many of us have had to struggle with more than trying to decide which of two TV shows to watch?

If you know what it means to fight for the right and to strive for justice—to give of yourself for others—then you know about the struggle for the prize and you can well appreciate the efforts of those who do likewise. You know already what I am about to say, because you have lived it yourselves.

I want to talk to you today about a man and a struggle for a prize—a man who saw injustice and did not turn away and leave it to someone else. I want to talk to you today about a struggle that still continues and the man who made the highest sacrifice in his dedication to that struggle.

On the third Monday in January of each year, we celebrate a very special holiday. We honor the life of a man who saw injustice; who witnessed firsthand the horror of discrimination; who suffered the sting of racism—someone who knew all that, yet did not allow it to defeat him. Far from deterring him, it made him all the more firm in his resolution to combat that injustice, regardless of the price he might personally have to pay. The desire for freedom that burned within him was a light that people could not help but see—and a beacon to guide all who were willing to follow.

The rights he fought for were not the rights of a special few. No, the rights he fought for were human rights—the rights of all humanity regardless of nationality or race or color. He fought for the right to dignity in an individual; he fought for the right to be judged on who you are and what you have done, not on your race; he fought that all people, everywhere, might have a chance to be what it was within them to become—based on ability alone, unhampered by man-made barriers that confined and smothered and killed. In short, he fought for freedom for us all.

I speak, of course, of Martin Luther King, Jr. Here was a man who, in the face of great violence directed both at him, personally, and at the civil rights movement he championed, chose to conduct his struggle on the principles of passive resistance, of nonviolence. While others screamed and shouted the rawest of insults at him and his followers—while others threw stones and pushed and shoved and beat and even killed—he stood his ground, he bore the insult, he withstood the pain without trading violence for violence, without the poison of hatred, without stooping to the tactics of the vicious and depraved. Time and again, he was attacked, and time and again he repulsed the onslaught—not with physical weapons, but with the weapons of peace, with the weapons of love.

Finally, it was an assassin's bullet that cut him down, that sent him to that rest he had often spoken of. Yet that bullet could not stop the cause in which he believed—the cause for which he had fought so valiantly and given the last full measure of devotion—his very life. Largely because of the struggle of Martin Luther King, Jr., civil rights legislation was passed with the teeth to enforce it, and Dr. King's self-stated dream of watching black children and white children playing together in an atmosphere unassailed by racial discord came one step closer to a reality.

So it is that we honor Dr. Martin Luther King, Jr. We honor his efforts and his struggle for the prize of freedom for all people everywhere. We honor the supreme sacrifice he made for the freedom of all people, everywhere. We honor the fact that his spirit is alive even today in the fight for equality and true justice for all. His fight was the fight for human rights that will continue while humanity endures.

Let us honor Dr. King and what he stands for now, on this special day, and in our hearts and minds and actions throughout the year to come.

> *SPECIAL DATA: This is an extremely serious subject and requires a serious approach; humor is definitely not appropriate in a speech for this occasion. Also, notice a very effective technique used here. Begin by talking about accomplishments and struggles, reserving the name of the person you are speaking about. Then, after all the accolades have been given, say something like, "I speak, of course, of . . ."*

102

TOPIC: *Presidents' Day and a Common Heritage*

AUDIENCE: *Suitable for an Adult or Student Audience*

Holidays are times during the year when we, as a nation, focus our attention on special people or special events. Such a day is coming up soon—and that day is Presidents' Day.

It is celebrated in February of each year, in honor of the birthdays of two great American presidents, both of whom played a very special role in our history. February 12th is Abraham Lincoln's birthday, and on February 22d we traditionally celebrated the birth of George Washington. Lincoln, as you are well aware, was president during the American Civil War and was the framer and signer of the Emancipation Proclamation, the document that formed the basis for the abolishment of slavery and the establishment of the concept of civil rights. Washington, often referred to in both literature and history as "the father of his country," led the Colonial troops during our American Revolution, persevering under great hardship, and leading them to eventual victory and the establishment of a new nation. He then served as the first president of that young country, the United States of America.

On Presidents' Day, we honor these two giants of our history, to be sure, but, in a larger sense, we also honor all those who have served this country as president. Most certainly, some presidents have been popular and some have been not so popular; we remember some for the great things they did while in office and try to forget others for the not-so-great decisions and actions they have been part of. Some presidents left office to live long and honored lives and some died in office—in some cases as victims of the assassin's bullet. On this day, however, in the true sense of the word, we celebrate them all, for they are all part of us, part of our common heritage as Americans.

Ours is a country, you see, where our leaders are not selected for us by a committee or by the might of a gun. Rather, ours is a land where we choose our leaders through elections, where we have the say as to whom we shall have represent us and our interests. Competition is part of that process of choosing our leaders, for if we had a choice of but one person, it would really be no choice at all. Within our heritage, however, is the provision for any number of people to stand for election to this, the highest post in our land. We are a land not of one culture but of many—and we are a people of many opinions, of many approaches to problems, of many different groups with differing needs and differing beliefs. No single individual can satisfy everyone's desires, and in every election there are several candidates who make known what they believe, what they stand for, and what they will do if elected. Based on this, and the extent to which we, as individuals, share the candidates' vision for America, we vote for one candidate. This is also a part of our common heritage, which we proudly celebrate on Presidents' Day.

Except for our Native Americans, each of us is descended from a family that came to American from somewhere else in the world, and each of us is rightly proud of what we call our ethnic heritage. Think of it, people from every country in the world have fought and struggled to come to America, where we continue to honor our heritage, while knowing that we have joined together as Americans as well, and that is wonderful to behold.

All of this we honor on this special day. For, make no mistake about it, when we honor our presidents, we honor our country, and we honor ourselves as well. We are a country of diversity, and the miracle is that out of that diversity an individual is elected who will serve us all—someone with whom we may not all agree, but whom we all agree to support. This is a part of our common heritage, and this, too, we celebrate on Presidents' Day.

Therefore, let us honor this special holiday—Presidents' Day—and celebrate our common heritage.

SPECIAL DATA: Holidays offer a special opportunity to educate our students, as well as giving them a chance to enjoy a hiatus from school. Speeches like this one for Presidents' Day can go a long way toward enhancing their understanding of what it means to live in the United States of America.

103

TOPIC:	*Spring and a Season of New Beginnings*
AUDIENCE:	*Suitable for a School Audience*

Does anyone have to tell you that there is something wonderful happening just outside the windowpane? After several months of short days and leafless trees and frozen landscapes, after bleak days and dark clouds and biting winds, after sniffling colds and numb fingers and slushy streets . . . there is something stirring in the air—something that brings with it a message we welcome in our hearts. Spring is on the way!

There are few things in this world that are as welcome as the coming of spring. Perhaps it is that we have all been shut inside for most of the winter months; perhaps, as some suggest, we have been deprived of sunlight for too long; perhaps it is the fact that the cold and dark have finally penetrated into us through the very walls of our houses. Whatever the case, the prospect of warmer days and the reds and pinks and yellows of flowers and the light green of new leaves and the sun high in the sky once more is enough to make our hearts leap; it is enough to renew hope and spirit and smiles and laughter.

Soon, you will be leaving school for spring break. Many will be celebrating such religious holidays associated with the springtime as Easter and Passover. Others will be taking trips with your families—some to distant places for vacations, others to see grandparents or other relatives. All of you will be enjoying the spring weather, breathing deeply of the spring air, and rejoicing in the promise that spring offers as an annual gift.

Yes, everyone loves spring and there is no reason why we should not, for spring signals not only the end of winter but the beginning of something new—new life.

Everything that has seemed dead and dry is suddenly alive with promise. On bushes, small green shoots begin to sprout; trees take on a coat of green to replace the gray-brown of winter; in the ground something is happening that is causing the once-frozen soil to split and push up, revealing the green growth underneath that strives for the sun and will soon dazzle us with beauty in gardens and fields throughout our land.

Truly, this is a time of beginning, a season of new starts, a period of renewal both in the land and in us. And that's what I want to impress upon you today, during the last moments of school before the start of the spring break.

Enjoy that break, with all that you will be doing; enjoy it whether you will be on vacation, with your families, or just getting outside to play. Have a wonderful time, but remember that this spring break is not the end of the school year, and when you return, you return to the final marking period, and that's precisely why your teachers and I want you to relax, have a good time, and refresh yourselves. We want you to come back here ready for that final push, ready, if you will, for a new beginning in which you will try your hardest to do your best, to learn the most you can, to grow to your fullest extent.

Just as now is a time of new beginnings in the land, let it be a time of a new beginning in your lives as well. Just as seeds under the ground will push upward and bud and flower, be resolved within yourselves that you will do your best in school to imitate the blossoms; see how much you can grow during these upcoming last weeks of the school year. Make no mistake about it, this spring means a renewal in you as well.

The coming of spring is wonderful, indeed, and your teachers and I are looking forward to it every bit as much as you are. You should also know, however, that we are equally looking forward to a new beginning in each of us, in every person in this school when we return.

The coldness of winter has passed and the glory of spring and of summer lie before us all. How we will make use of them is, in large part, up to us, just as how we handle our lives here in school is up to us.

Have a wonderful spring break!

Have a wonderful school life!

You deserve both!

SPECIAL DATA: If you are speaking at an assembly just before a spring break, or any break for that matter, remember that the students have their minds on the freedom from school rather than what you are going to say. This is not the time to introduce anything new; don't bring up new rules or procedures. The reminder to them to return refreshed to finish the school year is sufficient.

104

TOPIC: *Memorial Day and Those Who Remember*

AUDIENCE: *School Audience*

I have a challenge for you. Please don't shout out, but raise your hands if you can answer. Who can remember something special that happened, let's say, over a year ago. (*NOTE: If time is not a factor, you might want to call on one or several. If you wish to keep the time short, merely continue.*) That many! You see, that's one of the wonderful things about the human mind; it has the ability to remember.

Now, how many of you remembered something happy, a good memory? I see, just look at those hands. And did any of you remember something that was sad? Sure, I'm certain we all have something sad in our lives.

That's another thing about remembering, we have a choice sometimes of remembering something happy or something sad. If you choose to think about it, you can remember the time you went on vacation with the family and the fun you had, or that last birthday party when everybody you loved was there and you got that birthday present you always wanted, or that special day when you won the award, or the time when your team won that special game. If you choose to think about it, you can remember the time you were sick and couldn't leave your bed, or the time when you had to stand before your teacher and admit that you didn't do that project, or—even sadder—the day that your pet dog or cat had to be put to sleep. You and I, all of us, have the ability to remember something sad or something happy.

Sometimes, when we remember something very happy, we cannot help but laugh. Sometimes, when we remember something that is very sad, we experience that sadness, and we cannot help but cry. Memories are very powerful things.

On this coming Monday, the last Monday of the month of May, we will celebrate a special holiday known as Memorial Day. As the very name of it would seem to suggest, it is a day for people to remember—but to remember whom?

Some of you already know about the great war that took place between the states; you may already have studied about it in social studies. It was a terrible conflict, known as the Civil War.

During that war, many people died on each side, and sometimes families were even divided, with part fighting for the North and part fighting for the South. Oh, yes, it was very bad, and it was very sad. Indeed, when families and wives and children and even the other soldiers remembered their friends and relatives who had died in this great war, there was a deep sense of loss and a desire to somehow honor those who had given all they had to fight for that in which they believed so deeply.

That was why General George McClelland, a great Union general of that war, set aside one day as being very special. On that day, soldiers and civilians alike were to decorate the graves of their fallen friends and relatives and do them special honor. The designated day was May 30. It very soon became known as "Decoration Day," due to the decorating of the graves with flags and flowers. In the twentieth century, "Decoration Day" was changed to "Memorial Day," and the date was changed to the last Monday in the month of May. That is the day we will celebrate and the reason you will have a brief time out from school.

When the name and exact date of the holiday changed, however, the purpose of the day did not change. Some of you will spend part of this upcoming holiday placing flowers or other remembrances on the graves of relatives who have died, or attending religious services to remember them. Others may go to see some veterans organization present a special program or parade to remember and honor those who have died in war. Decoration Day may have changed its name to Memorial Day, but its purpose is still the same.

That is something you might want to ask your parents about. Perhaps some relative of yours—maybe a relative you never knew—fought and died in a war to keep this country free. If you find out that this is so, then be sure to remember that relative in some special way.

Memorial Day is a holiday, to be sure—a very special day that has been set aside for those who remember and for those who are remembered.

Let us honor these memories on this Memorial Day, certainly, and also throughout the entire year to come.

> *SPECIAL DATA: If you plan to give this speech to an adult audience, you can amend it to suit that audience; however, don't cut out the audience participation aspect. Children are not the only ones who enjoy answering questions or being part of a poll by the raising of hands. Used sparingly, it can be an effective speaking tool.*

105

TOPIC:	*The End of the School Year and What the Future Holds*
AUDIENCE:	*Students and Adults; Perhaps a Few Parents and Community Members*

You know, from the way some of you people were acting, I could suppose that something great was going to happen soon. Mrs. Goodhand, (*selecting a teacher in the audience*) can you think of anything that's going to happen. No? Neither can I. Now, personally, I can't think of anything that's coming up that could get us excited . . . except . . . except . . . No, it can't be; you can't be excited just because . . . just because three days from now school will end and your summer vacation will begin. That can't be it, can it?

(NOTE: At this point, you can engage in some byplay with an audience of children, asking, "What's happening three days from now?" and pretending you can't hear them, etc. It's great fun, but it does take a while for them to calm down afterwards.)

I hope you enjoy every minute of your summer break, and do you know why? Because you have earned it. That's right—earned it. You have earned it by coming to this school over the past year; you have earned it by studying and learning and growing in knowledge with your teachers; you have earned it by working hard not only at your studies but at the various projects and activities that this school has sponsored throughout the school year. Yes, you have earned that summer break, and not only I, but your teachers right along with me, wish that each second of your summer is filled with health and happiness and joy and laughter.

Let me tell you a secret. I hope your teachers enjoy the summer as well. I tell you, they have worked just as hard as you, and even harder, in leading you in learning and discovery and personal growth. They have been here before you arrived in the morning and stayed long after you went home. They have spoken with your parents, made special plans for you, taken you on field trips, and made learning fun. It is my sincere hope that they take a well-deserved rest and enjoy the summer every bit as much as you do.

(NOTE: You can, at this point, lead the students in applause for the faculty. Lead the applause by saying, "Let's show our teachers just how much we appreciate all they've done for us all year long," or something to that effect. You are the judge of what time permits.)

If the truth be known, even I am looking forward to this summer and to all the relaxation and joy it will most certainly bring, but I have to tell you, I'm looking forward to something else as well.

I know that we will all enjoy this summer, but each of us realizes that there will be a life after the summer. Perhaps we don't want to think about it now; perhaps we will push it to the furthest corners of our minds; perhaps we will try to wish it away, but the fact remains that while the summer will end our lives will go on. We are eager for that summer to begin, but we must also be mindful of what the future will bring.

After the sun and the summer, the vast majority of you will be coming back here. School will start, and once more you will be walking these halls and working in these classrooms, and I'll be welcoming you back instead of saying farewell.

You don't have to worry about that future; you don't have to be concerned about what it will bring, for if you really think about it—if you drop the fooling around and concentrate—you know that this is a good and enjoyable place to be. You know that, come the fall, you will begin to learn and care and explore and grow all over again. There will be new classmates, new classes, new teachers, and new adventures waiting for you all.

Of course, summer is a wonderful place to be, but so is this place. I will never embarrass anyone, but I know students right here, today, who have told me, come

September, that they were glad to be back; glad to be with their old and their new friends; glad to be where they can share and learn and grow. I'll even share a great, big secret with you now from my point of view—your teachers and I will be glad to have you back as well, because, you see, it just isn't a school without you. You will be leaving this place, but it will always be here. We will be here waiting for you, saying, "Welcome back! Won't you come in and stay for a while? We're glad to see you again!"

Enjoy your summer, but remember that this is what your future holds, and it is good.

You have a wonderful future ahead of you—starting now!

Have a great time!

SPECIAL DATA: As with the other speeches in this section, it's best to fashion a speech that conveys just one idea. If you have ever spoken before the start of the summer hiatus, you will know that one concept is about all even the best-behaved of student audiences can handle at this point. Stay relaxed and you will do just fine. A sense of humor helps, too.

106

TOPIC: *The Fourth of July and the New Patriot*

AUDIENCE: *Adult Audience—Possibly a Patriotic Group*

It must certainly have occurred to you, for it has come to my mind several times, that the framers of our Constitution would be absolutely amazed at what has come of their efforts could they return to modern America—if, by some weird fluke of nature or science, they could be transported into our day and age.

That makes for absolutely fascinating speculation. We can see, for example, Thomas Jefferson or Samuel Adams or Benjamin Franklin suddenly materializing in present-day Philadelphia. We watch as they dodge taxicabs, absolutely bewildered by these inventions that were undreamed of in their time, and absolutely agape at the skyscrapers and wonders of the modern world. The thought is an interesting and provocative one.

Given my particular bent, however, it is not surprising that I would have them chance by a school and step inside, to be given a tour. I would have them see it all, from kindergarten classroom to eighth-grade science lab; I would have them talk to the teachers; I would have them interact with the children. I would definitely have them sit in on a class or two while they were there; most certainly I would want them to do that.

I'm certain that Ben Franklin would want to attend a science class, Tom Jefferson might be interested in the class on writing techniques, and Sam Adams would definitely be comfortable in social studies; he would probably have a thing or two to say about it, and he might even end up teaching the class!

Now, since this is my fantasy, I can do whatever I want to do, and I would get to interview these three distinguished and historic visitors at the end of the school day, and, naturally, I would ask them just what they thought of a modern school. Is this what they expected? Was this what they had in mind?

I think I know the reaction I'd get. I think they would be both amazed and pleased to see the wide variety of children from so many races and nationalities and ethnic cultures, all working together and learning and growing and becoming better and better citizens for our nation's tomorrow. I think they would marvel at the wide variety of subjects that are taught, even at the elementary school level. I think they would be astonished at the care and counseling given to each individual child, at the attempt made to understand the individual child, at the work with the individual child to help that child develop his or her fullest potential.

I believe that at that point, they might ask me what date it was, and if it was the Fourth of July. I would have to tell them that it was not, since school is not in session in the month of July, and I would ask them why they inquired.

In my dream, they would reply that they asked if it was the Fourth of July because that was the day when they had proclaimed the Constitution of the United States of America for all to see; that was the day when they reached out with all their dreams and aspirations to lay the future before their fellow citizens of the new country, and what they had just seen was the fulfillment of those dreams. They had seen freedom at work, they had been to a school where the new patriot was being trained. For, make no mistake, the new patriot who understands democracy, and who will play a part in shaping that wondrous vision, is being educated now, not in terms of rifles and cannon, but in terms of communication and world skills. With that in mind, they would think that it surely had to be the Fourth of July.

To be sure, there would be those who would take exception to my dream and argue that this is not how our founding fathers would react. There are, sadly, individuals in today's world who will tell you that patriotism is dead, and the love of one's country a "primitive notion." When I look into the faces of our children in school, however, and hear them share with me their hopes and dreams for their futures and the futures of their classmates, I swell with pride that I live in a land that has, indeed, been called the "last, best hope for mankind." When I see that flag blowing freely against the blue, clear, and safe skies of our country, I realize the lie of all that "primitive notion" business, and the thrill of patriotism courses through my veins, and I thank my Creator as did our founding fathers for the blessings poured out upon this land. And I know that were they here, as in my dream, they would know the special significance of the Fourth of July is still very much alive, is still honored, is still a part of the rich heritage of this, our native land.

God bless this land and this people. May the Almighty continue to pour out His grace upon us, and may we continue to educate our sons and daughters as the new patriots of an even greater nation to come.

SPECIAL DATA: If you are ever called upon to give a Fourth of July speech, remember that here you are dealing with other than a school audience. You will, perhaps, notice some subtle differences from the ones before, which were intended for school audiences. Always suit your speech to your audience; that is one of the surest secrets of successful public speaking.

IN CONCLUSION

Holidays, whatever the deeper meaning behind them, are joyous occasions. Even when the holiday celebrates the supreme sacrifices made by others, the majority—the vast majority—of your audience thinks of a holiday as a happy time. Certainly, your approach to speeches for these holiday occasions should be one of optimism and happiness, pride and a forward-looking attitude. End all your holiday speeches on a positive note, with a look toward the future, and with a respect for the causes behind each holiday as well. Educate your audience where you can; leave them with something pertaining to the holiday on which to ponder; and be ready to enjoy the holiday with your audience.

Section 7

"All in One Room . . .": Speeches About Elementary Education

American public education has come a long way since the fabled and, in some cases, hallowed days of the one-room schoolhouse. Indeed, change and education seem to go hand in hand. The one-room schoolhouse served its community remarkably well, and there are even certain places where it still does. For the most part, however, the one-room schoolhouses in the largely agricultural communities of the previous century have given way to today's schools, serving children in communities of commuters, city dwellers, agricultural specialists, and suburban sophisticates. Public education has changed and will continue to change as society inevitably changes.

In this section, we'll talk about the components of elementary education—the things that change as well as the constants. Perhaps we'll discover a thing or two, and certainly, we'll have a laugh along the way.

TOPIC: *"This Place Is Haunted by a School Spirit"*

AUDIENCE: *Adult Audience—Parents; Community Members*

The story goes that the kindergarten student came home from the first day of school very, very excited and announced to his mother with a great deal of noise and conviction that he was not going back to "that place." When his mother presed him for a reason for his decision, the boy replied, "Today the teacher said that we would learn about school spirit, and I'm not going back to any place that has spooks!"

Well, if you ask me, I think that lad was being quite sensible, amazingly sensible. I know that I, personally, would not want to go to any place where I had to worry about ghosts and goblins! Would you?

Actually, if I must tell you the truth about this place, then I will have to tell you a secret; yes, this school, this place, is haunted by a school spirit. Absolutely, for there is a very well-defined spiritual entity in this place, and, with your permission, I'd like to take a few moments to tell you about it.

One clever person once defined *school spirit* as the feeling inside you that makes you feel totally nauseated when the other team scores, and I think there's some truth in that. Even here at the elementary school level, you can see it in Pop Warner football and Little League. You can see it at intramurals, and you see it in our children when they are at play on the school grounds. "See it" is a poor phrase to describe school spirit, because it is actually felt rather than seen. Be on the sidelines or in the stands for one of these games, and experience how quickly *"that"* team turns into *"your"* team." Then feel inside yourself just how necessary it becomes for *"your"* team to win; feel the pride you suddenly have in *"your"* school" and *"your"* students" and *"your"* players." Then, when you find yourself jumping to your feet and screaming at the top of your voice, urging, encouraging, willing that team on to victory, oblivious to anything that is happening except that *"our"* side" must win—that, my friends, is *school spirit*.

My personal introduction to school spirit came well over thirty years ago when I was a young elementary school teacher; my fifth-grade students were going to play a field day game with Mrs. Johnson's fifth-grade class.

Now, "Mrs. Johnson" is not her real name, and she has long since retired and moved away to a happy rest. While she was here during my early teaching days, however, she had a reputation as the sternest teacher in the school. Certainly, she was one of the most "proper" of individuals in terms of her culture and time. We worked together for five years, and she never called me by my first name once. In fact, she never said anything to me except, perhaps, a perfunctory "Good morning." Proper, if you know what I mean—*proper*.

There we were at the field day, and our fifth-grade classes were playing each other in softball, and it was the last inning, and the score was 7-6, in the other team's favor. All through that morning, I had been active, pacing just outside the base lines, shouting encouragement and direction to a loud, gangly group of boys and girls who were putting their fifth-grade hearts into winning this game.

On the other side of the playing field was an equally loud fifth-grade class who also wanted to win. Mrs. Johnson, their teacher, was hardly as phrenetic as I; she sat on a folding chair with a book open in her lap, raising her eyes occasionally to see that all was well with her charges.

Now we were in the last moments of the game and the score was tied. As I paced and fretted, I happened to notice that Mrs. Johnson's book lay closed on the ground, and Mrs. Johnson was on the edge of her chair, eyeing the diamond with eyes wider than I had ever known them to be. My class was at bat with one out left. If my fifth-grader could score, the game would be tied, and we would go into extra innings. If my player struck out, the game would be over, and Mrs. Johnson's fifth grade would win.

There was the pitch, my student swung, and it was a long, fly ball to center field. I was on my feet, yelling and shouting, when all at once, I stopped and gazed with wide-mouthed wonder at Mrs. Johnson, who was on her feet and jumping up and down. She had kicked away her book, and the pens she always carried in a pocket of her blouse were flying this way and that, and she was screaming . . . screaming, "Catch that ball!!!" Screaming? No, actually, she was demanding, commanding, and virtually willing that ball into the center fielder's glove with everything that was in her—body and soul! The fielder caught the ball, the game ended, and Mrs. Johnson's fifth-graders were all about her, and she was jumping and yelling with them, a strand of her perfect hair blowing wildly across her face. I don't think she ever looked better!

That . . . *that* is school spirit!

That is also what I find around this place, every single day of the school year. It is the feeling that I perceive in the teachers as they conduct their classes, knowing that they are giving the children under their care the very best education that each one of them is capable of receiving. It is that sense of dedication to something far greater than the individual that I perceive in all those who work in this school; they go far beyond that which is expected to shape the lives of the children that this school serves each and every day. It is the vivacity and enthusiasm that I perceive in all of the children, our students, who work here and play here and grow here—who are the singular most vital part of this school.

And school spirit is still more than all this. School spirit is that sense that lets you know that this is truly *your* school. It allows you to feel, to sense, to internalize the overriding truth that this is more than the place where you spend a certain number of hours each day—this is truly *your* school; it belongs to you; it is part of you as much as you are part of it; it is a true component of your life, and you savor and appreciate and cherish that fact.

That is school spirit; that is what every good school inspires; that is what is part and parcel of this school. School spirit? Why, this place is haunted by school spirit everywhere you look!

And I, for one, am very proud of it!

SPECIAL DATA: *A speech like this is appropriate for any function that is honoring the school. In the place of the phrase "this school," you can insert the name of your school in order to personalize it. Moreover, if you have a particularly well-known story of school spirit in your school, this is the place to use it. Be positive, as with all speeches of this sort, and mean what you say, and it will be a fine tribute to the "spirit" of your school.*

108

TOPIC: "My Three-Decade 'Stretch' in the Elementary School"

AUDIENCE: Suitable to an Adult Audience; Parents and Colleagues

When I was a child, I could hardly wait for school to be over, and as that last day of the school year approached, I faced it with an odd mixture of anticipation and dread—anticipation in the sense that I was looking forward to the summer without the teachers and the books and the assignments, dread in the sense that it was on that final day of school that we learned who got promoted to the next grade. While I was never in danger of not going on to the next grade, back then, the fear of being "left back" was very real in my mind.

Of course, they allowed me to continue, and I must really have liked it, because I just kept coming back to school ever since. I went from elementary school to high school, to college, and when I left the role of student behind me, I came back as teacher and, finally, administrator. It has been thirty-five years since I left school and started being an educator. Thirty-five years—that's over three decades, and what a time it has been!

It is inevitable, I suppose, that when you have reached that number of years, people will come to you and ask you about the significance of what you have gone through over those decades—what you have seen and experienced, and what you have made of it all. Certainly, that has happened to me, and I tell you, it has made me think.

Thirty-five years—three-and-a-half decades—and what have I seen; what has it all meant; what have I learned?

I remember, very early in my career, that lovely November afternoon when a light breeze blew outside my classrom window and hurried a few orange and red leaves along the pavement. I remember that my class was taking a test and a silence hung over the room.

Then the principal came on the loudspeaker to announce that in Dallas, Texas, our president, John F. Kennedy, had been shot and killed. I recall how those words were like bullets entering our own bodies. The test stopped; all activity stopped, and the principal asked that everyone stand and observe a moment of silent prayer for our fallen president. If I had thought the room was quiet before, now the silence hung heavy and deadly. You could hear the breathing, and then one child began to sob softly. I went to her and held her, fighting back tears of my own, tears I would share with many others in that school on that day.

I suppose that was what we call "being a witness to history," and if that is so, I just kept on being a witness as the history of the era unfolded before me. Not only was I a witness to history; I lived and experienced the aftermath of that day in November. I confronted preteenaged children high on marijuana, talked to blue-spectacled junior hippies who would sit and grin at me during the flag salute—the ones who, when I asked them why they didn't participate, told me, "because we don't have to"! Although you are free to disagree with me, I feel that I was witness to the death of innocence in our children under a media assault that has eroded values at the most basic level of all—that of our children.

I have come to believe that children are a mirror of our society, and as our society has changed, I have watched our children grow and change with it as well, sometimes for the better, often for what I believed to be the worse.

I would not have you think that the picture is dark, however, for along with every negative, there is always a positive; I have watched children develop a heightened awareness of their society as a whole and their community in particular, and I have seen in children heroic acts of love and goodness. I am no pessimist, and I am a child advocate. I do see in our children the hope for our future, whether that makes me a wild-eyed optimist or not.

It has been my privilege, over these thirty-five years, to witness and be a part of it all. Sometimes shocked, sometimes distraught, sometimes worried, sometimes amazed, sometimes encouraged, and frequently overjoyed, I have watched and taught and been a part of the lives of these children, and if I must make sense of it all—if there must be something I have learned from it—then I have an answer for myself, an answer that will satisfy me as I look back.

In all that time, one thing has been consistent and remains consistent. It may not be earth-shaking, but here it is—kids respond to love. From the first to the last; from the loser to the winner; from the worst kids I ever had to the best and most shining examples, kids have responded to love, do respond to love, and, I am certain, will continue to respond to love as long as there are parents and children; as long as there are students and teachers; as long as the human spirit continues to reach out into the world.

In my three-decade "stretch" in the elementary school, I have experienced much and learned much. I hope I will remember what I have learned, but it will be secondary to the love I have experienced from the children who shared these premises with me, some of whom have their own children in school even now. That love remembered is what has made the thirty-five years tolerable; that love given and received has made them glorious.

It has been superb. Thank you for being a part of it all.

> *SPECIAL DATA: This speech is part of the retirement speech of an educator who was, indeed, witness to quite a lot of educational change; you will have your own experiences to relate. If you should be asked to reminisce about your time in education, concentrate on the positive aspects of it rather than assuming that your audience would be interested in the "war stories" that we can all tell. By all means, voice your own opinions, but end your speech on a positive note, with an uplifting truth about teaching and education in general. If you do that, you will certainly be on the right track for any audience.*

109

TOPIC: "Community and Communication—Guides for the Elementary School"

AUDIENCE: Community Audience, Including Parents

The story goes that a very successful businessperson bought a special gift for his mother. It was a parrot who could speak seven different languages. Moreover, because of this unique quality, the bird cost $10,000.

The bird was sent via a special messenger to the man's mother, and two days later, he called her. The first thing he asked his mother was how she liked the bird.

"Oh," answered the mother, "it was delicious. I made a casserole out of it, and your father and I each had second helpings."

"What!" exclaimed the woman's son. "Ma, that wasn't a chicken! That bird cost *ten thousand dollars*! It could speak seven languages!"

"Oh, yeah?" his mother returned. "Well, tell me this: If that bird was so intelligent, how come he didn't say something?"

Now, there is a moral to that story, and the moral is not to ask the chicken its opinion before you eat it. Rather, the moral I see is that the best accomplishments in the world will remain unrecognized and unheralded if they are never told; if they remain a secret; if no one else gets to know about them.

Those of us here at Dwight Road Elementary may not speak seven languages, and our plumage may have gotten a little gray around the pinfeathers (at least for some of us), but we are definitely not ready for the stewpot! In fact, I know for certain that there are many things to crow about in our school. I know the glorious plumage we can spread—the good that we do; the children that we help; the learning that we foster; the growth of which we are a daily part. I know this place and our commitment to the children of this community. And, like those of the bird of that story, our accomplishments should be recognized. To me, that means presenting our school as it is—showing our community what is right about Dwight Road Elementary.

Toward that end, we at this school are constantly open to our community. Never has a parent or community member come to this school without being attended to; shown openly what we do; given whatever information he or she required. We are proud of what we do as an outstanding elementary school in our community, and our community is welcome to see what we are doing right.

That does not mean that things will never go wrong, or that we will never have needs. When that happens, however—when there is a need that only the community at large can fill—we come to you honestly, place the problem before you, and ask for your help in righting the situation at your school, perhaps asking for your input on a new curriculum or your work for the passage of a budget. We come to you that we may work together for a common goal.

That same spirit carries over to the education of the sons and daughters of this community, for when there is a problem with a child—whether that problem is personal, social, or academic—then we all have the problem: the school, the parents, and ultimately the community. If, through communication, the community and the school have built a firm relationship that will last and a trust that will prevail, then that problem doesn't stand a chance. That problem will be overcome, and the child will be the winner, along with every person in this school and every community member.

Therefore, if communication is the key to this success, then let us promise and covenant that we will start today to establish those firm bonds of community.

Do we have problems? Do you see someting in us that disturbs you? Are we, perhaps, missing something you want to bring to our attention? Is there something you don't understand?

For the sake of us all, and particularly for the sake of the children of this school, don't allow those doubts to stay inside where they can grow and fester and posibly poison the whole system. Do not be like the expensive parrot who ended up as Sunday dinner. Rather, come and tell us; let your concerns be known. You will be heard, we will listen to what you have to say, and you will come away with your questions answered to the best of our abilities.

Please, don't wait until you have a question or a concern. If we are doing something right, please let us know about that as well. We do the best we can, and we take our lead from you, our community. Tell us what we are doing right, and we will continue along that avenue of action.

Has your child grown, matured, or changed in some positive manner during his or her stay at Dwight Road Elementary? Tell us about it. Have you been particularly pleased with a program, a special activity, a particular service of this school? Tell us about it. Has one of our staff been especially helpful? Is there a very special teacher in your child's life? Has one of our educators done something that has inspired, uplifted, encouraged, or helped your child to grow?

If so, I would ask you to do only three things: Tell us about it! Tell us about it! Tell us about it!

If we can rely on one another to communicate what is in our hearts, then I assure you that we will have a true community—a place where we know one another and communicate and cooperate for the good of our children.

SPECIAL DATA: The truth of this speech is evident to any educator. If there ever was a day when the school could remain autonomous, it is long over. The members of the community have the right to be involved in the schooling of their children, and they are increasingly demanding that right. The key to a productive school-community relationship often lies in the area of effective communication.

110

TOPIC: *"Elementary Education in the Twenty-First Century"*

AUDIENCE: *Adult Audience of Community Members, Parents, Educators*

I like to fantasize sometimes that there were public schools back in the Stone Age. In that fantasy, I am Principal Og, all dressed up in my brand-new saber-toothed tiger skin outfit, supervising a cave full of little cave people as the cave teachers teach them the proper drills for staying out of the path of the brontosaurus and avoiding all forms of conflict that would alienate the tyrannosaurus rex. A very good idea, indeed.

In yet another dream, I stand in my best silks as I become principal of a school in Colonial times, just slightly ahead of the American Revolution. In this vision, I believe that I am teaching my charges the proper method of pouring tea. The fervor of my dream convinces me that the students have to be taught about tea, so they can be ready for the Tea Party they will be holding soon in Boston Harbor!

Now, while these are certainly fantasies, they are part and parcel of what education will be like in that fast-approaching twenty-first century.

When I started in education, more years ago than I would care to remember, the word "computer" was something relegated to a few scientists who had built something using "vacuum tubes" that could do some basic mathematical processes.

I even remember hearing one scientist proclaim that it would be a long time—if ever—before the computer could be used with the general public, for in order to do the functions that might be required of it in the business or scientific worlds, the computer would have to be the size of the Empire State Building (at that time the largest building in the world) to contain all the tubes and electronic equipment necessary to do the job.

Ladies and gentlemen, that same computer the scientist was talking about then can, today, fit in the palm of my hand. What's more, that hand-held computer can do a thousand times more than the first creations that took the entire floor of a building to house.

What is the point of all this? Well, twenty years ago, the schools taught computers only as part of very innovative science fiction stories. Today, right now, you would be hard pressed to find a school in any area of our country that did not teach some form of computer familiarity, at least—and computer facility in most cases. Many schools have computer labs, where students perfect their skills and gain the knowledge necessary to become functioning members of tomorrow's society. Today, allowing a child to finish school without some familiarity with computers is virtually unthinkable.

We are *not* speaking here of colleges, or even high schools. The best time for children to start learning about computers is from the very youngest age, and the elementary schools of our land produce very happy elementary school students who, quite frankly, are much more conversant with the computer than many of their parents.

Which leads us to the coming century. What will education be like in the twenty-first century? What will the schools teach at that time? From my fantasy examples, the answer is obvious. The century itself will determine what the schools will be teaching and doing. Schools have always stood ready to adapt to the needs of the societies in which they existed—the societies they served— and I am very sure that they will continue to do so in the societies of the future. As they have throughout history, the schools will be there to train the citizens and to prepare them to meet the challenges of their time—to fill the needs of the community.

We don't have to go "techno-crazy" and imagine a bleak time when the computer replaces the teacher and children are ensconced in individual cubicles, staring at blinking monitors, being "taught" by a programmed disk and an electronic image. That will never happen, for while computer learning programs have been and are a great asset to learning in the hands of a teacher, the individual teacher cannot be replaced by a machine that knows only the correct and incorrect answer.

As one of our elementary school students once told me, "A computer can't hug you when you get an 'A'!"

What will elementary education be like in the twenty-first century? I don't know the particulars. Indeed, I know of no one who will be able to paint you a picture in anything more than shadows, but I do know that there will be one fixed point in that ever-changing universe called the future. That one fixed point is that whatever is needed, the schools will be there to provide it.

Now, that is something of which we may all be sure.

> *SPECIAL DATA: Like the weather, the future is a constant topic of conversation. The question of what elementary education will become is often hotly debated in seminars and all sorts of gatherings of educators. The truth, however, is that inevitably, the school will step forward to meet whatever needs the time and situations will demand. This speech has some frivolous examples, and one very serious example, of how it works.*

111

TOPIC:	*"What Parents and Teachers Will Never Know"*
AUDIENCE:	*Suitable for Parents or Educators*

If you were to ask children about school, ask them what school is made up of, they might give you a number of answers. Some might say that school consists of teachers and chalk and yellow paper and paste and crayons. Still others might say that school is recess and opening windows with a big pole and having lunch in a cafeteria. Still others might incorporate books and notepads and big pencils and even computers.

Yes, it would be quite a list. There would, however, be one item on that list that we have not mentioned so far. That item is . . . tests.

Call it a quiz; call it an enforced review mechanism; call it a standardized evaluation instrument—it's a test. We give a lot of them around here, in virtually every class. Some of them are written, and some of them may be as informal as the teacher's asking a specific student a specific question on a specific subject, but we give tests.

Testing is a natural part of all teaching, whether it is done formally as here in school or as informally as one child's teaching another how to hit a ball or ride a bicycle. "Now, tell me, why do you keep the bat off your shoulder? What do you do when you want to stop the bike?"

We ask questions; we test those who are being taught, and we do it for a very good reason—in order to teach a person effectively, we must know what that person knows and, consequently, what she or he still needs to know that we may teach.

With all the testing that we do; with all the asking of questions upon questions, there is a great deal that we know about the child we teach. There is, however, one thing that we don't know—one thing that we will, most likely, never know.

We will never know when the penny dropped.

We will never know the moment when learning became real, when the child realized that it was not a game, but a very vital and real part of life—that time when the child took a bunch of facts and made them a living part of his or her very being.

How does a child learn to speak?

William Gibson's play, *The Miracle Worker*, is the story of the early life of Helen Keller, who, although blind, deaf, and mute, would go on to achieve greatness and prove a sterling inspiration to all individuals with disabilities. This play, however, deals with her early years when her teacher, Annie Sullivan, tried to make contact with the all-but-uncontrollable child through the use of the manual alphabet pressed into the child's hand. It was a long, hard struggle, for, at first, the child had no idea of what was happening and, at best, conceived of the various positions of the manual alphabet as no more than a game for the fingers.

In one scene of that play, Helen's mother asks Annie Sullivan how long it will take, and Annie replies by asking Mrs. Keller how long it takes a baby with unimpaired hearing to learn to speak. How many words, she asks, does a baby have to hear before there is a realization that those sounds mean something? How many times do you say "water" before the child associates that sound with the liquid it desires? A million times? Two million?

The time comes when that "miracle" happens—that breakthrough realization—and after that, the child will never be quiet again. The same thing must happen in school if the child is to succeed both in school and in life.

A child comes to school, and at first, it is overwhelming. There are new people, other children, many things to do; much that is expected of the child; people telling him what he must study; people telling her what she must do. If that child is to succeed, there must come a moment when the whole thing makes sense. There must come a time when the child realizes, if not in words then in concept, that this is not an extended video game, that this is not a clever battle between him or her and the teacher or school, that this is not a place where the law forces you to spend so many hours per day.

Does it happen after the hundredth teacher contact; after the thousandth home-work assignment that a child's parent has supervised; after the ten thousandth question asked, example given, fact explained? I don't know, and, indeed, that may be something that we as parents and teachers may never now. Even the child may never fully recognize the point, but, for the vast majority of our students, thankfully, it does happen; it does come.

When it does happen, for that child, nothing will ever be the same again. From that point on, it all makes sense; *education* has ceased to be just a word, but instead has become a very real and very valuable part of that individual's life.

No, we, as parents and teachers, may never know when it will happen, but that is all the more reason for us to keep trying; never to give up; never to cease teaching just one more time. Yes, we may never know, but as Henry Adams once wrote, "A teacher affects eternity; he can never tell where his influence stops."

For the sake of our children, we can never stop trying—never stop giving each child the insight that will eventually make learning real.

We simply never know!

> *SPECIAL DATA: If you have ever taught a child who seemed truly not to care about education, then you know how challenging and frustrating that may be compared with teaching a child who is actively engaged in his or her own education. This speech emphasizes the point that the child who cares is the child who succeeds. It can also be used as an appeal for increased cooperation between school and home.*

112

TOPIC: *"So You Want to Become Involved in the Elementary School"*

AUDIENCE: *Audience of Parents*

My grandfather used to tell an interesting story. In fact, he told it so many times that, in all honesty, it ceased to be interesting to us in the family. Nonetheless, he kept on telling it.   This is how it went.

When my grandfather was a young man, he came into some money, legitimately, I must hasten to add. In any event, there he was with $200, a veritable fortune in those days, and he was looking for a place to invest it, a place where that money could grow, because, after all, that was why he had come to this country; that was part of the American Dream.

Now, as my grandfather told it, he was offered a stock investment that he considered very carefully. He claims that he was offered stock in something called the Ford Motor Company at the dizzying price of one dollar per share. Again, according to Granddad, he thought long and hard—and decided against it! It was too risky, he decided—too unstable. He chose, instead to invest his money in . . . you guessed it . . . a chain of livery stables!

Well, you know the rest. Ford Motors skyrocketed and prospered and doubled, tripled, quadrupled its worth and on and on and on.

The livery stables? Well, they went the way of the horse and buggy.

You know, I don't know that Grandpa ever fully got over that. Each time he told the story, it would become a bit more embellished, and the tone of his voice would become a bit more plaintive, a bit more hollow with the ringing echo of an opportunity missed; a chance tossed aside; a treasure abandoned. Oh, the missed opportunity! Oh, the regrets and the self-recriminations! If only he had become involved at the time!

Now, I do not have a stock offer to make to you this evening. I'm not selling real estate or mutual funds or combination juicer/blenders. If, however, you have ever bemoaned a missed opportunity to be an active part of your child's school . . . if you have ever said, with an appropriate ring to your voice, of course, "Oh, how I wish I could become involved in the elementary school!" If you have ever done either of these things, or even thought them, then, ladies and gentlemen, do I have a deal for you! You want to know how to become involved with the elementary school? Well, sit back, because I'm about to tell you

First and foremost, don't wait to be asked. As in most things of value, you must set out and take hold of it. Sitting at home and bemoaning the fact that no one has ever asked you to help out at the school will produce nothing. I'm here to tell you that if you want to become involved, there is a place for you, just as soon as you take that first step. Don't sit at home and wait to be asked; volunteer today!

Next, understand that a very good way to start your involvement with the school is by starting to attend the PTA meetings. Again, the PTA will not come to you, but if you come to the meetings, I can promise you that at each and every one, there will be ample opportunity for you to become involved in a myriad activities with this school. We are very proud of our PTA, and they have much for you to do. Start attending those PTA meetings today!

Third, contact your child's teacher. Classroom teachers in this school can and will use you in a variety of situations that require your help on field trips, at special activities, and in the classroom itself. Even if those positions are already filled, your child's teacher will have valuable suggestions on how you can become an active part of this school. Contact your child's teacher.

Fourth, contact school personnel; you can contact me personally, or inquire in the main office of the school. New needs spring up here every single day. What may not be needed today may be a pressing need tomorrow. We will gladly tell you how you can be of help. Contact this school. Finally, always keep in mind that there is much to be done, and in a very real sense, it waits for you to do it. Our teachers, our staff, everyone in this school works hard, and there is still much to be done. One extra pair of hands will help to get it done all the more efficiently and quickly. A hundred extra hands will help even more. There is, indeed, very much to be done, and perhaps you are the one to do it.

There is a saying, "You reap what you sow." As a volunteer in our elementary school, you will find work that will challenge you, that will take your time and effort, that will involve you and your skills. You will spend many hours being actively involved in this place.

For this, you will be paid nothing.

There will, however, be rewards that one cannot calculate on an adding machine nor deposit in a bank account. There will be such intangible rewards as the smile of a child, the look of wonder on the face of a student who has suddenly learned under your guidance, the knowledge that those laughing, vibrant children are enjoying themselves and learning because of your efforts. There will be a knowledge that is yours alone . . . a knowledge that you were a part of it all.

And, I can promise you, you will never become like my grandfather, years later bemoaning an opportunity gone forever.

So, you want to become involved in the elementary school?

OK, there's a sign-up sheet right over there.

Who's first?

SPECIAL DATA: This speech is good for an initial gathering of parents at the beginning of a new school year. So many parents have been known to say, "Well, we'd like to do something for the school, but nobody ever asked us, so . . ." People like to be asked. In this speech, you inform the parents about how they may be involved and you invite that involvement as well.

113

TOPIC: *"Can Children Be 'Killed With Kindness?' Taking a Hard Look"*

AUDIENCE: *Parents (good for educators as well)*

On many of these occasions, I have stood here and outlined plans for various projects, inviting you to participate in what the school was doing, giving you new insights on many topics that were of vital interest to the home and to the school.

Tonight, I want to communicate to you a most important fact.

Tonight, I'd like to give you a foolproof method of destroying a child.

Oh, I don't mean physically, of course, but I have a plan whereby you can destroy a child's future totally, completely, and without compassion, and look good while you're doing it.

And, what's more, it is a plan that will work with every child, any child . . . yes, even your child.

Actually, it's a four-step process that has been used over and over again to the detriment of many a child over many years. It is a process that will continue to be used, and children will continue to suffer under it. I want to tell you about it tonight, so you will know the proper method of destroying your child.

Here it goes.

Begin with step one: Give the kid everything he wants. This is essential. Never make the child wait for something or save for something or do without something he may desire in order to benefit someone else. Convince the child that the world revolves around her and that the important things in life are what she wants. Never allow the child to consider the needs or desires or feelings of others. Allow, "I want it

. . . now!" to become the battle cry. Convince your child that what he or she wants is the only important thing in the world.

This will, by the way, have some very interesting benefits for you. You see, by getting your child everything he or she wants, you can substitute your money for your time. You don't have to become involved at all in your child's upbringing. You can go your merry way, never have to spend time with your child, and call it kindness.

The next step to the destruction of your child is very important. Overall, make certain that you give your child *no* responsibility. That's right—*no* responsibility. Now, you can say things like, "He's only a child!" or, "She needs to enjoy her youth!" or whatever else you may care to utter to reinforce the fact that you give the child no responsibility.

That means that your child never has to wash a dish, never has to make a bed, never has to hang up an article of clothing, never has to put away toys or do any objectionable task such as taking out the garbage or mowing the lawn. Remember, such an action might convince a child that he or she bears responsibility for his or her own actions. How silly. We wouldn't want that to happen, now would we? Remember this second golden rule in the destruction of a child—never give a child responsibility.

The third rule is very important, too. Never, never, never allow your child to take the consequences of his or her own actions. If your child has done something that other, narrow-minded individuals might consider wrong, such as, let's say, hurling a rock through a neighbor's window, then defend your child, lie for him or her and say your child was a thousand miles away at the time. Above all, never allow your child to take the consequences. Never suggest that the child fix the window or work to pay off the expense of fixing it. Never demand that the child apologize for the incident or do yard work for the people or something to make up for it. Just defend without the facts; convince the child that it's not his or her fault, and above all, never punish the child for doing something wrong. After all, we wouldn't want to impinge upon his or her freedom to throw rocks at neighbors' windows. Kids will be kids! You wouldn't want to punish them just because they were having a little fun, would you?

Now, here is the final step in the destruction of a child, so please be certain that you listen carefully and get it right. You must, at all costs, avoid discussing or addressing all hard or difficult issues until the time when the child asks about them. *Do not* discuss with your child such topics as God, morality, sex, drugs, honor. Morality, for example . . . isn't that something they teach in churches and synagogues and the like? Never tell the child there's such a thing as right and wrong; that might inhibit the boy or girl. Sex and drugs—hey, are you comfortable talking aout those things? After all, they're only problems for other people's kids, aren't they? If you wait until *they* ask *you*, why you might never have to tackle the problem at all. Besides, they'll find out about sex and drugs soon enough. Isn't that what the street is for?

Every single one of these rules will ensure that you have avoided all involvement with your child. What's more, you can even take your noninvolvement and defend it by calling it kindness. Of course, your child may not turn out too well, but think of all the comradeship you will have with your son and daughter as you go through one adult crisis after another.

You will, however, have proved an adage my grandmother used over and over again.

"You know," she would sometimes say, "one of these days you are going to kill me with kindness."

Well, no argument there.

SPECIAL DATA: If a speech like this is to be effective, there must be a clear understanding with your audience that what you are saying is the direct opposite of what you are recommending. This is conveyed in a number of ways with body language, tone of voice, and other nuances of presentation, and the ridiculousness of the material. It is a given that parents want what is good for their children, not to "destroy" them. If you have the rapport with your audience that is needed for this speech, after a very few lines they are fully aware that the content is satiric. Used properly, this can be a most effective and dynamic technique.

114

TOPIC: *"Keeping the 'Elementary' in Your Child's Education"*

AUDIENCE: *Suitable for Parents and Educators*

Two students were talking.

"Really," stated one, "I can't see how you can maintain that Shakespeare wrote his own plays when both internal manuscript evidence and corroborative documents clearly indicate the fine hand of either Marlowe or Bacon."

"Indeed," answered the other, "I contend that any attempt to vilify Shakespeare as a rampant plagiarist is nothing more than mere intellectual snobbery . . ."

At which point the first student turned to the other and whispered, "Be quiet, here comes the teacher. Recess is almost over, and we're supposed to be playing hop-scotch!"

Yes, you laugh at that story, and we all do. Our first thought is that these students are, perhaps, college or even graduate students, discussing some fine point of literature. When we find out that they are elementary school students at recess, the incongruity makes us laugh. The story does, however, point out something I'd like to explore with you for the next few moments.

I sometimes wonder if, in our push to bigger and better education, we have not succeeded in taking the "elementary" out of elementary education.

I once knew a fifth-grader who really needed the services of a social secretary; she already had a schedule that would have made the First Lady or the Queen of England look like pikers in comparison. This child was engaged in everything. She was at the top of her class academically and was president of the student council. She did peer tutoring, acted in all the school's variety shows and every class play that was put on, was an office aide, and, upon occasion, served as an aide in the library.

All of this was school related, but her schedule didn't stop with school. Outside school, she took classes in ballet and tap dancing, took piano lessons, worked in a special program for young community volunteers, and played on a community girls' field hockey team.

In the office, we laughingly said, "One of these days, this kid is going to get an ulcer." We were not so amused when she collapsed in school and had to be taken to the hospital with multiple stress-related ailments. Here was an elementary school child, but there was not one thing "elementary" about her or what she was doing.

Perhaps it would be a good thing to take a look at exactly what that "elementary" in "elementary education" really means. "Elementary" means that this is the place to learn the basics. This is the place where you will not only learn the readin' and writin' and 'rithmetic of the old song, but will prepare a foundation for all your later learning. You will not, for instance, learn microbiology, but you will come out knowing what a microscope is and wanting to know more about its use.

"Elementary" means that this is the place to learn how to socialize and get along with all sorts of other people. Here, you first come into contact with people who are not your family, who do not think that everything you do is wonderful and special. Given the proper guidance and the attitude of teachers and classmates, you learn to get along with almost everyone—a very valuable lesson—absolutely necessary for both survival and success in today's world

"Elementary" means that this is the place to learn to love school— to acquire a love of school and learning that will carry through into later life. Virtually every teacher has heard and understands the old saying that you cannot make a child learn who does not want to learn, and you absolutely cannot stop a child from learning who has the burning desire to do so. It is part of the elementary school's purpose to instill that love of learning that will prove such a powerful incentive throughout the child's entire academic career.

Each child is an individual with unique and separate abilities and temperaments. I have had many parents, over the years, ask me, or ask the teachers in the school, about how much is enough.

"Do you think my son can handle school and Little League?"

"If my daughter takes that part in the school play, is her homework going to suffer?"

"Keisha wants to take a paper route."

"Barry would like to join the Community Kids Program."

"What do you think?"

I have given an answer to all of these questions, and I will give one now. It may not be the answer you want to hear, but I have become convinced that it is the only answer possible: It depends upon the child.

How much an elementary school child should take on, both inside and outside the school, depends entirely on how that child is constituted. I have known children who have thrived on busy schedules and who are unhappy when their day isn't as full as it can be. I taught one such girl who is now a thriving business-woman in our community—still as busy as ever, still a friend of our school, and (very important) still happy. I have known others who have crumbled under the pressure, and when that happens, no one comes out a winner—especially not the child.

Remember the "elementary" in elementary education. Is your child actively engaged in learning the basics that he or she will need for a lifetime? Is your child learning to socialize and become a part of a cooperative comunity where each plays a valued part and each is respected for what he or she is and is becoming? Is your child becoming more and more interested in learning and displaying a love of school, even though vacations and breaks are welcomed by all?

If so, then these activities may be built upon and added to. If, however, the additions begin to erode the "elementary" processes, then something has gone wrong. For example, the moment that your son or daughter begins to complain that school has become a real "downer," because the homework and the classes are just eating into the dance lessons or the community team, then perhaps it is time to reconsider the team or the outside lessons before the homework is sacrificed for activities that have replaced the "elementary" and made it secondary.

Such activities as music, the arts, sports, and community involvement have been and will continue to be a part of virtually every student's life. That is not in question. If the outside comes into conflict with the "elementary" process and threatens to override it, that process will suffer, and when that happens it is inevitable that the child will suffer as well.

Let us do something radical. Let us use our own good sense in each individual case, but above all, let's make certain that we keep our children's elementary education . . . elementary!

> *SPECIAL DATA: Feel free to substitute an example from your own experience, in your school, for the one we used as you personalize the speech for your audience and circumstances. The topic is one that concerns many educators, and is certainly something you'll want to address.*

115

TOPIC: *"The Elementary Legacy—Strap On Your Armor Before You Leave"*

AUDIENCE: *Suitable for Parents; Teachers; Community Members*

Do you like movies about medieval times? I do. I'd love to get myself a suit of armor. I'd also love to direct one of those movies, let's say the scene where the knight goes out to fight the dragon. Just picture the scene: Off goes the knight to fight the dragon, and there's the dragon, ready to barbeque the knight. The brave knight comes right up to the lair of the beast, enters the dark cave and disappears into the gloom.

But, we're not worried, are we? We know that knight has everything he needs in order to slice up that scurvy beast. Just then, the knight's squire comes running down the mountain path, holding something in his grasp. "Sir Knight!" he exclaims. "Sir Knight! Come back! You forgot your armor!" About that time, we hear appropriate screams from the cave and the dragon begins sending out invitations to a dinner party featuring filet of knight as the entree!

Well, as you may have guessed, this is not a frivolous story. I see it as a rather sobering tale of the legacy of the elementary school. In this analogy, the dragon is the world that waits outside these walls; the knight is your daughter, your son, and the armor—the armor is the elementary legacy without which no child should leave this school.

Which of the many dragons will your child be facing? Will it be the drug dragon? The crime dragon? The sexual harrassment and abuse dragon? These are just a few, but there are many more; you can surely add to the list.

These dragons wait for your children—for your sons or daughters, off on a quest for a good, happy, and productive life, and bound and determined to conquer every dragon in sight.

The elementary legacy is the armor that they will wear into the fray. The elementary school has always provided this armor to everyone who has come here and who has sat still as it was being fitted—for make no mistake—the elementary school's job is to provide the armor and that armor is always tailor-made.

That armor consists of all the academic basics, neatly tied together in a utility package called "knowledge." The coat, called "coping skills," is hand-fitted as well. It is woven day by day within the schools and it allows the "knight" to meet up with all sorts of obstacles and overcome each one. Finally, the knight stands in a pair of very solid boots, known as "personal growth." These boots allow the fighter to stand firm before all the onslaughts of the "dragon."

In the past, this armor has been provided for many, many individuals. It started in elementary school then, and it continues in elementary school today. Whatever the future holds, the elementary school will continue to provide the armor for each successive generation of "knights" who venture forth from the relative safety of these walls to meet —face to face—the fiery dragons of this, our world.

This is the elementary legacy; it is available to each and every child who enters this place. No matter how perfect the armor may be, however, it remains useless if it is not put on before going into battle. When I was a child, I would run outside to play, completely oblivious of the weather, rain or sunshine, cold or warmth, and my mother would always yell after me to wear my hat. Was it a thousand times my mother yelled after me?

Between us, between the home and the school, we can fashion an armor that will give the knight-child a good chance at overcoming the dragons of this world, and with parents and educators working together, we might even have a chance of seeing to it that the armor is worn, in the sunlight and in the rain.

Let us tell our children: This is the elementary legacy; this is your armor! For your own sakes, strap on your armor before you leave!

> *SPECIAL DATA: This speech is useful for a program on education in general or elementary education in particular. To personalize this speech, you might want to give some actual examples (with names changed, of course) to illustrate former students who both did and did not "strap on their armor."*

IN CONCLUSION

This section is meant to speak to the value, content, and structure of elementary education. If one thought comes through, we hope it is that these speeches are written and delivered by people who are very much a part of the educational scene—people who know schools and students, and teaching and administration, and the running of a functioning school.

This is important for a number of reasons, not the least of which is that, at times, you will be speaking to people whose only experience with elementary education is that they took part in it so long ago, they have all but forgotten what it was like. Now, they have children of their own in this place, and they really do want to be convinced that you know what you are doing; that their children are in very good hands; and that they can have security and peace of mind in entrusting their children to your care. Your enthusiasm and your knowledge of the elementary school and the entire educational process will be of great help in establishing rapport. Let them see your knowledge and feel your enthusiasm, and that audience will be on your side and the side of elementary education as well.

*S*ection 8

"*Parent* Is an Active Verb . . .": Speeches That Reach Out to Parents

Teachers and students may constitute the makeup of the school, but it is the parents who can make or break a school or a school system. A community of parents who constantly vote down the school budget can leave a system tottering on the edge. Groups of parents who are dissatisfied with the school or who are upset about something related to the school can make the school a very uncomfortable place to be.

On the other hand, a school that possesses the support of its parents and the community is a place where education sparkles and success is a daily event. With the parents of a community behind you, there is absolutely no end to what may be accomplished for your students—for your school.

In this section you will find speeches fashioned to reach out to parents on a variety of levels—all aimed at getting parents both involved and enthusiastic about the school. For the most part, these speeches can be used individually, or as part of a series, for example, at successive PTA meetings.

Now that's an investment that pays a big dividend!

$$\boxed{\textbf{116}}$$

TOPIC: *Parents and Teachers—Partnership or Panic*
AUDIENCE: *General Audience of Parents*

(NOTE: This speech is an appeal for parental involvement in the education of their children and in the day-to-day operation of the school.)

Let me begin by telling you from my heart how very happy and gratified I am to see so many parents here this evening. I truly believe that this is a beginning, a beginning of a wonderful and productive relationship between you, the parents, and us, the school.

You know, there are people who view their children's education as a twelve-year war fought on the battleground of their children's lives. They begin with an adversarial attitude, and they maintain it all along the way. Nor does this apply only to parents, for there are teachers who feel the same way, and who look upon any parental contact as an invitation to a duel.

Fortunately for you and for us and for the children of this school, you will not find that attitude in this school. Very simply, we will not allow it. We are not in a twelve-year panic; we are in a twelve-year partnership, with the benefit of the student as a common goal.

Here at Dwight Road Elementary, we are advocates of involvement in the school by the parents of our students. We believe that this is an outstanding characteristic of those schools that are acknowledged for the high quality of their performance throughout our land. Research continues to be conducted on schools at all levels and under all circumstances, and time and again that research has very clearly demonstrated that the involvement of parents is a real key both to a child's success in school and to the genuine success and excellence of the school itself.

Christopher Cross, one-time Assistant Secretary of Education for Research and Improvement, wrote, "We can no longer afford to have parents disengaged from the education of their children. We cannot expect others to perform those duties, and we cannot expect children to do well without the guidance, the tutoring, the nurturing, and the commitment of parents. To do less is to consign our nation to an ever-increasing decline into economic and educational oblivion."

Certainly, I and the entire faculty of Dwight Road Elementary believe this to be true. The question that remains is, how do we go about making it happen? How, in short, can we enhance parental involvement here at our school?

Perhaps the first step would be to let you, as parents, know just how important it is for you to talk to your children about school and school work and to become much more involved with your children's school life. When you ask your child, "What did you do in school today?" you should never accept the classic answer, "Nothin'." That simply means, "Nothing that I want to tell you about now." Pursue the matter; get to know what your child is doing; become familiar with what is going on with your child in school.

Next, it is up to us in the schools to work hard to create more opportunities for your involvement, which could well include specialized programs to help you see your children through school. Those opportunities might include courses in such varying topics as how to work with your child on homework and even how to start preparing for college—yes, even here at the elementary school level.

Finally, we in the schools must encourage parental conferences. It is through communication that the school and the home will join together for the benefit and good of the child. Through these conferences, parents and teachers unite as partners in the education of the child. Through these conferences, the child becomes the center of all aid and attention, and that child's success is both augmented and assured.

There is an age-old story that I first heard as a very young teacher. The story goes that a child who wanted to go over to his friend's house after supper knew that his parents generally did not like him to go out in the evening. Therefore, the first thing he did was to go to his mother.

"Mom," he said, "may I go over to Joey's house after supper? Dad says it's OK with him if it's all right with you." Immediately thereafter, the boy sought out his father, saying, "Dad, may I go over to Joey's house after supper? I talked to Mom, and she says it's all right with her if it's OK with you."

I believe that the name of that game is "Divide and Conquer."

This "Mama-Papa" game may have advantages for a child who wants to "put one over" on his or her parents in a home situation, but I will tell you that it is absolutely deadly when applied to the home and the school. As long as the home and the school are kept apart; as long as there is no communication between home and school; as long as the one has no idea of what the other is doing; as long as this process continues, the student can get away with whatever he or she wishes. The student may be a very happy child—that is, until the reality of failure sets in; until it is too late to remedy the situation.

With cooperation and parental involvement, the student is guided both at home and in the classroom, and that student emerges the winner. In fact, we are all—everyone of us—winners!

So, here we stand, and our hand is stretched out to you. Let's not panic; let's resolve to build a partnership that will survive throughout your sons' and daughters' education—a partnership in which everyone wins.

> *SPECIAL DATA: Many parents are eager to participate, but hold back from fear of being considered "interfering" or of not being wanted. It has been proven over and over again that the positive involvement of parents in the operation of the school and the education of their children is a real factor in unqualified success for both the student and the school. In this speech, you let the parents know that, and make a logical appeal for their involvement. Any speech that speaks plainly to an audience, and speaks to the problem directly, is certain to engender a positive response.*

117

TOPIC:	*The Elementary School and Your Gifted and Talented Child*
AUDIENCE:	*Parents of Gifted and Talented Children*

(NOTE: This speech is aimed at a specific segment of parents, in this case the parents of gifted children, thus the differences between this and the previous speech.)

Good evening, folks. Please allow me to welcome you to this gathering.

Getting right to the point, you are here because your children have been identified as falling into the Gifted and Talented classification, and we'd like to take some time tonight to tell you exactly what that means and what we, as a school, have to offer your children.

There are a number of ways to look at the gifted and talented child, and one way is by the following comparison to milk. Allow me to explain.

When I was a child, we had milk delivered daily to our front door. It came in glass bottles, with, as I recall, waxed paper tops. The milk was pasteurized, but it was not homogenized; that is to say that the fat or cream particles were not evenly mixed with the milk liquids, as they are today. If you allowed the milk to stand for even a short time, the cream separated and came to the top, while the liquids stayed at the bottom. Indeed, on cold winter days, the cream would freeze at the top of the bottle and push the cap up so that a column of cream stood out of the neck of the bottle. Sometimes, you would come out on a frosty January morning to find the cat licking the cream like a popsicle.

Now, stretch the analogy for a moment and allow your gifted and talented child to be the cream in that milk bottle. The two schools of thought on G&T students have always been related to that milk. Some feel that the cream should be allowed to rise to the top, separated from the rest of the bottle, to be skimmed off as rich treasure. Others think that the cream should be mixed into the rest of the bottle in order to make the entire bottle all the more rich.

Should the G&T student remain in the regular classroom, ready to help other students, ready to lead the class into new avenues; ready to provide incentive, direction, and help for those who may be falling behind? Should the G&T student be taken out of the classroom and placed with others like him or her in order that they may all go forward at their own pace and investigate areas of study that would not be within the reach of a class in a regulation classroom? These are the two viewpoints with which we must contend.

I have heard it said that with the G&T student, you could take the child, place him or her in a good library and come back at the end of the term to find that the student has learned as much or more than if he or she were in the class. I want to tell you now that that is the biggest fallacy about the gifted child that I have ever heard!

"To educate" means "to lead out." With all of our students, that means leading out of the state of not knowing and into a state of knowledge, whether that knowledge is academic, social, artistic, or philosophical. This implies—no, it insists upon—a leader who is trained to handle the specific needs of these very special children, and one who is particularly sensitive to their needs. It demands a teacher who can take these eager, quick, agile, and hungry minds and see to it that they are fed the diet on which they can flourish and grow strong.

The U.S. Army has a recruiting slogan, "Be all that you can be!" Well, you'll find no argument with that slogan here!

One of our tasks here at Dwight Road Elementary is to prepare your children for the future—for the world that they will face outside this school. That means giving them all that they are capable of receiving. Our approach is somewhat of a mixture of the two philosophies about which I spoke before. We do not propose to take your children out of the classroom and make them "special" or "set apart." Rather, we intend to augment their regular classroom learning by taking them out for a special class on a regular basis. In that class, they will be challenged and introduced to fields of study that will open up their eyes and minds and allow them to be, in the words of that slogan, "all that they can be!"

I'd like to make one thing clear. Being in a Gifted and Talented program should be a rewarding experience, not a punishment. Because these children are brighter, they should not be loaded down with work. What we aim at is not more work, but different work, designed to sharpen the abilities they already possess.

And you, as parents, will play a very vital part in this process. Your G&T child needs your support and understanding every bit as much as, if not more than, any regular student in this school. Your child needs to know that you are proud of him or her. Please do not assume that Gifted and Talented children do not need your reinforcement, your encouragement, your continuing interest and support. They need you to be there, to understand what they are going through, to be interested enough to ask about what they are doing and be involved in their projects, research, and learning.

All children must study and learn and grow within the protective framework of the home and the school. It is equally essential for G&T children as they work toward their true potential in this ever-changing world.

Together, that is a goal we can achieve!

> *SPECIAL DATA: In this speech, you give specialized information and enlist parental support for the program that involves their children, in this case a Gifted and Talented program. Keep the tone conversational, as if you were explaining something to several acquaintances. It is always well to take this approach when you are addressing a smaller group. Assume that you are being regarded as a friend who is there to help your audience. Should any resistance surface during the encounter, you can always handle it then and there, but start off as friends, and the chances are that you will end as friends as well.*

118

TOPIC:	*When Something Goes Wrong—How to Talk With the School*
AUDIENCE:	*A Group of Parents*

I was reading the newspaper the other night, and my husband (or wife) came by and looked over my shoulder at the page I had open before me. "For goodness' sake," he said, "what are you doing looking at the Obituary section?" "It's the first place I turn to," I told him. "Nowadays, the only time I get to see our friends is when we gather at the funerals of other friends!"

Come to think of it, that is much the way in which many of us view our relationship—the relationship of the home (that's you) and the school (that's us). For a great many people, both in the home and in the school, the only time that we ever come together or have contact is when there is a problem—when there is trouble.

That's rather like the young lad on the farm who had not uttered a word for the first eighteen years of his life. Doctor after doctor had said that there was nothing wrong with the boy, but he simply would not speak. Then, one night at the dinner table, he looked up at his parents and said, "These are the worst mashed potatoes I ever tasted!"

"You can talk!" exclaimed his parents. "Why didn't you say something before?" "Up till now," answered the lad, "the mashed potatoes were all right."

Don't let it be that way with us. Don't wait until something has gone really wrong before you contact us with your concern.

I once took a phone call, and a person on the other end of the line screamed, "I want to know what you're going to do about it!" "Do about what?" I asked. "Well," answered the caller, "if that's your attitude, I'm going to take this to the school board!"

Please, don't wait to contact the school until a minor problem has become a major incident. Handle it while it's still a candle flame rather than a forest fire.   Let me give you a few positive steps that may be taken toward that goal.

First and foremost: Contact the teacher involved. If there is something concerning your child that you don't understand; something that you perceive as a problem, don't just think about it—get the facts. Contact the teacher involved. I promise you that a call to a teacher in this school will be answered just as soon as possible.

I can also tell you from a background of many years in elementary education, that fully eighty to eighty-five percent of all problems are solved by this simple expedient. That's right, immediate contact between the home and the teacher will set things straight in almost all cases. Of course, even after that contact, there may still exist misunderstandings or areas that will need to be reconciled, but in the vast majority of cases, the problem ends there—no longer an obstacle to understanding and cooperation.

The next step, if that first procedure does not satisfy, is to contact the guidance personnel of this building. Why would you want to do that? Simply because they are trained to arbitrate problems—that's their job. Guidance can set up a face-to-face meeting between you and anyone else in this school. What's more, they can be there to ensure that everything runs as it should. What a great alternative to sitting alone and allowing doubt and suspicion to build to the point where the real problem is obscured and untouchable!

Finally, if you receive no satisfaction anywhere else, you can call the administration of this school. I am very aware that part of my mission is to act as an aide to you, the parents of the children. If you contact the administration, I can promise that we will hear you out, listen impartially to what you have to say, and work unrelentingly with you to bring the problem to a satisfactory solution.

Let me tell you the story of a man who looked out at his lawn one day and realized that he needed the use of a garden hose. He thought a moment and remembered that he had seen his neighbor using a bright green hose just the other day. The man knew what he would do. He would go to his neighbor and ask to borrow the hose.

On his way over to his neighbor's house, the man began thinking. "You know," he said to himself, "I borrowed a rake from my neighbor last summer, and I believe it's still in my garage. I'll bet he remembers that I didn't return that blasted rake. As a matter of fact, I'll bet he's been sitting there all winter, just thinking about that rake he lent me that I never returned. Maybe he's sitting there, waiting for me to ask to borrow something, just so he can slam the door in my face and not lend me that hose!"

At that point the man had reached his neighbor's door. The neighbor, seeing him on the front porch, opened the door and said, "Hello, Fred. What can I do for you?"

"Well," the potential borrower snapped, "if that's the way you feel, you can just keep your blasted hose!"

Doesn't that sound like the phone call I told you about a while ago?

Let's not be like the man with the hose; let's get ready to work together and communicate as we both strive for solutions when something goes wrong, because when a problem does surface, you don't have the problem and the school doesn't have the problem, but we share the problem, as we will share in the solution.

Is there a problem? Let's talk.

SPECIAL DATA: While this speech most definitely gets across a particular point of view, it also teaches the group the procedure to be followed when something goes wrong. Note that along with presenting the procedure you give quite a bit of explanation of how and why it works. Never merely tell an adult audience what they have to do; to do that is to invite instant resistance. Your instructions stand a better chance of being followed if you give the procedure and explain at the same time why following it will help to expedite the matter.

119

TOPIC:	*Becoming Involved With Your Child's School*
AUDIENCE:	*Group of Parents*

The story goes that two relay teams had a race, the winner of which took home a rather rich prize. The two teams were neck and neck throughout the entire race, and now it was nearing the final laps. Finally, one team pulled ahead, and as they neared the point where the baton would be passed, that team was a full twenty yards in front.

The leader ran up to the next runner and held out the baton to that final runner. That person just stood there, with arms folded. "Take it! Take it!" screamed the runner with the baton. "Please!" exclaimed the other athlete. "If I take that from you, we'll have a relationship, and I really don't want to get involved!"

As ridiculous as that story may be, for many people it is not a story but a way of life. Have we not all heard stories of people who have been injured or assaulted as people walked by, preferring to refuse to acknowledge what was going on rather than allow themselves to become "involved"?

Unfortunately, that may be the way some parents feel about the school. Oh, not that they are allowing harm to come to their children or the place where they spend spend so much of their day, but the rationale goes that the school probably knows what it's doing, anyway, and they really wouldn't want me sticking my nose in there. Such an attitude will certainly keep anyone uninvolved. It will not, however, do one single thing to enhance the child's education.

Why? Well, let me make it very clear. Research has been going on for some time regarding this subject, and the evidence shows that when parents are actively engaged in the formal education of their children, student achievement improves. What's more, it rises in all areas.

That's not speculation on my part; that's documented fact. What's more, this rise in achievement relative to parental involvement isn't just at the level of the elementary school. Of course, you are going to see it throughout your child's stay at Dwight Road Elementary, but what research has shown is that the positive results of your involvement continue throughout high school.

Remember that the home is the very first educational environment for every child. Later, the child will leave home for a percentage of time each day to attend school. At the end of the day, however, the child goes home.

Now, if the home and the school offer two differing environments, with two different sets of rules, the child quickly learns that once out of the school building, he or she can "turn off" education. He or she comes through the door, the books get tossed in a corner, on comes the stereo or the CD or the one-eyed monster, the TV. This is home, and it has nothing to do with school, and certainly nothing to do with that educational process that has gone on during the previous hours of the day.

If, however, the home and school are involved with each other; if the parents know and are even a part of what is going on at school, then the home becomes an extension of the educational environment, and the process continues. That age-old question, "What did you do in school today?" may not even have to be asked; you will know. What's more, you will be there to guide your child in the direction he or she needs to go.

We cannot afford to view the home and the school as separate entities. Indeed, just the opposite must apply, for we are well aware of the importance of the home in the processes that go on in this school. Let me give you one example that applies to us here at the elementary level.

One of the basics that the school aims to teach is the process and skill of reading. Reading is absolutely essential to every child as well as every adult. We take great pains, therefore, to do everything we can to make sure that the child learns to read and learns to read well.

Do you know who learns best—with the fewest problems? With, statistically, the greatest ease? Do you? The answer is . . . the child who has been exposed to reading at home before he or she ever sets foot in the school. Yes, the child who is in an environment where books are prized; where the child is read to—this child learns best. If your involvement continues at all levels of your children's education, the benefits will just keep on coming.

Helping your child with homework is fine and good and laudable, but I would urge you to do even more than that. If you can, become a part of this school, whether it is helping out as a classroom parent, reading to many youngsters at story hour, supervising class projects, or any one of the many opportunities that this school offers.

At each of the PTA meetings we have had over the past several months, I have continually urged your involvement in our school. I have told you how it can be done as well as what can be done. Tonight, I have tried to show you why this is so important, why I will keep on emphasizing the importance of your cooperation, and how pleased we in the school would be to have you.

Come in to have a look at us; we want you to see how good we are. Come in and check us out; we're willing to show you what we do and what we have. Come in and ask what you can do to be involved in this school; we'll gladly tell you. In fact, we'll gladly sign you up on the spot; we're ready to get you started just as soon as you want to.

Let me say what I firmly believe—something I have said before and definitely will say again—when the home and the school are positively involved with one another, everyone is a winner! And your child wins most of all!

SPECIAL DATA: This speech tells parents why their involvement in the school is so valuable. You can get more information on this subject from the NEA or your state educational association. They can also lead you to other sources. You can use this speech alone, or as part of a series of speeches (as is indicated in the speech itself), perhaps in combination with speech 116 or speech 118. Parents really can make a significant difference in a school; don't hesitate to inform them of their part in the process.

120

TOPIC: *Is There Life After the Elementary School?*

AUDIENCE: *Parents*

(NOTE: This speech informs parents about a very important skill every child needs, and tells them how they can play a part in passing it on.)

Burning questions —questions that boggle the minds of even the greatest philosophers—have been asked by introspective and sensitive minds since time immemorial. These are questions like "Why am I here?" and "What is life all about?" and "What's my purpose?"

Another question is dear to the heart of every parent of a child in this building: "Is there life after the elementary school?" The answer should be very encouraging. Yes, there is life after the elementary school—for you *and* for your child.

I know, because I have sat where you are sitting now, that having a child in elementary school and being actively involved in the process fosters an obsession on that process. Car pools, lessons for your child to be taken to, lessons for your child to be picked up from, class parties, class plays, that part for the science project that your child forgot to tell you about that he or she needs by tomorrow morning—all of these are a part of what I perceive as "the elementary school two-step."

The time will come, however, when your child will leave this school; the day will come when Dwight Road Elementary fades into the background and the high school and college and the business world pop up before them, waiting to enfold them and try them out.

When that happens, one of the most important factors that will help to determine their success and adjustment to these new lifestyles will be something that, we hope, they have learned from you and us here at the elementary school level—namely, how to get along with others. In the diverse world they will face after this school, our children will have to know how to get on with a wide variety of people; they will have to know how to cooperate for the good of the group. That's why we place such an emphasis on that aspect of learning.

You can drop by a classroom and see students seated at their desks, quietly engaged in learning on an individual basis, and that is proper and valuable. It should be noted, however, that a great many learning activities in the classroom also involve group work, with the student not only taking in information, but also learning how to cooperate and function as a valuable part of the team—in other words, learning how to get along with others. Even in the highly competitive world of business, while competitive ambition has its place, it is the ability to work with the team and cooperate for a common goal that will be a factor in most people's success.

Achieving this cooperativeness is neither automatic nor easy. Quite often children fail to appreciate other people's viewpoints and have some difficulty in dealing with people who are different from them. To overcome this difficulty, the school and the home must work together; the result will be of immense benefit to our students when they enter that life after elementary school.

One leading family counselor phrased it like this, "If your son or daughter has high self-esteem, he or she will make it in the world." The child who has a sense of personal worth; who feels good about himself or herself; who is unafraid to enter new situations; who does not worry that failure will prove him or her less a person of value—that child, in the counselor's words, "will make it in the world."

That's where we come in—parents and school. These feelings of self-esteem don't develop automatically in the individual. Rather, they develop and are developed within our relationships to other people. A child who grows and flourishes in a place where he is encouraged; where her efforts are recognized; where he is cherished; where she is important—this is the child who will develop the self-esteem that will carry him or her through life after elementary school, through school and right out into what we all know as the real world.

We do it together—the home and the school. You can tell a child that he is loved and you can tell a child that she is capable, but unless he or she believes it, there is no progress. Your involvement in this school; our frequent contact with the home; parents and teachers taking notice together of what is right with the student—all these and more go toward convincing the child that we care; that the home and the school are engaged in a process of working together for that child's ultimate good; that the child is good and capable and worthy of love.

We're not just saying it—we're doing it!

It starts here and now, and it starts with us. Would you like some ideas on how to build your child's self-esteem? We have those materials available. Would you like to be in the classroom when your child gives that science presentation? It can be arranged. Would you like to be there on that softball field when your son or daughter runs into home; would you like to be there to put your arms around him or her—to tell your child how proud you are, even if he or she just struck out for the fourth time? You can be there.

Be involved with the school; together we can work at building your child's self-image into something that will allow him or her to face that life after elementary school, and to face it with a smile. Now, isn't that something worth working for?

SPECIAL DATA: Many children suffer from low self-esteem, and there is not a single teacher who denies its detrimental effect upon a child's achievement. While there may be an occasion where the school alone can reverse the situation, in the vast majority of cases, it is a combination of home and school working together that produces the best results. This speech may be used as part of a general series at successive PTA meetings, or as part of a longer program on the involvement of the parent in the school. Don't hesitate to change it to reflect your own educational needs.

121

TOPIC:	*That Candle in the Window Is Burning for You*
AUDIENCE:	*Parents*

Let's get right to it.

Studies continue to show that the value of education is impressed upon students when they see their parents and other family members actively engaged in support of the school and the school program. Let's take a look at some of the benefits.

In almost every case, student achievement is higher; the student not only has the school looking at what he or she does or does not do, but the home is there as well, encouraging and motivating. Of course student achievement is higher.

Next, there is a significant improvement in school attendance. If nobody cares what you're doing in school, why bother to even be there. With the active participation and cooperation of the home and the school, everyone cares that you are in school and learning, and that learning will be reinforced at home. Oh, yes, school attendance improves.

Third, an improved student sense of well-being emerges. There is a sense among students that things are OK— that all is well or under control. After all, if the two single biggest and most powerful forces in your life, your home and your school, are in it together and have it all under control, then of course it's OK!

Another very real benefit is that student behavior gets better with increased cooperation between home and school. For centuries, it seems, educators have known that most students exhibit two standards of behavior—one in school and one at home. Home behavior is, as a rule, preferable to the behavior away from home, but the reverse can be just as true. When the home and school are working together and those two institutions are intertwined, student behavior understandably improves in both places.

Both students and parents have better perceptions of classroom and school. Students whose parents are involved in the school tend to believe that the school is working for them, a perception that brings about increased achievement and satisfaction.

Teachers constantly report that homework is completed and handed in on a more regular basis when the parents become involved with the school. Now that parents are informed and participating, they are more aware of what work is required outside of school, and that work is forthcoming from students.

Next, it is reported that hopes are higher for the educational careers of students, and students have higher goals for themselves educationally. As the perception of the school as a place that is approved, supportive, and safe continues to grow, students begin to feel free and secure enough to formulate realistic and energetic academic plans.

Now, this next benefit should, by now, come as absolutely no surprise to any of us. As parental involvement continues, students get better grades. Everybody is on their side now; it's their school now; they can do it. They get better grades.

It has been said that familiarity breeds contempt, but I'm not too sure of that. When parents become involved in the school, they become familiar with the school and its personnel—particularly their child's teachers. Instead of contempt, however, research shows that greater parental satisfaction with teachers comes with involvement. If we get to like each other, we go to great lengths to get things done, don't we?

Finally, researchers have found that successful family involvement actually brings about a special productivity in the time that parents and children do spend together. In short, parents and students find themselves growing closer together, and the time they spend together takes on a higher quality.

The power that parent and family involvement has to positively influence student success is without question. Years of research have shown us the benefits—many of which I have outlined for you this evening. That's why we have had this series of talks; that's why we at Dwight Road Elementary are constantly inviting you to be an active part of this school; that is why it is worth all the effort invested in developing effective involvement programs.

When I was a child and we visited my grandmother, we would always have a wonderful time. Invariably, however, as we were leaving for the ride home, Grandma would say, "I'll leave a candle in the window for you!" That statement confused me. After all, what did I need a candle for? Anyhow, what good would it do me in the window where I could never get to it? I tell you, it simply didn't make sense. Then I asked my mother.

She told me that in the days before there were electric lights, the nights were very dark; people had to rely on moonlight or starlight alone for guidance. Imagine yourself, she told me, walking or riding a horse and making for home in that inky darkness, uncertain of where you are. Now look, up ahead—there, in the darkness. It's a pinpoint of light that grows brighter as you make your way toward it. Someone has been expecting you and has placed that lighted candle in the window to guide you through the night—to guide you home.

That was the true meaning of the candle in the window. We want you to know that there is a candle in every window of this school. If you are uncertain or "in the dark" about this school or how your involvement can help, then come to the window, come to the light; come to this school, and we will take you in.

Look at that flickering candle in the window. Don't you know? It's burning for you!

SPECIAL DATA: The research cited here is based on a 1991 study that still has relevance today. If you want to turn this into a longer speech, you can easily expand on any of the benefits mentioned. You might also combine it with speech 119 or one of the other "involvement" speeches. Suit the speech to your time, your purpose, and your audience. If you really believe that parental involvement is a good and desirable thing, then your speech will convey that belief, and it cannot help but bring results.

122

TOPIC: *What You Don't Know Can Destroy You*

AUDIENCE: *Parents and Comunity Members*

"What you don't know can't hurt you," the old saying goes. I suppose that's true, under some circumstances.

I remember being on a picnic once with a number of family members, including Aunt Helen. Aunt Helen was one of my favorite aunts, but she definitely had her problems. While she had a number of problems, the one that applies in this case was that Aunt Helen had a very desperate and very real fear . . . of insects. Many people dislike insects, particularly the bigger ones, but Aunt Helen had a fear of them—from the largest monstrosity from the depths of the jungle right on down to an ant without the letter U.

There we were on the picnic, and everything was going well. Aunt Helen was wearing a particularly colorful blouse, and I was admiring it when one of the spots of color began to move. I blinked my eyes, and the spot of color moved again. I took a tentative step forward.

There, on Aunt Helen's sleeve, was one of the fuzziest and most colorful caterpillars I ever saw. I looked at Aunt Helen, who was busily engaged in putting out the goodies for the day and talking to my mother.

"Aunt Helen," I said, "I have something to tell you." She turned from what she was doing, gave me a great, big Aunt Helen smile and said, "Sure, honey. What is it?" Well, you know what I told her. Her eyes darted down to her shoulder, and even as I watched, the smile faded, and she began to shake. No, not just shiver, but actually shake. Her lips moved, but no words came out; her eyelids began to flutter. Her eyes began to drift upward. I did what most kids would have done. I reached over and grabbed the caterpillar and sent it to caterpillar heaven, if such a place exists. I got rid of it. For the rest of the day, I was Aunt Helen's favorite, and the next day, she took me out for ice cream.

Later, talking about that small incident in the country, my father would remark, "What you don't know can't hurt you." In that case, I suppose it was true. As long as she was unaware of that caterpillar, life was wonderful and Aunt Helen went about her business in relative happiness. It was only when she became aware of the presence of the insect that her life fell to pieces.

While the old adage may occasionally be true, to assume that it is true in every case, or even in the majority of cases, is to invite disaster. I have had over thirty years' experience with children and parents and teachers and school. In my opinion, based on that experience, not only is it untrue that "what you don't know can't hurt you," but if I could change that statement in every book in which it appears, I would write, "What you don't know *can destroy you.*"

Of course, I could tell you stories, true stories, that would prove that point. I could tell you of children who got started on drugs in the elementary school, because they were "blissfully ignorant" of the poison they were taking in—because they believed the monsters who got them started. I have attended the funeral of an elementary school student who didn't know that you weren't supposed to get into a car with a stranger. I could tell you of girls who have been embarrassed, shocked, and even edged into hysteria because they were unaware of the natural changes that were taking place in their bodies, because no one had prepared them for those changes. I could tell you of children who walked into danger without knowledge of that danger; their ignorance did not protect them, but merely led them, to use another cliché, "like lambs to the slaughter."

On another plane, this applies equally well to you, the parents of the children of this school, and us, the teachers and administrators of this place. If we stay in our own domains—parents in the home and teachers in the school—then we will know nothing of each other. Opinions we form about each other will be based on wild speculation at best. When problems arise, and arise they will, we will each act separately, based only on what we do not know, each of us in our separate sphere, attacking a problem that may or may not exist with a perspective that may or may not bear any resemblance to what actually *is.*

Excuse me, but that is a formula for disaster!

If a child who does not know that he should not get into a car with a stranger is at risk of serious harm; if a child who has no idea of what that funny powder will do to her is a catastrophe waiting to happen; if these situations are true reflections of what not knowing can bring about, then the home and the school, operating on a lack of knowledge, pursuing what each believes is best for the child, are heading for disaster.

What you don't know can't just hurt you—it can destroy you and your child.

If we are to succeed together; if we are to produce a child who may be termed "educated" and ready to function in this ever-changing and often inhospitable world; if we are to work for that goal that we most certainly share, then we must work together, and we must work together based on mutual trust, mutual respect, and mutual and accurate knowledge.

Make no mistake, it is by getting to know each other that we will come to respect each other, understand each other, and work effectively with each other toward the betterment of your child and of every child in this school.

You already know the way. Throughout this school year, at each of these meetings, we have explored parental involvement in the school. At these meetings, we have looked at the benefits to the school, the home, and the students when parents take an active interest in their children's education, we have learned the myriad ways in which you can help out in this school; we have even spoken of the problems that can arise through lack of communication and subsequent lack of understanding; and, most important of all, we here at Dwight Road Elementary have opened our doors and opened our hearts, issuing a sincere and heartfelt invitation for your involvement.

I am delighted that so many of you have responded. Those who have can tell you, I am certain, that the results have been very positive for them and for their children. I have received this assurance from many of the parents, many of the teachers, and many of your children—the students of this school.

What you don't know can destroy you—I think we have proved that statement. If so, then it must follow that what we do know—know about the school; know about the curriculum; know about the plans of our teachers; know about the hopes of our parents; know about the needs of our students; know about each other— what we do know will build the firmest of foundations on which to build the tower of your son's education, your daughter's future.

Since we are into clichés this evening, how about this one: Ignorance is bliss where 'tis folly to be wise. Let's amend it to read this way: Knowledge is truly bliss when 'tis disaster to be ignorant of what is going on and affecting our lives and the lives of our children.

Now, there's a cliché I can live with.

How about you?

SPECIAL DATA: Most schools hold a series of PTA meetings or parental gatherings throughout the year. In this speech we see the conclusion of a year-long series that stressed parental involvement in the schools. This speech, like earlier speeches in this section, can stand on its own, or it can be incorporated with many of the others to make a longer and more detailed speech.

IN CONCLUSION

Research shows that positive parental involvement reaps enormous benefits for students, for the home, and for the school. On the other hand, lack of communication between the home and the school has been known by many of us to produce negative, and sometimes very disturbing, results. The speeches in this section are intended to reflect those findings.

While these speeches were given in a series, over a number of parental gatherings, you can adapt them to suit your individual needs; combine them in the ways suggested in Special Data sections, or use any of them alone.

Most important: Assure your school parents that they are welcome, that they are needed, and that working together will benefit everyone involved—their children most of all. The results are bound to be positive!

Section 9

"Tough Times; Tough People . . .": Handling Troublesome Issues

The saying, "Tough times don't last, but tough people do," is a comforting thought in times of trouble, and as anyone who has been around professional education for any time will acknowledge, those "tough times" do come.

From race relations to drugs, from censorship to the troubled child, from sex education to those who seriously disagree with the school, troublesome issues are no longer confined to the college campus or even the high school. Today, even the elementary school can be the scene of some "tough times."

Let's see how we can approach some of these troubling, and troublesome, issues.

123

TOPIC: *An Elementary Look at Race Relations*

AUDIENCE: *Parents; Educators; Community Members*

In one elementary school I know, two girls were the best of friends. Not only did they do their homework together, they did everything together. In fact, they were inseparable. To understand the point of this story, you must know that one girl was black and the other was white.

One day, the teacher noticed the two girls arguing rather vehemently in the back of the room. Before she could get back to them, they were on the way up to her with a question.

"Ma'am," stated one young lady, "we want you to settle a question for us. We want to know what color is better?" At that, the teacher's heart sank. Taking a deep breath, the woman, a veteran teacher, began to explain to the pair about race and judging people on what they are and not the color of skin or nationality or . . .

At one point the girls interrupted her. "But, Ma'am, we know all about that. We've known that for years." "Then, why . . ." "Well," answered one girl, "she says we should wear green dresses to the dance, and I say we should wear yellow. What we want you to tell us is . . . which color is better?"

While that story is true (I got it from the teacher involved), I wonder if it is truly reflective of race relations as they exist in our schools today. It would be ever so fine if it were, but in reality, it may be an exception that is far from the rule. I think it is fair to say that race relations have not yet reached the point where we can all work with, evaluate, employ, and enjoy people without ever noticing their color or race. If we take an honest look at our society as a whole, we must see that we still have a long way to go.

On an individual basis, as in the story of the two young ladies, perhaps we have. At least here, in the elementary school, we try . . . we try.

Our goal is not a race-less society. At one time, the prevalent philosophy was that America was to be the great "melting pot," where we all gave up our heritage in order to melt into one big, all-encompassing category called "American." Today, our goal has changed to that of a society where cultural diversity is celebrated.

That's what we do here at our elementary school. We do not try to eliminate or supress our differences. Rather, we celebrate them. We all celebrate our heritage, whatever it may be, and in so doing, we learn from one another. In celebrating our differences, we learn of our common heritage in humanity.

It is most important that we start here, in the elementary school. This is the time for children to receive that direction that will steer them through life—to teach them how to honor our diversity while we revere our similarities. Our goal is to produce children who look upon race as something to be honored and celebrated—never something to hold a person back.

We all know that the issue of race relations is a complicated and frequently emotionally charged issue, but if we can do anything to help us all arrive at the philosophy of those two girls, it is a worthwhile task to undertake. In any event, we can never stop trying.

Let's look forward to the day when arguments about color are confined to the color of dresses. For the sake of our children and their future, we must try—and keep on trying.

> *SPECIAL DATA: Don't wait until there is a racial crisis at your school to give a speech like this. Martin Luther King Day is an ideal time to use this speech, but it can be used as well for any program on civil rights, the history of our country, education for the future, and the like. The anecdote is true, so you may use it with assurance, and it does reflect the essence of what we hope to achieve.*

124

TOPIC:	*What We Don't Say About Child Abuse*
AUDIENCE:	*Originally for Educators; Possibly for a Community Audience*

Usually, I like to start each address with something humorous. This is an exception. This evening, I am going to talk to you about one of the most painful subjects that fall within my duties to handle. This evening, I want to talk to you about child abuse.

Perhaps a good place to begin would be to examine for a moment what child abuse isn't. Some people have claimed that in a rush to deal with serious cases of abuse, the law has all but negated the parent's right to discipline the child.

I am not trying to deny you that right—not at all. A parent has a right to discipline his or her child. Indeed, there is reason to believe that a parent who does not discipline a child is guilty of child abuse as well. A child needs direction, and that direction does not come naturally; it has to be instilled.

No, we are not talking about a child being denied a privilege (watching TV is not an inalieanable right) or being sent to his or her room. We are not talking about that at all.

I have seen firsthand, and tried to keep it out of my dreams, the results of true child abuse. I will not sicken you with explicit details, but I have dealt with bruises and broken bones from being beaten with chains, cigarette burns on the arms and buttocks, and children who could not sit down because of sexual abuse. The victims of this abuse were children in the elementary school. They came from every conceivable economic background—from every possible social stratum. In fact, their only common point was their suffering.

I have also dealt with children who have been abused in school. I'm not pulling punches here, for this is far too serious a subject to worry about hurt feelings. I would much rather see a feeling hurt than a child. A child who is stood up in front of a class and publicly humiliated by the teacher is being abused. A child who is placed in the hallway of the school without supervision—as a punishment or even for such an innocuous reason as the taking of a test —may be subject to abuse in that hallway, where 62 percent of all bullying occurs (N.A.S.S.P., March, 1995); that child is being subjected to child abuse. A child who is denied access to the school nurse or the lavatory facilities is being subjected to child abuse.

Let me be very quick to tell you, every teacher in this school is aware of this, and we all work very hard to see to it that the specter of child abuse of any kind and under any interpretation simply does not exist in this school. Each teacher and administrator in this school is, collectively and independently, a child advocate, and we continue to work for an environment where each child is treated with respect and dignity and the ability to learn is unimpaired.

Certainly, there are laws on the books against child abuse, but what those laws don't tell you is that they are virtually powerless to prevent it. These laws may deal with offenders once they are caught, but that is after the fact. The child still hurts; the effects still linger; the damage is still done. That's what the laws do not tell you, and that is also the reason why this place—the elementary school your children attend—puts so much time and energy into programs of awareness about abuse like the one you are about to see this evening.

I hope that we will all come out better informed. If there is even one person in our audience this evening for whom this subject is relevant; if one person learns something to pass on to someone who needs it; if one of you learns to recognize a symptom and spots it and reports it; if one child—one child—is spared the horror of child abuse, is spared the physical and mental suffering, is spared the guilt and shame—will it have been worthwhile? Will it have been worth your attending?

You know the answer, and you know how concerned we are for your children—as concerned, I assure you, as you are.

After all, that's why we're here.

SPECIAL DATA: The subject of child abuse must be addressed seriously, and with delicacy. It surely goes without saying that only general incidents of child abuse, like those mentioned here, can be spoken of. Very few people, including the faculty of any school, disagree with a "get tough" attitude on child abuse. This speech was used as a lead-in to a program on the subject (like the opening speeches in Section Three), but you can easily modify it to stand alone.

125

TOPIC: *Sex Education in the Elementary School*

AUDIENCE: *Parents; Educators; Community Members*

My child came to me one day and asked that question all parents wait for. He asked, "Where did I come from?"

I was ready; I tell you, I was ready. I got out those books I had bought, I sat him down, I explained everything on what I considered to be his level of understanding. It took a long time. Finally I was finished.

"Now," I said, "does that explain where you came from?" "Yeah," he answered, "Tommy says he came from St. Louis, so I wanted to know where I came from, but just wait until Tommy hears all this!"

Which brings us to the subject of sex education. I want there to be no mistake about it; I'm talking about sex education on the elementary school level.

Before we begin, I would like to give you my personal view on sex education. I have affirmed in the past as I affirm now that sex education is the prerogative of the home. I firmly believe that parents bear both the right and the responsibility to inform their children about sexual matters. *(Note: If this is not your view, by all means omit it, or substitute your view.)*

I still remember, however, when I was a child. I don't recall how old I was, but I was certainly in elementary school. One afternoon, I asked my father what it meant to "have sex," a phrase I had heard from some other children. My father looked at me and sighed—and then told me to go to the dictionary and look up the word "intercourse." I looked it up, and it stated that "intercourse" was "commerce between nations." I came away more puzzled than I had been before. It was a long and difficult time, as I recall, until I was set straight. I was set straight where the vast majority of the children in my era got their sex education—in the street, by other kids. Misinformation was rampant, and when I finally learned the truth, I held onto a germ of resentment for having been lied to for so long.

Don't get me wrong, I loved my father to the day he died, and I came to sympathize with the feelings he experienced, coming from a background where such things were never mentioned at all. If there is a point to all this, it is that while I believe that sex education belongs in the home, I find that in many, perhaps most cases, it is not being carried out. As always, the school prepares to step in to fill the need.

Children need facts and truth; few would disagree with that. The trouble starts with the fact that sex education is a highly charged subject, both emotionally and morally. Consequently, people on both sides of the issue are vehement about what they believe to be the best approach to the subject. Some claim that the only way we are ever going to solve such pressing issues as the AIDS epidemic is to give children full knowledge of the processes involved so that they may take precautions to avoid contracting AIDS. Others claim that teaching a child about sex without teaching morality is akin to placing a loaded gun in the hands of a two-year-old and telling him or her to go play with the rest of the kids on the block.

If we are going to be realistic, the debate is going to go on for some time. I say this because I have met with both sides and both sides are, in my opinion, sincere—absolutely sincere—in their beliefs. I certainly don't have an answer, but I do have a speculation.

Perhaps this is where that cooperation between the home and the school should come to the forefront. Perhaps this liaison between the two most powerful forces in a child's life might finally work out exactly what "sex education" means and should be in the elementary school. Perhaps the day will come when the school will teach the "facts" about sex with a certainty that the home will supply the personal morality that is needed.

These are speculations, of course, and I am eager to hear your views. One thing, however, is certain. If they don't get it from us, they will get it from somewhere else. Who should tell our children about sex—the parents and the school, or the street?

That's a choice we have to make!

SPECIAL DATA: Admittedly, sex education is a very touchy subject, and whatever your personal opinion, it is well to handle the subject with great sensitivity. Above all, you must be convinced of the merits of whatever you are proposing and speak with honesty and fervor. Even if people in the audience disagree with you, they can still come away convinced of your personal integrity. That can be a great advantage when you are dealing with a program of sex education in your school.

126

TOPIC: *The "Drug Dragon" and the Elementary School Child*

AUDIENCE: *Parents; Educators; Community Members*

Over the many years that I have been an educator, a number of people have asked my opinion about several topics connected with school and education. Once, one person asked me what I thought was the greatest detriment to the school and to the education of our children.

Well, that was quite a question—certainly one that made me think. I believe that I am able to answer it now, and I also believe that there is no better time to state it than here at the beginning of this program tonight.

The singular worst, most destructive, curse ever placed upon the youth of our country is, without question, drugs.

I have known a girl who stole money from her parents, arranged for her parents' home to be robbed, bullied children into giving her money, looked for every opportunity to steal from her classmates and her teachers, and generally cared for nothing and no one except where her next drugs were coming from. This was a child who was addicted to drugs. She was ten years old.

You must understand that drugs constitute a "Dragon," a truly ravening beast intent on destruction, the destruction of our youth. There was a time when drugs were a problem with only a small segment of our society. That is no longer true. The hot breath of the Drug Dragon has infiltrated every stratum of society, every area of our land, every age level—right down to elementary school children on the playground.

No one is safe; no one is immune. That means every child in the world, including yours, is a potential meal for the Drug Dragon.

Can we conquer the Drug Dragon? Sad to say, the answer is that we probably cannot destroy the beast completely, but I'll tell you this, we can certainly injure the beast right down to the very core. We begin here and now. In school, we have a number of antidrug programs already in place; some of them are mandated programs, and many of them are special programs that have been set up by parents and teachers working together for our children. There are also programs for parental awareness of the problems, detailing various approaches to these difficulties.

In addition to these, it must be addressed in the home —this pitched battle with the Drug Dragon. Children are very quick to pick up all sorts of attitudes, particularly from their parents and teachers, so let's begin by telling our children that all drugs are bad. Tell them that any drugs aside from those that a doctor gives you are not to be played with or fooled with. Be sure to tell them that there is no such thing as a "recreational" drug.

Now, you can argue that last point with me if you wish, but before you do, let me tell you that I have seen small children who came to school stoned from the drugs they found their parents using. I'll also tell you of children who called for help only to be ignored by parents who were busy with those same "recreational" drugs. So, come on, tell me that there is nothing wrong with recreational drugs, and I'll listen politely and then do everything in my power to turn you in!

You know, that Drug Dragon is far too powerful for one, single person to fight. Together, however, we can fight, we can present a united front, and we most certainly can deal a mighty blow to that beast. Let your children know your attitude about drugs and the slimy creatures who would get them started on drugs. Please don't assume that your son or daughter is too young to be in danger. Tell them of your opposition; love them enough to really make that opinion known; support what your children learn about drugs in the programs given in school, and—most important—let your actions be the loudest speaker of all.

Don't just tell your kids about your opposition to drugs; show them. Together, we can deal a mighty blow to the "Drug Dragon" that threatens to consume our children, but that's the way it will definitely have to be done—together.

> *SPECIAL DATA: Drugs are right at the top of every educator's list of worst things that can happen to children. With this speech, you impress on your audience the importance of working together to assure that the children will not be targets of those marginally human specimens who would push drugs on the playground of every school in your community if they could. The words and attitudes are tough; that's because it is a tough subject!*

127

TOPIC: *Censorship in the Elementary School Classroom*

AUDIENCE: *Suitable for a Mixed, Community Audience*

Two protestors had to leave the protest line, and they met coming around a corner. One carried a large sign that read, "I'm For It!" while the other had a sign stating, "I'm Against It!" They smashed into each other and both went sprawling, along with their signs.

"What's your position?" shouted the first. "No fair!" the other countered. "You tell me what you're for, and whatever that is . . . I'm against it!"

To live in a democracy is to take into consideration the views of all. We don't have to agree with those views, but we must get along with all people, whatever their views may be. Sometimes, this is very rewarding, as it is when we celebrate our differences or honor various leaders on "special" days. Sometimes, it is downright impossible, human nature being what it is.

When a particularly touchy or emotionally charged subject is introduced into the elementary school, you can be certain that there will be controversy. Not to go into specifics, but this always brings to mind the controversies that have come about over certain curriculums and, of course, sex education. All this has led to charges of censorship in our school and the classes that we teach. Are we, indeed, censoring the materials that our students receive?

Well, of course we are. We have always exercised some form of censorship in our classrooms, and we most likely always will. In subject matter, we decide what materials the student will learn at what time; we will not have a student study anything that is beyond his or her ability to comprehend it. To introduce materials too soon is to guarantee failure. In concepts, we understand that some students have the ability to handle abstract concepts and some do not. Often, this is age related, and we are not about to introduce concepts to children that they do not have a chance to fully comprehend. In interpersonal relations, we exert censorship as well. We do not think that it is just "self-expression" when one child calls another by a racial epithet. We censor that; we do not allow it. Yes, we will censor that; we will censor speech and behavior that carry hate and cruelty and poison into our school.

But that's not the point. The point is that someone has to take charge and say what is and is not rational and appropriate for our students. The place for that, however, is not in the classroom. Our teachers teach within guidelines established by the Board of Education, and the administration of this school continues to be vigilant in seeing to it that those guidelines are adhered to.

Should you, or anyone for that matter, care to disagree with those guidelines, or care to disagree with how this elementary school adheres to those guidelines, then I tell you that the place for that disagreement is not before our children and is definitely not at the cost of the interruption of our children's education.

The place for controversy and a demand for change is in the offices of the School Board. The place is in personally organized groups who will make an active and proper effort to change that which exists. The place is in the voting booth as you work in support of those candidates who will support your ideas.

To understand this process is to understand the difference between law and anarchy, and it is also to understand what we want to teach our children with regard to what the right to disagree is all about and really means. Whether censorship does or does not exist in this school, and whether or not you agree with what is or is not being taught, there is a process for you to deal with it.

Above all, right now the elementary clasroom is a place of learning. Whatever your opinion, let's remember that and abide by it.

> *SPECIAL DATA: Sometimes, even on the elementary school level, there are people who will say that you are teaching the students too much about a subject, while others contend that you are not teaching enough. When such a controversy comes, the best you can hope for is that those who are dissatisfied will take their concerns to the proper places to discuss them in an open forum. Keeping cool and maintaining a strong approach like the one demonstrated here will carry you through those trying times.*

128

TOPIC:　　　*The Elementary School, the Home, and Effective Discipline*

AUDIENCE:　　*Parents; Possibly Members of the Community*

When something goes wrong; when an incident involving your child occurs, you want it handled and you want it handled effectively. In many cases, that means punishment for those involved in the incident.

I remember one parent whose son had been involved in throwing balls of paper on the bus, thereby proving a distraction to the driver and the safe operation of the vehicle. According to the driver's report, the boy in question was one of the major paper throwers. The very next afternoon, I got a call from the parent, telling me how unsafe and potentially dangerous the situation was, and how he would support whatever punishment I decided upon.

I responded that I thought that was quite good of him, considering that his son was one of those to be punished. "Oh," he added quickly, "There will be no need to punish my son. I've always taught him to be sensitive to other people, so I'm certain that he'll learn his lesson if you merely suspend everyone else on the bus!"

Children make mistakes and often must be punished in order to enforce the fact that what they did was wrong and totally unacceptable. Without that reinforcement, the behavior continues and has a tendency to escalate, as the child probes to find his or her boundaries.

Children expect to make mistakes, and they expect to be punished. Certainly, in this school, children expect to face consequences when they do something that is obviously wrong. They know, for example, that they are not allowed to run in the hallways, and they know that if they do so, they may face an office detention or, for a continuing infraction, a Saturday detention. I once had a child walk into the main office, drop her books on the counter, stomp over to the row of chairs outside my office, and plop down in one of them.

"Did someone send you to my office?" I asked. "Not yet," she answered, "but after what I did, it's only a matter of time. I figured I'd avoid the wear and tear on everybody and come without being asked!"

You see, children do expect that they will be punished, but they will be upset if they consider the punishment unfair or inappropriate. A child runs in the hall, and I assign that child a detention—no problem. A child runs in the hall, and I assign five Saturday detentions and suspension until such time as the parents can come in—overkill, and totally inappropriate for a first-time offense. Two children run down the hall, and based on nothing else but personal whim, one is let go and the other punished—many, many problems follow. It is the fairness of the punishment that adds to its effectiveness.

You, as parents, and we, as the school, must understand that situations concerning your children and punishment are going to arise. As I've told you many times, we want you involved in your child's education, and this aspect of it is no exception. Indeed, our faculty understands that when a problem begins to unfold with a child, the first line of attack on that problem is to contact the home.

If we do have that contact, then the likelihood that the offending behavior will never be repeated is great. If, for instance, a child does something wrong in school, and the home reinforces what is being done in school, then the child becomes aware that the two most important and influential entities in his or her life are solidly together on this, will not accept what has been done, and the behavior had better be changed.

Let us always remember that the object of punishment is *not* vengeance, *not* retribution. Rather, the goal of effective discipline is to amend, to change, and to bring back to the proper pathway the behavior of the one who has offended.

Of course, I would be less than realistic and less than truthful if I said that this works in 100 percent of the cases with which I have dealt. Of course not—not everyone can be reached. But, I have seen it happen, and I've seen it happen time after time. I have seen children turned around when the home and the school worked together to achieve effective discipline that will alter the child's life in a positive manner.

Perhaps it won't happen overnight, but surely we share this goal for our children. Working together, we can attain it. For the sake of our children, we can do no less than try.

SPECIAL DATA: Discipline in school, perhaps particularly in the elementary school, often becomes a bone of contention between parents and the school; facts may be totally ignored. Quite often, the school has one story, one set of facts, and the parents have another story, the one told them by their son or daughter. If home and school are communicating, and if there is a spirit of trust between the two, they both have the same set of facts, and there can be no basis for dissension.

129

TOPIC: *How Do You Handle the Child With Problems?*

AUDIENCE: *Those Involved With the School; Parents; Educators*

There is a wonderful poem by John Godfrey Saxe entitled "The Blind Men and the Elephant," in which six blind scholars go to examine an elephant in order to "see" what it is like. One touches the elephant's tail and proclaims that the elephant is like a rope; another touches the beast's leg and tells everyone that it is like a tree; still another touches the elephant's ear and pronounces the elephant to be like a fan. So it goes. Each thinks the elephant is something different, although all of them have touched the same animal.

One particular "elephant" in the lives of all of us is the problems that will arise. It is not a question of *if* they will come, but rather it is *when* they will come. When they do, a great deal will depend, as in this poem, upon our approach to the problem— the way in which we touch it and deal with it in our lives.

Now, let me introduce you to a very basic fact of school life. There will, in any given elementary school, be children with problems. That's not being pessimistic; that's not being negative; that's being absolutely realistic and truthful. These problems may range from behavioral difficulties right on up to serious learning problems, but problems have existed, do exist, and will continue to exist within the elementary school, and these problems must be addressed. Let me tell you how we handle problems here at Dwight Road Elementary.

First, we find out what the problem is. As a saying I once heard goes, we do not go off to hunt the grizzly with an unloaded rifle. We depend upon such variables as teacher perception, observation by a supervisor or someone from administration, whatever test material we may have, and any relevant information from other sources. Before we do anything else, we get our facts straight.

Next, we involve the parents. We will not wait until it falls upon you like the proverbial "ton of bricks." From the very beginning, you will know. I can promise you that whatever problem may be facing your child, it will not be the child's problem; it will not be the school's problem; it will not be the home's problem; it will be our problem—one we will think about and handle together.

Third, we plan to handle the problem. Neither of us does this alone. Together, and with the aid of those specialists who can suggest proper avenues of approach, we try to formulate a plan whereby the child's problem is addressed efficiently and effectively. When we set out to help a child, we want to know what we are helping with, what needs to be done, what tools we have to do it, and how we are going to set about it. That means not only here in school, although we will certainly do our part, but at home and in the hours outside of school as well.

Finally, we work at it. Perhaps this is the merest fantasy, but I have the belief that problems have a tendency not to go away. It's as if a problem wants to stay around, and it is going to take concerted and consistent effort to budge that problem, to root it out, and to dispose of it totally and completely. It can be done, but it is going to take hard work on all sides. We have never been afraid of hard work.

Let's not approach the problem from a hundred different points of view, like the blind men of the poem. Let's be united in our desire to help; united in our confidence in each other; and united in our attitude that, together, we can help to solve the problems of our children.

Around here, we believe that we can make a difference, and we do! Over the years that I have been in education, I have known cases of failure and stories of success, and I will tell you, I have witnessed more success stories than failures.

With cooperation, with shared intent, with common purpose, we can handle the child with problems and work toward the solution of those problems that keep a child from achieving all that he or she may be capable of attaining.

We believe we can make a difference. And—we do!

SPECIAL DATA: The problems we are addressing in this speech are not of the type in which the child forgot to bring milk money twice in a row or was sloppy on his or her homework one day. Classroom teachers handle those problems on a daily basis. Rather, this speech addresses those problems that seriously affect a child's learning, whether from an academic or behavioral standpoint. The involvement of parents in these cases is of the utmost importance, and with this speech, you are conveying that fact.

130

TOPIC:	*Special Education in the Elementary School Setup*
AUDIENCE:	*Parents of Those Involved in the Program*

It has been stated that all people are created equal. Despite the poetry and the beauty of the sentiment, experience with life often teaches us that all are not created equal, just equally. Certainly, we all start out life in the same manner; however much the circumstances of our birth may differ, we came into this world equally. After that, however, the differences began.

As children begin to grow and develop, we begin to see many differences emerge. We see some children excel at one thing or another; we see some children who achieve self-sufficiency at a very early age; we see the curious and the content; the affable and the affected—a microcosm of society as a whole. There may be a child somewhere who does not need help in the process of growing up, but in our experience, virtually all children need our care, our help.

Every child we teach; every child who comes through these doors and into this elementary school; every child in your home and at your dinner table and in your heart; every child—is special.

You might say that here at Dwight Road Elementary, we specialize in "special" education, and we are very proud of that fact. The term, "special education," has other connotations, however, beyond the uniqueness of each child. It connotes the process we have for dealing with those children who require more help and guidance than it is possible to give within the confines of the traditional academic classroom. When children require this special attention, we are ready to step forward and help. Indeed, we have the facilities and the trained individuals who dedicate their lives to just such an endeavor.

You must understand that the concern and care we show our special students is the very quality that sets us apart from a factory or a business. The factory seeks to produce a product; something uniform; every one just the same. It stamps them out by the hour. Business seeks to make a profit for itself, and it is in terms of that profit that the success or failure of that business is assessed and rated. We are not so concerned about getting the product out, or making a profit; we are concerned with the process. We look at success —at individual victories in the process—not at how much is or is not accomplished. Our emphasis is not on producing something called "a student"— someone who is the same as every other student—but in seeing to it that each child does the best he or she is capable of doing, gets the help he or she needs to be a part of it all, and functions as a very special part of life.

It is not always an easy task. We work, we fail, we pick ourselves up and try again, there is a breakthrough and a success, and we rejoice with the effort and the success. Our compassion, our humanity, our community demand that we treat all our children as special, because they are! It is our task to provide very special educational guidelines and assistance to whose who are most special of all in our schools and in our hearts.

Let's get started.

> *SPECIAL DATA: The topic of special education can be especially touchy for many people; therefore, you must handle it circumspectly. Parents of special children, like any parents, appreciate honesty, a cooperative attitude, and genuine concern for their children. Talk to them in a straightforward manner, and you will establish a rapport that will serve you well in all future dealings involving their special children.*

131

TOPIC: *Handling Concern About the Elementary Curriculum*

AUDIENCE: *Parents and Community Members*

A boy came up to his father and asked for some help with his science project. "I need some things," the boy explained. "I need two eagle feathers, a jar of grape jelly, a pair of pantyhose, a 9-volt battery, and a 1967 nickel. Do you think you can help me find these things?" "Son," answered the father, "I don't think that's the question. The question is, what are they teaching you in that school?"

Now, there's a question that has been asked many, many times over the years. Sometimes it has been asked in curiosity, and, frankly, many times it has been asked in anger. That's what I'd like to investigate in these next few moments.

If a school, any school, is to be effective as a place of learning and growth, it must have a curriculum. There is little disagreement there. A curriculum may be likened to a road map for travelers; it tells us where we are, where we are headed, and the general route we are going to take to get there. There is disagreement, however, as to what is in the curriculum—what side roads we are going to take and where we are going to stop and explore along the way, to continue our analogy.

Within recent years, the curriculums of schools from colleges right on down to our own elementary school have been set upon and attacked and denounced by people and groups representing many diverse opinions.

I could go into specifics, but that would only take up time. Read your evening newspapers or look at the television news shows, and they will give you an idea of the various conflicts that are going on around the curriculums of schools and school systems across our nation—from the big cities to the small towns. Putting it concisely, some say there is too much and others claim there is too little. This applies, of course, to a myriad topics, from sex education to social studies revisions. In a pluralistic society, such diverse opinions are inevitable; they may be a part of the process that has made us great, or the price we pay for democracy—I don't really know.

I can say, and mean it, that I admire the dedication and the steadfastness of the beliefs of these individuals and groups who work so diligently for the causes in which they have placed their trust and their faith. Faith like that can, and often does, move mountains.

I will add, however, that there is a forum, a public forum, for the voicing of their dissent and their concern, and I gladly point these individuals in that direction. The campus of this elementary school is not that forum. This school will not be interrupted, nor will any child be made uncomfortable or frightened, because of the actions of those protesting the curriculum or any other aspect of this school or educational system.

Yes, we cherish your questions and concerns, but we cherish the peace and learning of our students even more. For the sake of our children, we can learn to work together, even if our opinions sometimes separate us.

> *SPECIAL DATA: There comes a time when you must take a stand. You can certainly try to recognize all sides of the question, but at some point you must draw that line and refuse to step beyond it. This speech acknowledges that there may be reasons for opposition to the curriculum, and it even acknowledges that the opposition is in good faith, but it refuses to allow the school or the school grounds to be utilized as a place for dissent or demonstration.*

132

TOPIC:	*Examining the Right to Disagree*
AUDIENCE:	*Adult Audience*

There was a budget crisis at a business, or so the story goes, and the executives decided to ask the workers how to cut down expenses to avoid having the entire business go under. There were, of course, many responses.

When all the replies had been tabulated, the company announced that the workers had been unanimous in saying that the way to save money was to cut salaries. They were equally adamant that the salary cutting was to be in a department other than the one in which they worked. In other words, everyone who responded wanted to save money by cutting the salary of some other person!

In a way, that sometimes applies to people who disagree with us. We understand, in that rational part of our minds, that the world is filled with people who are going to disagree with what we do, what we say, and what we believe. We are even willing to grant others the right to disagree with us as long as they know that we are right and they are wrong, and provided that they don't make any noise about it. Maybe that's human nature; if we didn't believe in the opinions we hold, why would we hold them; why would we fight for them?

In a democracy, *all* may disagree. In a democracy, all may freely express that disagreement. That applies to society as a whole, and it applies to this school. But I will warn you about something—you had better check your facts first; get it straight before you come in to get on with it. Before you accuse me or the teachers and staff of this school of anything besides dedicated service to your children, make sure that you know what you are talking about, and that you are disagreeing rather than slandering. Saying that you believe that school funds could be better used is disagreeing. Saying that there was culpable misuse of school funds is something else, and you had better have the evidence to back up that statement.

Time and again, I have said to anyone who would listen that I am proud of this school and what our students and teachers accomplish here on a day-to-day basis. I have invited you to come into our school and see for yourselves just how good we are. I have implored you to become actively involved in your children's education, and I have shown you how and taken the hand of each parent who wished to take that step.

Those who are now involved know what is going on here, and when they speak, they speak from knowledge and from personal experience. When they disagree, they disagree based on fact and belief, and never from unsubstantiated opinion.

Of course you can disagree. That is your right, but if you do, come to me before you do or say anything else. Let's see if we can settle it quickly, and get on with the real business of this school—educating our children.

> SPECIAL DATA: Let's hope you never have to give this speech! If you encounter such a trying time, you want to deal with it. Vocal opposition to the school from some segments of the community can result in negative publicity or dissemination of rumors. Your no-nonsense attitude here, urging your attackers to stick to the facts, encourages truth and equity, and condemns unsubstantiated rumor. It also attempts to teach the proper way of handling disagreements between the public and the school should they arise in the future.

IN CONCLUSION

If some of the speeches in this section seem to have a hard edge to them, remember that this section is about handling those hard and troublesome issues that unfortunately do arise, even in the elementary schools of our land.

When trouble comes—and it most certainly will—the educational leader must be prepared to take a firm stand according to his or her belief or knowledge. The laws of common decency dictate that we show civility to everyone, and the dictates of our democratic setup offer everyone a right to dissent, but you will get nowhere— *nowhere*—trying to accommodate every opinion and viewpoint. Not only can't it be done, but the result for you will be frustration and possibly a weakening of the school structure—something you most definitely do not want.

So, keep your opinions firm and founded in truth, stick to your beliefs, try to be courteous with everyone, and remember that your primary task as an educator is to see to the education of the children in your charge.

Let that be your concern, and you will never go far wrong.

Section 10

"The Ten-Month Tango . . . ": Special Speeches for Special School Events

We once heard a school year referred to as "the ten-month tango." Lasting from August or September through May or June, depending on where you live, it does, at times, seem a complicated series of steps we take to get through the intricate "dance" of each school year.

Complications in our successful performance of that "tango" are often caused by the myriad situations, dilemmas, and circumstances that arise during any given school year. Some of them are anticipated; some of them are totally unexpected; some are easily solved; others tax our ingenuity and creativeness. All are issues that must be faced.

The speeches in this section are offered for your use on the occasions of all those special school events that occur during that "ten-month tango."

Keep dancing!

133

TOPIC: *Retirement of a Long-Time Educator*

AUDIENCE: *Friends; Colleagues; Community Members*

If you expect me to rise before you this evening and proceed to roast our honored guest, then you are going to be vastly disappointed, for that is not what I am going to do.

I could engage in funny quips and jokes, and I know that Mr. Adams would be one of those laughing the hardest. Over the years that I have known him, I have continued to be impressed by his warm, affable, and at times quite pointed sense of humor. He has learned to laugh with life, and, consequently, the Human Comedy laughs with him and is carried on by the many students who have come to appreciate and cherish his quick wit. I could joke with him, but I won't.

If you expect me to stand before you and read testimonial after testimonial to the teaching effectiveness of this teacher, you will again be disappointed, for I do not intend to do that.

I could, of course, for when the news of Mr. Adams's retirement after so long as a teacher in this system was announced, letter after letter began to flow in from former students and all those who had the privilege of being taught by Mr. Adams or being his colleague or in some way being associated with him over the almost four decades since he came to this township. I could read testimonials, but I won't.

If you expect me to come before you and tell you that with his retirement after so long and cherished a stay in our school system, this school is losing a magnificent educator who, like certain beverages, has grown better and better with time; if you expect me to tell you that this school will miss the affability, the concern for each individual child, the dedication to his profession that has been the hallmark of his career; if you expect me to tell you that I personally will miss the day-to-day contact, the smiles, the shared joy and the shared burdens, the assurance of striving together for something worthwhile that our acquaintance has meant; if you expect me to tell you that, you are right. That is exactly what I am telling you.

The term "educator" is often used loosely, but I know of no one who deserves that title more, with all the honor and glory attendant to it. Ladies and gentlemen, I give you Mr. Harold Adams.

> SPECIAL DATA: *Of course, in telling the audience what you are not going to tell them, you have told them anyway. It's an effective and dynamic way of getting your point across.*

134

TOPIC: *Acceptance of Your Own Retirement*

AUDIENCE: *Friends; Colleagues; Community Members*

What can I say? Part of me feels as if it were only last month, or at the most last year, that I walked through the door and into the first classroom that was truly mine—truly my responsibility. I guess there must have been a long weekend in there somewhere, because suddenly, here I am and it's several decades later, and you people are buying my husband (or wife) and me a lovely dinner and saying all those inflated words and describing someone I'm not even sure I know.

I suppose it was inevitable, and several days ago, someone asked me if I had learned anything from those years of teaching. Certainly, that has made me think, for that is not a question that can be seriously answered off the "top of one's head." Had I been flippant, I might have answered that over these years I have learned to bring my own lunch and avoid eating cafeteria food at all costs and go into the principal's office only when she's smiling. These answers would have been calculated to be "cute," to be frivolous, to avoid a real answer that would reveal the very bottom of my soul.

What have I learned? Among the tests and the lesson plans, the smiles and the tears, the successes and the failures; the kids who made your heart leap with joy and those who made your heart break with sorrow—what have I learned?

I think, if there is one message that has come through with amazing clarity, it is that there is one, and only one, quality in the world that is always right, always proper, always a part of the solution and never a part of the problem.

And that is *love*. Yes, love.

In all the years, with all the children, in the myriad dealings with parents and colleagues and administrators, I have never known love to be brushed aside. The love that has been given to me by you tonight and over the years by all the students I have known has touched my heart and will truly be my sustenance in the days to come.

I love you all, and I thank you.

SPECIAL DATA: You could, certainly, make this speech much longer by detailing incidents that you recall from the years past that "prove" your points. Beware, however, of making a thank-you speech that is too long. It is always best to leave an audience wanting more.

135

TOPIC:	*Eulogy for an Educator*
AUDIENCE:	*Family; Friends; Community Members; Dignitaries; Former Students*

In his famous essay, seventeenth-century essayist John Donne, wrote, "Every man's death diminishes me, because I am involved in mankind. Therefore, send not to know for whom the bell tolls; it tolls for thee."

That is probably one of the most sobering passages ever written, and certainly one of the truest regarding the human condition. It applies especially to us gathered here today, with great sadness and a sense of abiding loss.

Julia Harrington Molino was a person who was deeply involved in humanity. She loved on many levels of understanding and was adorned with many titles. She was variously known as wife, mother, grandmother, church member, choir soloist, community worker, tireless volunteer, past president of the local chapter of the American Cancer Society, author of poetry and children's stories, dear friend, and . . . of course . . . teacher.

It was under that last title that I knew her best; it was under that last title that hundreds and hundreds of fortunate children knew her best; it was under that last title that scores of grateful parents and community members knew her best; it will be under that last title that I will miss her the most, that her students and all those she served so well will feel the greatness of the loss.

Her presence was a palpable part of Dwight Road Elementary School. Her talents and her insights helped to shape policies and curriculums; her care and concern and willingness to put out tremendous energy for each child in her class helped to shape a countless number of lives that will be the better for knowing her, for having fallen under her gentle, dynamic, and loving teaching. She was a *teacher,* and how we loved her.

John Donne wrote, "Send not to know for whom the bell tolls." Listen well, and you can hear the hollow ring that emanates from our hearts.

We know only too well for whom the bell tolls; we know it tolls for us.

SPECIAL DATA: The technique illustrated here is a good one; take a line from a poem or other literary piece of which you are particularly fond and expound upon it as it applies to the particular situation. There is a depth of meaning in poetry and other literature that can help to make a trying time a bit more understandable and give a great deal of comfort.

136

TOPIC:	*Eulogy for a Student*
AUDIENCE:	*Family; Friends; Teachers; Community Members*

There are times when words are insufficient to bring forth the fullness of the heart. How can we possibly express in words and sentences what rests in our souls at a time like this?

I can say that our school is steeped in a sense of loss that permeates the fiber of the place. Joyousness has left the halls; the school day is somehow incomplete; a place in the playground stands empty, waiting for the laughing child who will not be there today or tomorrow or ever again.

In the time he was with us, Timothy Bailess left a legacy of smiles and a mind full of lasting and positive memories. I can close my eyes now and see him as he tumbled through the doors of the school, his energy and his enthusiasm a real and vibrant entity that could not help but infect you as well. I can truly remember those dark eyes sparkling in the afternoon sun as he waved at me from the school bus, or the pride and passion he exhibited when he showed me what he had accomplished and learned in class one bright October afternoon. His memory will stay with us as long as schools and children are an integral part of each other.

Our hearts go out in deepest sympathy to Mr. and Mrs. Bailess. We cannot ever fully know the depth of suffering within the heart of another, no matter how much we try to empathize—but we can imagine. If we, who knew him school-time, day-to-day, can be devastated by his loss, we dimly perceive the pain that burns within your souls.

I can say these words—with my lips and with my mind. What I cannot express is the depth of the sorrow for the loss of that child who smiled and brightened my day.

All I can say is goodnight, Timmy—we love you.

SPECIAL DATA: Oh, how difficult it is to speak or give a eulogy for the death of a child! It will always be a process that will try your very soul. Try to be sensitive to the anguish of the parents, particularly; try to understand; and try to give your audience a living memory to carry with them.

137

TOPIC:	*Eulogy for a Parent*
AUDIENCE:	*Family, Friends, Colleagues, Community Members*

Eric Barton was a friend of this school system, this school, every child in it; and, I proudly add, he was my friend as well. In these capacities alone, he proved to be a tireless worker, a vital factor in positive change, an energetic child advocate, and a friend who was always there, whenever he was needed.

All these things he was to me, to Dwight Road Elementary School, and to the children who daily attended that place. Yet, he was more . . . he was much more.

He was a beloved husband—his wife Barbara working beside him on many a project for our school and community. He was a dedicated and loving parent of two children who were graced to have him as their father and whom we, at the school, are very happy to have in our classes. He was a man to be admired; a friend to be cherished; a husband and a father to be loved.

And now . . . too soon it seems . . . he is taken from us, and we gather in shocked amazement to try to put into words what may be known only in the sanctity of our individual hearts. We try to make sense of those words we heard so recently—that he had been taken from us—words that cut so deeply and so swiftly to the heart of our sorrow.

May what he has done become his legacy. I was in a position to know the depth of his feeling for the children of this school; I knew the many times he stretched forth a hand to help everyone from the smallest child to me; I knew of the sensitivity he could express to make everyone feel a part of the solution.

I don't pretend to have answers, but I do know that love given receives love in return; I do know that kindness paves the way for kindness yet to come; I do know that mercy and tenderness are never given in vain.

I knew Eric Barton, and that was a privilege.

SPECIAL DATA: It is never wrong to outline the accomplishments of the deceased. Remember, however, that you are expected to do more than merely give an impersonal biography. The accomplishments you mention should be relevant for your audience, and for you—should show how your life was enriched by knowing the deceased.

138

TOPIC: *Memorial Service for an Educator*

AUDIENCE: *Colleagues; Friends and Family*

It has been a year now since one ordinary day was turned into an extraordinary time of sorrow by the news that a colleague, an outstanding human being, a close and personal friend had been taken from us. Indeed, it was a day that none of us shall soon forget.

And that is why we gather together here today. We gather to pay tribute to the memory of Mary Tillotson; we gather to give our respect to a person of honor and dignity and dedication to the profession she loved; we gather to remember.

I ask that we stand now (*pause until all are standing*), and I ask that we bow our heads for a moment of respectful silence, and in that time let each of us remember her; let each of us speak silently the fullness of our hearts; let each of us cherish her in our own way. Come, let us remember Mary Tillotson.

(*The moment of silence should last about 20 seconds at most. Then continue your speech.*)

Thank you; please be seated (*wait until all are seated*).

We remember so clearly, don't we, that it is difficult at times to believe that she will not be walking through the doors of the school at any moment and heading for her classroom to sit with her ever-present mug of coffee, waiting for "her kids," as she called them, to come bouncing into the room, or waiting for some colleague to come to her, as so many of us did, for her help or assistance or advice. Her spirit was the spirit of the educator; she was a teacher both in and out of the classroom, and that spirit is sorely missed by those who knew her.

She is not with us, but allow us, for a moment, to imagine that she is. To her, we say, "We miss you, Mary; we miss you as do the children whose lives you touched; as does this entire school. We honor your memory, and want you to know that you rest in our love."

> SPECIAL DATA: *Few things affect a school as much as having a teacher die suddenly, and it is our sincere hope that you don't have to go through that. It is inevitable, and particularly if the teacher was highly respected or liked, that there will be some sort of memorial service, possibly right in the school. This speech is appropriate for such a service.*

139

TOPIC: *Memorial Service for a Student*

AUDIENCE: *Classmates; Parents; Teachers; Family*

(*In this memorial service, the speaker is dedicating a plaque to the memory of a former student who died tragically.*)

If the measure of your worth lies in what your passing means to those with whom you worked and shared your life, then Boydd Williams was, indeed, a young man of exceptional worth, and it is he whom we remember this day; it is he whom we are here to honor.

That the students of this school miss him is clear to those of us who work here every day. They knew Boydd as a classmate, and half a year after he was so tragically taken from us, they still talk about him; they still feel his presence as they go about their day. Boydd was one of them, and he is most definitely missed.

Boydd is missed by the faculty and administration of this school, as well. He was here from kindergarten through most of his fifth-grade year, so almost all of us got to know him, and all of us miss him. He was filled with enthusiasm, eager to learn, and a delight to have as a student, a fact attested to by every teacher in this school whose classroom held this lovable, likable, energetic child.

We gather today, some six months after the accident that took his life, to pay tribute to his memory. We do that by cherishing his memory in our hearts, and by dedicating this plaque in his memory. This plaque was thought up by our own student council and was paid for by contributions from our student body. It reads, "In Memory of Boydd Williams, a fifth-grade student in this school. You were with us but a little while, and yet we remember . . . we remember."

This plaque will have a permanent place on the wall of our school.

In Boydd's honor, look at it . . . and remember.

SPECIAL DATA: Remember that when you are doing something like dedicating the plaque in the speech above, you are not merely addressing the students of the school. There will undoubtedly be a number of adults present, particularly from the deceased's family and possibly even from the press. Also, if this is to be an assembly, hold it with the upper-grade children only, as the younger ones might not be able to appreciate it.

140

TOPIC: *Memorial Service for a Special Person*

AUDIENCE: *Teachers; Parents; Friends; Family; Dignitaries*

(In this speech, you will be announcing a special program or fund in the name of the deceased.)

James Wexler was a very special person. Anyone who knew him knew the truth of that statement. While he was not an educator in the sense of being a certified teacher or administrator, still his life was bound up in education. Indeed, over the absolutely amazing twenty-six years that he served on this township's Board of Education, eleven of those years as president of that group, he had touched the lives of countless numbers of students and teachers.

Under his leadership, this township's schools grew from a place with three elementary schools and a single high school into the fine community of education that it is today, with two major high schools, three middle schools, and ten elementary schools to serve our youth.

That was a very proud achievement for Jim Wexler, because it was always the children who were his first concern. He was their voice, their advocate; he believed sincerely that he could make a positive difference in their lives, and, as someone who often worked closely with him, I will tell you that he made a very profound difference, indeed.

Now, a year after his death, those of us who knew and respected him and who shared his vision of education for every child in this township have established a memorial that we believe would have pleased him very much. This day, I take pleasure in announcing the "James A. Wexler Memorial Scholarship Fund," this fund to provide annually a full first-year college scholarship to one girl and one boy from our community to aid in their continuing education.

Even in death, the name of James Wexler continues to be synonymous with growth and education and excellence for all children.

Now, that is a memorial of which James Wexler would have heartily approved!

SPECIAL DATA: If you are involved in something of this nature, make certain that you publicize it thoroughly—not to get publicity for you, but to let as many as possible know about the fund. There are bound to be those who wish to contribute.

141

TOPIC: *Testimonial for a Teacher*

AUDIENCE: *Adults; Colleagues; Parents; Community Members*

(This testimonial is to be given during a program honoring a teacher who has been given an award.)

Now, I ask you, why would anyone want to give Judy Abbot an award? I mean, just because she is a dedicated educator who has served the children of this community with twenty-one years of her life, is that a reason to give her an award? I mean, just because she has sacrificed countless hours of her time both inside and outside of school to work with, encourage, and develop the young minds under her tender care, is that a reason to give her an award? I mean, just because she has been instrumental in formulating curriculum, establishing a specialized reading program for children with reading difficulties, and making the school a special place where children want to be, is that a reason to give her an award? I mean, just because she is a friend who never lets you down, a surrogate parent and guide to all the children who so frequently run to her embrace, a teacher who refuses to give up on the hardest and most recalcitrant of cases, is that a reason to give her an award?

Well . . . yes! I guess those are pretty good reasons to give an award to anyone, and particularly to Judy Abbot, who personifies the very best qualities that we, as a society, believe a teacher to have. Yes, those are very good reasons; very good reasons, indeed, and I join everyone here in rejoicing in the presentation that will be made very shortly.

The many, fortunate children who have passed through her classroom and through her expert and loving care, her colleagues who have always recognized in her that special "something extra," and all of us who know and work with her stand testimony to exactly how deserving she truly is.

Believe us, Judy, the honor is ours.

SPECIAL DATA: Notice that in this technique you ask the question, who would give the teacher an award, and then you answer it quite completely. Be sure, however, that your audience knows that you are using a special technique, and not truly questioning her worthiness. This is best done with a twinkle in the eye and a smile to the recipient.

142

TOPIC: *Testimonial for an Administrator*

AUDIENCE: *Colleagues; Audience Typical of a Testimonial Affair*

Ladies and gentlemen, I truly believe that a night like this one was inevitable. In fact, no one can say that I didn't warn her that this was likely to happen. I don't know how many times I told her that if she didn't stop being the best principal in the township; if she didn't stop being involved with what her kids were doing and visiting all those classrooms to be a part of all that happened in her school; if she didn't stop opening her door freely to everyone, from a child with a problem to any adult who just wanted to talk—I told her that if she didn't stop these things, a time would come when her friends and colleagues would demand a dinner in her honor and force her to sit there and listen to people say nice things about her in front of her instead of behind her back!

You see, Ellen, you didn't listen and just kept on being such an outstanding administrator that . . . well, here you are! Don't say I didn't warn you!

Actually, it wouldn't have mattered if I had told her all those tongue-in-cheek things I just mentioned, because anyone who knows Ellen Fleishman knows that she is single-minded in doing what she believes is best for her kids, her faculty, and her school. Over the years, she has worked diligently and spent countless hours on curriculum and budgets and requisitions for the good of her school without ever sacrificing her most delightful task—being with the children, helping each and every child in her school.

She knows every child in her school by name—and, I may well suppose, just as many parents. That is the mark of someone who cares, and Ellen Fleishman is a person who cares. Indeed, that is the hallmark of her administration and the legacy of her career that we honor here tonight.

My goodness, Ellen, no wonder you got a dinner!

SPECIAL DATA: This speech was given to honor one administrator's 25 years in education, but you can modify it to suit your needs. It is similar to the last speech in that the humor is derived from the direct opposite of what you are saying. This one, however, is a great deal broader than the previous speech, and is readily recognized as humor.

143

TOPIC: *Testimonial for a Special Parent*

AUDIENCE: *Community Members; Dignitaries; Family; Friends*

Every parent whom I have ever met as principal of this school is a special parent, for the vast majority of those I do meet are parents who have volunteered to be a part of their children's education by becoming a part of Dwight Road Elementary School.

Tonight, however, I would like to single out one such parent from the many. Certainly, all of you here tonight have worked long and hard for the good of your children and your school, and in no way do I want you to think that your efforts have gone unnoticed or unappreciated, for that is simply not true. What you, all of you, have done this year is nothing short of magnificent, and I am thankful for you.

There is, however, a very special parent here this evening; a man who has served the past two years as PTA president; a man who has given unsparingly of his time and considerable talents toward the betterment of our school; a man who is known by the students, teachers, and other parents as someone who truly cares—cares about them.

With this meeting, his tenure as president of our PTA comes to an end, but, if I know him the way I think I know him, this will not be the last we will see of him in our school. He will be here helping out; being a true friend to education; providing a sterling example to the youth of Dwight Road Elementary School, and making this place a better place to be.

He would never say these things about himself, of course, so that's why his fellow parents have asked me to voice what is in their hearts. May this small honor be indicative of the great esteem in which we honor you in our hearts.

Join me, please, in recognizing a very special person—our PTA president, Mr. Roger Galley!

> SPECIAL DATA: *It is always fitting to pay some special attention to those who help the school in so many ways. The final PTA meeting of the school year is an appropriate time. In a real sense, they are the mainstay of the school's success in the community in which you must live and function. Make your speech enthusiastic and your praise genuine, and all will go well.*

144

TOPIC: *Testimonial for a Student*

AUDIENCE: *Students; Family; Faculty; Community Members*

I would like to welcome all our guests this afternoon, and I am particularly pleased to see and greet Mr. and Mrs. Lopez. We are so glad you could be here, because we are going to be talking about your son—and all of it good!

Perhaps it is a sad fact of human nature, but all too often, we have a tendency to dwell upon the negative, sometimes to the exclusion of that around us which is positive and good. It is the problem that holds our attention, not the things that flow smoothly, presenting no difficulty along the way. Anyone in my position could fall into that habit; it's easy to concentrate on the difficulties with students that came across my desk. Indeed, we could concentrate on the fights, the undone work, the misbehaviors—and the things that may not be discussed— and lose track of the fact that the vast, vast majority of our students continue to learn and grow and do the work and flourish here at Dwight Road Elementary School.

That is why it is so exciting and so happy an occasion when I can present to you a student like Rudy Lopez. All you need do is to look into Rudy's sparkling and alert eyes to know that here is a very special young man. Talk to him for a moment and you are convinced of that fact. Live and work with him as we do here at the school, and you will find yourself believing that there is hope for tomorrow, if tomorrow contains people like Rudy Lopez.

Today, we are going to present to Rudy Lopez a special award for a very special accomplishment, and that is something very fine. But, we want him to be aware that what we are most proud of is the fact that he is our friend and a credit to his school.

Rudy, that's a job well done!

SPECIAL DATA: This speech can be given as part of a program to honor the outstanding achievement of a student. You might want to go into some detail about the accomplishments being honored. Be effusive with your praise, and let the positive be emphasized. Your hope is that other students will want to emulate this student's performance.

145

TOPIC: *Speech for an Elementary School Graduation*

AUDIENCE: *The Graduates; Friends; Family; Faculty*

Good evening. It gives me the greatest pleasure to be able to greet the (*give the year*) graduating class of Dwight Road Elementary School. It has taken you six years (seven if you count kindergarten) to get to this point, and here you are, ready to leave elementary school and, after what I hope will be a wonderful summer, enter into the world of the middle school.

Now, I want to make it clear, I want there to be no mistake about it; you are here because you have earned the right to be here. It has been quite a long time since Mom or Dad took you by the hand to the kindergarten class and left you with that strange person who would lead you into the wonderful world of play blocks and finger paints.

During the years from then to now, you have grown physically; some of you could hardly reach your teacher's knee, and now a number of you are taller than some of your teachers. But that is not the only way in which you have grown, for over these years, you have grown in mind as well. When you started school here, you could neither read nor write nor add together two numbers and get a sum. All this you now do with relative ease. Not only do you know these basics, but with each passing day you have gotten better and better with them, and you have used these skills to learn even more of the world about you as you investigated history and science and art and music. With each new item you learned, you learned that there was more to investigate—more to know.

Now you are here at the end of one stage of your education. It is the end of only one step in a long journey, however, as you will discover next year in the middle school. Because you have come through here, you are now ready to enter there.

May God bless your journey.

SPECIAL DATA: In general, all graduation speeches should be kept short and to the point. This is not a college commencement, where a celebrity is to speak upon invitation; this is an address to mark the occasion, without making parents and students restless. Be concise.

146

TOPIC: *Short Speech for a Kindergarten "Graduation"*

AUDIENCE: *The "Graduates"; Parents; Teachers; Family*

(Kindergarten "graduations" are great fun, excellent photo opportunities, and greatly enjoyed by parents. Here is a very short speech appropriate to the occasion.)

I have to say, don't they look wonderful? (*Wait for applause to subside.*)

Girls and boys, this afternoon is very special, do you know that? It is very special because you have worked so very hard, and now it is time for you to be finished with kindergarten and to start the first grade. I can promise you that you are going to have a lot of fun in elementary school, and I can promise you that you will learn many, many new things as well. You will like your teachers, and I can tell that your teachers are going to love you.

Right now, though, it is time for us to tell you how proud we are of you and all you have done over this past year.

Now, how many of you did the best you could do in kindergarten? Come on, raise your hand if you worked hard—if you are a good student. (*Wait until all hands are raised.*) Well, look at that! You all worked hard. You know, that's a very good thing.

Do you know what people do when they like the hard work that you have done? They clap their hands to show how much they like it.

You did something really good this past year, and we really like you. So, this is for you, the Kindergarten Graduating Class of (*Date*) of Dwight Road Elementary School.

Well done! (*Lead applause.*)

SPECIAL DATA: If a regulation graduation speech must be kept short, just consider the length a kindergarten attention span will tolerate. Also, adjust your language to the level of understanding that is appropriate here. Speak to your audience, and you will never go wrong.

147

TOPIC: *Speech on Parent-Teacher Conferences*

AUDIENCE: *Parents; Teachers; a PTA Meeting Prior to Conferences*

Let us suppose for a moment that you had paid tuition to take a course at a local college (*or name a local college*), and that you had arrived at the classroom several minutes before the class was to begin. You got out your notebook and pen and got ready for the class to begin.

At the proper time, a well-dressed gentleman or lady entered the room and sat at the teacher's desk. You were all set to begin, when suddenly the instructor closed his or her eyes while sitting bolt upright in the chair. While you uncomfortably listened to the teacher's breathing, he or she did not move. In fact, for the next fifty minutes there was no motion other than the slow breathing. Then a bell rang and he or she rose and left the room without a word to the class.

Would you feel as if you had learned nothing? I am certain that is what I would have felt under the circumstances, but upon reflection, I don't know how true that is. I think we may have learned a very great lesson. I believe we learned that where there is no communication, there is no learning. That is true of that imaginary class, and it is true of education in general.

Very shortly, parent-teacher conferences will begin here at Dwight Road Elementary. The very basis of these conferences lies in the communication that will take place. We expect the teachers of this school to be frank and open with you, just as we expect those same qualities from you in return. If we can truly communicate our concerns, our observations, and our hopes and plans to one another, not only will we have learned from each other, but our children will be headed for an educational future of learning and fulfillment.

Come on—we can talk!

SPECIAL DATA: The purpose of this speech is to lay a foundation for a free exchange during parental conferences. If it is given in a speech that reaches a great many parents, or even in a newsletter format sent home to parents, this can be effective in getting the cooperation we all desire.

148

TOPIC: *Transition to a New Policy or Program*

AUDIENCE: *Faculty Members—A Faculty Meeting*

Mom and Dad questioned their child after his first day of school. They asked him about his teacher, the classroom, the other children, and what he had done in class.

To all the questions, the lad answered enthusiastically and avowed that he had had a "wonderful" time.

"I'm sure," Mother remarked, "and I'm certain you'll enjoy it even more tomorrow." "Tomorrow?" said the little boy as his bottom lip began to tremble. "You mean I have to go through this thing again?"

Well . . . yes, son, I'm afraid you do; I'm afraid we all do. In fact, if there is any one thing that is certain about education, it is that it is a continuing process; we keep at it over and over; each day, we go through this thing again. The saving grace, however, is that we don't go through the same thing each day. We educate for our society; we educate for tomorrow. Society and tomorrow keep changing, and we in education keep up with those changes. We must, for that is our responsibility; that is our job. In fact, I suppose one might say that the certainty of education is the fact that education undergoes change.

You will hear this evening about a new program that will begin shortly right here at Dwight Road Elementary. This new program will mean a change for many students and teachers and, by projection, for parents as well. As this program is detailed tonight, I know that you will give it your attention and your dedication, because, in the final analysis, it is you who will make it work.

Yes, we have to go through it again, for education does not stop, but continues to develop and flourish along the way.

Let's hear how we can help it grow.

SPECIAL DATA: Anything new, whether a policy or program or course or curriculum, is bound to meet with a certain degree of resistance. This is to be expected. In a transitional speech, therefore, what you aim at is understanding and tolerance. You want an attitude that says, "Let's give it a fair chance."

149

TOPIC: *Transition to a New Administrator*

AUDIENCE: *Faculty Meeting; Possibly Community Members and Parents*

(In this speech, the principal is leaving to take a post in Central Administration and is introducing her replacement as principal of the school.)

Talk about your mixed emotions! I thought this would be easy, but now I not so sure.

For many, many years (*name the exact number if desired*) I have served as principal of this school. While there were times that might euphemistically be called "rocky," and while there were disagreements along the way, and while everything did not always run the way I had planned or the way I would have wished it, still, the vast, vast, vast majority of the time I spent in this building was joyous and invigorating and filled with wonder, thanks to an ever-changing, ever-wonderful student body, a host of supportive and cooperative parents, and the most talented and dedicated faculty it has ever been my privilege to know.

I am leaving now to take the post of Assistant Superintendent for our township. I firmly believe that in so doing, I will be entering a position where I may help even more students and see to it that our teachers have all they need to teach in the forceful and enlightening way I have come to know so well.

I leave, but not before arrangements have been made to leave this school in capable hands. You see, I wanted to have someone come in here who understood the process and had full appreciation for the people who made it work; I wanted someone to take my place who could appreciate just how hard everyone works around here and how effectively they handle the problems that do arise, and handle them before they become the tidal waves that threaten to engulf this place; I wanted to find, in short, someone who would love and cherish and care for this place as it has been my privilege to do over these many years.

I am about to introduce you to just such a person.

SPECIAL DATA: Adapt your speech to your particular situation. You can continue, of course, with details about the new administrator, always keeping things upbeat and positive, and finally the introduction of the new principal (in this case). Remember that you want to leave with everyone just a bit sorry that you are going, but not so distressed that they will not cooperate with the new administrator coming in. A rather delicate balance is called for.

150

TOPIC: *Transition From One School Year/Grade to Another*

AUDIENCE: *Students and Faculty Members*

Well, did you enjoy the summer? (*Wait until the reaction has died down.*)

You know, it seems to me that it was only last week that I was standing right here, telling you to have a great summer and asking you to be careful. Now, here it is two months later, and we are about to begin a brand-new school year. Now, I know it's natural to want to keep on with the sunny days and the play and the fun times that summer brings with it, but time never stands still. It is right; it is proper; and it is good that school begins.

Be honest with me and with yourselves—this morning when you came to this place, you met some friends you hadn't seen all summer, and you were glad to see them, weren't you? This morning, you went into your new classroom, and you were anxious and curious to see what it was like in your new grade and to know who your teacher would be this year, and it made you a little happy to be able to do that. This morning, whether you knew it or not, or expressed it or not, there was a feeling of pride that you were in a new grade in this school, a feeling that you had "made it through" to this new school year and this new grade.

Of course we are expecting you to work and study and learn, but we are also expecting you to have a good time here, a time when your bodies will grow and your minds will grow with them; a time when you will think and a time when you will laugh.

We have many wonderful things planned for you over this coming school year. What happened last year is over and done, and the great things that will happen during this school year are just waiting.

That's right, they are waiting . . . waiting for you!

Come on, let's get started.

> *SPECIAL DATA: This speech is best given to an assembly of students on the first day of the new school year. Children really do like to come to school, and there is a part of them that is glad when summer comes to an end and the new school year begins. After all, school occupies a major portion of their days; it is part of them and they are part of it.*

IN CONCLUSION

Many things that happen in public education are unique to a teacher, a school, or a situation, but just as many things occur during any given school year that are common to educators throughout the nation. That is the basis of this particular section.

The topics listed here are general, such as "Testimonial for an Administrator" or "Eulogy for an Educator," while you will be faced with a specific set of circumstances involving the administrator to be honored or the educator who has died. You will have to take time to adjust and modify each speech to your particular needs. The value of this book is the general outline offered to you.

Whatever you come up with, make certain that you deliver the speech enthusiastically. The best-constructed testimonial will become meaningless if delivered in a monotone or without apparent emotion of any kind. Indeed, in these speeches, particularly the eulogies and memorials, you want to show that you are concerned—that you do care—that it is real and meaningful to you.

Adapt the speech to your particular needs and deliver it with honesty and feeling, and you cannot possibly go wrong.

Part Two

A Complete Guide to Preparing

and

Delivering a Dynamic and Effective Speech

While every effort has been made to cover as many topics as possible concerning education, the situation will inevitably come that defies classification. When this happens, you will have to write that speech yourself, and that can often prove troublesome, especially since the demands upon our time as professional educators leave us little to spare for such projects.

Moreover, whether you prepare the speech yourself or have adapted one from this book, you will, eventually, have to stand up and give it. When that happens, situations may arise to threaten the effectiveness of your speech by causing difficulties that must be attended to immediately. These problems in public speaking can often be so challenging that they destroy a speech's impact if they are not handled properly.

The last two sections of this book deal with preparing an effective speech "from scratch," so to speak, and delivering it in a dynamic and positive manner. In addition, you'll find some advice on handling those irksome problems that sometimes arise.

Based on years of practical experience, the answers to public-speaking questions found here will, we hope, serve you well.

$\mathcal{S}$ection 11

P*R*E*P*A*R*E for a Winning Speech

Over the years, we have written hundreds of speeches, and after a while we discovered that there was actually a formula for writing these speeches that not only was effective but produced a dynamic speech—one that carried out its intended purpose. That formula is shared with you in this section.

We call it the P*R*E*P*A*R*E formula. Obviously, each letter stands for a particular step in the process of writing a winning speech.

Let's take a closer look at the process.

"P" Is for PINPOINT—Effective Ways to PINPOINT Your Topic

So, you have come to the point where you have been asked to deliver a speech, and now all you have to do is write one! That's certainly enough to give us all a moment's pause, but let's look at it realistically,

The first "P" in the P*R*E*P*A*R*E formula stands for the word "PINPOINT." Now, the point of a pin is extremely small, yet, as almost everyone can verify, extremely sharp as well. With this in mind, you are able to take the first step toward preparing your speech.

Suppose you are asked to speak next Tuesday evening. Immediately, there are some questions that *you* should ask, and the absolutely first question should be, "What do you want me to talk about?" "Oh," comes the response, "just talk about education."

Don't let it end there, because if you get up to speak about "education," the chances are good that you will give a loose, rambling speech, probably overlong, that will make your audience restless, and that is exactly what you don't want to do.

Therefore, you now begin to PINPOINT the topic of your speech, and you do this by continuing to ask questions. Here are some to be asked:

What is the composition of the audience? It is important to know this, and just a bit of reflection will tell you why. It is one thing to address a gathering of educators and quite another to be talking to a group of parents or a community association. Not once are we suggesting that you tell each group something different, but suppose you were to speak on "Education and the Elementary Curriculum." While you might cover the same material in each speech, we think you will agree that the material will be presented differently before each of the audiences mentioned above.

An audience of educators would understand certain terms that a group of parents might need explained to them. A community group might be primarily interested in how taxes are affected by new curriculum. Teachers might want to know if they will have to wait for new materials or if the budget is going to include the traditional field trips. Know your audience in order to pinpoint your topic for them.

How much will your audience know (or think they know) about the topic before you speak? A piece of advice that has served us well over the years in speaking before people was this: "Start at point one and work your way through to point ten, one number at a time!" In other words, don't assume anything; start at the beginning and work your way to the end in a straight line. Generally, this is good advice, but in pinpointing your topic, you'll want to know where that starting point is, for that knowledge can save you considerable time and effort.

"The Elementary School: Why We Do What We Do"—Now there's a fine topic. Homework is a part of all school, isn't it? We've *never* had to explain to a group of teachers why homework is important or why the school insists that it be done. Rather, the educator's group might want to concentrate on the disciplinary policies of the board of education as they relate to the elementary school and the personal willingness of the administration to back up a teacher's decision in the classroom. A group of parents, however, might be eager to hear about homework and how they can help, while not finding much relevance in classroom or intraschool dynamics. What does your audience know? What do they think they know? Pinpoint.

How does the program coordinator conceive of your speech? Entertainment? Information? Persuasion? What does the person who asked you to speak want your speech to accomplish? You don't want to prepare a speech on the impending crisis in elementary education and the doom that will fall should the current budget be defeated, and arrive prepared to give that speech, only to find that the dinner is one to celebrate the winning season of the township soccer team. As you walk through the door, the chairperson whispers to you, "They're in a great mood tonight! You're going to get lots and lots of laughs! Everybody's so happy!"

Therefore, find out what they want from your speech, and you can pinpoint exactly what is needed.

What is the maximum and minimum time you are to speak? If there were a master rule that we could impart to each prospective speaker, it would be on a poster board, on the wall of your office, in heavy black marker:

BETTER UNDER THAN OVER!

If you leave an audience wanting to hear more, they'll probably invite you back to speak again; if you leave an audience looking at their watches, yawning occasionally, and doing a great deal of shifting in their seats, then don't worry about having to speak there again.

Every audience has a built-in "time limit," after which they get restless. This depends on many variables, from how good the dinner was to how many people spoke before you or will speak after you to what you are speaking about. The best speeches are those that end before the audience gets restless.

Find out how long you are expected to speak, and stick to it. If you have too much to say in that allotted time, then (we're talking about good speeches and not wounded egos, right?) don't talk about so much! If you have a favorite speech that covers five points, and they are giving you fifteen minutes, then how about taking one of those points and making it crystal clear? If they really like it, they'll invite you back to tell them about the other four points.

"Better under than over!" That's tremendously good advice. Pinpoint that topic until you can successfully place it within the time allotted.

Where will your speech fit into the total program for that evening or afternoon? Common sense dictates that you will prepare a different speech if you are to be the featured speaker or the only speaker than if you are to be the speaker who introduces the main speaker. This applies in terms of the length of your speech, the goal of your speech, and what you may and may not cover within your speech (you do not want to cover something the main speaker will be covering five minutes later).

Therefore, know where you fit in, and, if necessary, contact other speakers (particularly if you are to introduce one of them); cordinate your efforts. Pinpoint your topic so that your speech fits in perfectly with your part in the program.

Finally, in pinpointing your topic, you should ask any question that you feel might have a bearing on the content of your speech. This attention to detail will help you prepare the right speech for the right audience at the right time. Would you, for example, give a forty-five minute speech if you were speaking just *before* dinner was to be served? Would you give a serious speech at a parent-child banquet where Santa Claus's appearance was to follow yours? Pinpointing your topic—and preparing for the atmosphere surrounding your speech—is your first step on the road to success.

"R" Is for RESEARCH—How to RESEARCH Your Topic Effectively

Now that you have successfully PINPOINTED your topic, and you know what you are going to talk about, what kind of speech you will be delivering (humorous, informative, etc.), how long you will be speaking, and where you fit in to the entire program, you may begin.

But not quite yet . . .

You may be the type of person who can speak, as the expression goes, "off the top of your head." That's fine. You may be a person who knows a great deal about your profession or any number of topics. That's fine. You may be one whom people consider good-natured or humorous, or "a funny person," and be able to have an audience roaring with laughter. That's fine. All of that, however, will count for nothing at all, if the audience perceives, or thinks it perceives, that you are misinformed about your subject. Put far more bluntly, it won't matter if you are the best speaker in the world if your audience believes that you don't know what you are talking about!

Understand the following: The greatest experts do research *before* they make pronouncements. The best speeches given (and that includes humorous speeches) are those that are fully researched—that present current, solid facts. All this means that you should and must do RESEARCH for your speech, whatever or wherever it may be.

But, you may well say, I know the subject I'm to talk about, I remember the facts; I recall hundreds of funny stories; one or two will pop into mind when I need them. Trusting to memory is risky at best, and disastrous at worst. People who claimed absolute authority within a single field of knowledge have been stopped dead on the dais by a question that required facts or statistics that they did not have at hand and that eluded their memory. That is a most embarrassing situation to be in, and it is made all the sadder by the fact that it could have been so easily handled by doing just a little research *before* the speech.

Before you do any research, however, you must know some facts, and to get them, you must ask a few more questions.

What will your audience want to know? Try to anticipate here. Put yourself mentally in the place of your audience. If you were hearing your material for the first time, what would you want to know? Try to be honest, or give your topic to someone who knows little about it and ask the person to compile, or, to tell you several questions that the topic inspires. If you know what your audience is likely to want to know—the questions they are likely to ask, then you will be able to do your research and answer those questions with dispatch.

What kinds of questions will they ask? Will your audience be on your side, or are they likely to be hostile? Will the questions they ask be argumentative (possible, for example, if you are speaking for the passage of a budget that is being criticized by some citizens' group)? Anticipation of the kinds of questions to be asked will be a guidepost to the type of research you will need to answer those questions to the satisfaction of the majority of the audience.

What kinds of humor will the audience appreciate? You are not a professional comedian, and your task as a speaker is not to stand up and tell joke after joke. A speech without humor where it is appropriate, however, can be very dull and can immediately dispose an audience to stop listening to you. Humor and its use can be a delicate subject, and the wise speaker tempers the humor used to the situation and the audience.

Are you speaking about a person? If it is known that you are a friend of the person, your humor can be much more broadly based than if you are merely an acquaintance. Should you avoid "put-down" humor? Is there a place for the comic "insult" that so many entertainers get away with? These are questions that only you are able to answer; your research should include knowing the audience for whom you are speaking and what they would or would not like.

There are a number of sources for appropriate humor that is geared to the educator as a public speaker. Two books, *2002 Gems of Educational Wit and Humor* and *Educator's Treasury of Stories for All Occasions*, both written by the authors of this book, contain a great many stories, anecdotes, quips, and incidents that not only are appropriate for any audience, but that reflect the current educational scene. Check your bookstore or your local library.

What is likely to antagonize your audience? Unless you have a need to suffer or your integrity demands that you make known a particular view unpopular with your audience, you should avoid any area that might be likely to upset your audience. For example, don't speak at a convention of vegetarians on the delights and benefits of sirloin steak!

That does not mean that you must compromise your beliefs, but it does mean that you should use common sense and avoid antagonism wherever possible. We all admire the obvious intelligence of the person who agrees with us. If you can, find out what will upset an audience, and, again if you can, try to avoid it..

What would please your audience? If you were ever in love, think back to that time and ask yourself what you did for the object of your affection. Did he like classical music? Do you remember when you got that special CD he wanted and placed it on his dinner plate under his napkin? Did she like daisies? Remember the day you sent her sixteen dozen daisies at work so that they arrived every half hour? You did those things to please the one you loved.

We are not suggesting daisies for your audience, but do a little research and find out what will please the audience you are addressing. Will it be a group of parents? Perhaps you can find a way to mention the names of several of their children; perhaps you can allay their fears about the rumor they heard about that program being cut; perhaps you can tell them that they are doing a good job and that the school appreciates them. These are small things to be sure, but you will find that it is often the small kindnesses and considerations that are the most remembered and appreciated by your audience.

Research your audience; find out what pleases them; and, if you can, do it. Once you have determined the answers to these questions, you can begin to do the proper research.

Remember that you must compile the exact information you need. If you are going to speak about a person, find out about him or her. If it is a current issue, review the past issues of the local newspaper or go to the library or office and get the exact data that you require; if you need anecdotes, stories, or humor that is appropriate to your audience and the situation, go to the books mentioned earlier or visit your library for something similar.

One last hint—when you find the answers or the information for which you have been looking, be sure to write it down, and keep it as a written part of your speaker's notes. Don't rely on your fickle memory.

Keep in mind that the quality of your research often determines whether your speech will be a success. The dividends that a well-researched speech provides will more than make up for your effort.

"E" Is for EXAMPLE—Using EXAMPLES for Dynamic Impact

Remember the proverb, "One picture is worth more than a thousand words"? It's true, isn't it? When you see a picture of something or actually witness someone doing something, it is infinitely superior to many, many words of explanation or description.

Good speakers have known that for centuries, and virtually all good speakers use EXAMPLES in their speeches in order to prove points or to clarify their message. Using a good example allows the audience to "see" what you are speaking about. When they understand, they are better disposed to continue listening to you.

Yes, examples can really be of help to you when you are giving a speech, provided that they adhere to the three following rules for the use of examples:

1. The example must be appropriate.

2. The example must be understood.

3. The example must be universal.

Let's take a closer look at all three.

1. The example must be appropriate.

To be appropriate, the example you use must truly make the point that you want it to make. Using an anecdote, however clever or delightful, that has no bearing on what you are saying will only confuse your audience.

Suppose that you know this really funny story about a bus driver in the city trying to make change for a man who has only a five-dollar bill, and it is rush hour. The point of the story seems to be that you can handle only one thing at a time if you wish to get the job done effectively. Let us say that the first time you heard it you nearly fell off your chair from laughing so hard. You are so impressed with it, let us say, that you can't wait to tell it during that speech you are going to give at the PTA meeting.

The meeting progresses, and you are introduced to speak about some changes in next year's fifth-grade curriculum. You begin by explaining that there will be some changes for the new fifth-graders, starting at the beginning of the next school year. There is an audible sound as parents shift their weight to lean forward and listen. "And I'll tell you about that in a moment, but did I ever tell you about the bus driver who . . ." you say, and you continue with your anecdote—the funny anecdote, the one that can't miss.

There is no reaction except faces with highly quizzical looks. "What's that got to do with my daughter and next year?" you hear one parent murmur. "Is that person saying my son can't handle more than one subject in school?" asks another.

Of course, this is only an example, but we hope it is appropriate and that you get the point. You must make certain that the examples you use are suited to the points you wish to make during your speech.

2. The example must be understood.

When we state that a good example must be understood, we mean that it must be fully comprehended and understood by everybody, or at least the vast majority of the audience. Let us give you an example.

In one school there were two teachers who, as it happened, had been childhood friends. When they were both assigned to the same school, they were delighted and renewed their long-time friendship. Indeed, they were soon inseparable, eating lunch together, sending notes to each other at times during the school day, spending free moments talking in the hall or classroom. They were both very well liked, and their friendship from childhood on was well known.

One day, they were to be introduced at a gathering of teachers and parents in recognition of a special project on which they had worked. The principal stepped forward.

"Here they are," said the administrator, "the Castor and Pollux of the educational world!" What? Castor and who? What does he mean? What is she talking about? Calling them "Castor and Pollux" is fine, *if* your audience knows that Castor and Pollux were two friends in Greek mythology who fought together in the wars of that day and were considered inseparable. Then it makes sense.

Unfortunately, not everyone keeps current on Greek mythology. If your audience does not understand your analogy, then the analogy is totally lost, and your audience acceptance rating has just slipped a notch or two.

3. The example must be universal.

Avoid "inside" jokes. An inside joke is a story or anecdote that is funny only to a limited number of people, because they share some specialized knowledge that others in the audience do not.

One day, a bat got into our school—we have no idea how. Once inside, it flew up and down the south hallway, causing children to scream at glass-shattering levels and all classes to be kept inside the classroom until further notice.

One of our teachers (we'll call him Mr. Borden) was a great outdoors type, and before the police and other municipal services could arrive, Mr. Borden went to the south hallway, took off his shirt, caught the bat in the shirt, took it outside, and let it go.

Two months later, during an introduction of teachers on a certain grade level, Mr. Borden was acknowledged. "We really like Mr. Borden around here," the speaker continued, "even though we think he is a little 'batty' at times." Several teachers in the audience snickered. Later, several parents in the audience privately inquired when Mr. Borden had had his mental problems. Was it a nervous breakdown? Is he currently under treatment?

Make those examples universal; all those who hear them should understand them for exactly what they are. "Inside" jokes lead only to confusion and antagonism, and they are better avoided.

Examples can be a great aid to any speaker, and they are easy to use properly. Always try to put yourself in the place of the person in your audience who knows the least about your subject, and address your examples to that person. Ask yourself the following questions, based upon the three rules for examples.

Is this example appropriate to my speech? Does my audience understand the point I am making because of this example?

Is this example clearly understood? Does my audience need any special knowledge to understand it? If so, am I certain the members of the audience have that knowledge?

Is the example universal? Will it be understood and appreciated by everyone in my audience? Have I reached out and included everyone, rather than just a specialized few?

If you can answer these questions in the affirmative, then you will have a highly dynamic speech, with examples that everyone in your audience will appreciate and remember!

"P" Is for PRESENTATION—Giving Your Speech the Best PRESENTATION Possible

Once you have written your speech, logic tells you that you will, eventually, have to deliver it before a real, live audience. Therefore, this phase of preparation, giving your speech the best possible PRESENTATION, is a vital step. Even the very best planned-out and crafted material will fall flat if it is not presented in such a way that your audience appreciates it for what it is.

A certain gentleman was a very intelligent and erudite speaker who truly had very good and positive things to say. He had spoken many, many times, and was fairly well known in our district. His speeches were always finely crafted and finely honed to say precisely what he wanted to say in the best possible manner. In fact, he was an almost perfect speaker—except for a nervous habit.

He adjusted his tie. By itself, that is no great, glaring flaw, but frequently, *very frequently* during his speech, he would reach up with his right hand, grasp the knot of his tie, and adjust it. No one ever thought to bring this to his attention. After a while, and particularly if he was giving a long speech, this could become especially annoying and distracting.

One day, it was discovered that an entire segment of the audience had not heard a word of this gentleman's speech, because they had made a small wager on how many times he adjusted his tie during this speech, and they were busy keeping count instead of listening to what was being said in the speech. Eventually, this speaker was gently told about his idiosyncracy, and he was able to remedy it and continue speaking before many different groups.

The point is, *everyone* needs to work at presentation.

It doesn't matter whether this is your first speech ever or your hundred and first, you should never set foot before an audience until you have thoroughly rehearsed it—until you are as sure as you can be that you are giving it the best presentation possible.

Presentation breaks down into three areas:

1. How you stand before an audience

2. How you speak before an audience

3. How you appear before an audience

How you stand before an audience is very important. Stand before a full-length mirror, and take a good look at yourself as you deliver that speech. Do your best to see yourself objectively, as others might see you when you speak. Ask yourself these questions:

Do I stand still? Move too much? Hug the podium? Walk around the stage? Does my stance project a sense of nervousness?

Do I maintain eye contact? Do I pick out individuals and stare at them excessively? Do I consciously try to avoid contact with my audience? Am I too stiff? Am I so informal I look as if I'm about to fall down?

How do I handle my notes? Does it look as if I am reading my speech? Is it obvious that I have prepared for this event? Am I happy doing this?

Do I use proper gestures? Too many? Too few? Are my movements natural or wooden? Do my gestures help in the delivery of my speech? Do I have any nervous habits?

Make a fair analysis of how you look as you stand before an audience and deliver your speech. If this analysis is fair, then you will find areas to work on that will help you form a dynamic presentation for a memorable speech.

How you speak before an audience is an essential part of any speech, since a speech is basically an oral effort. Here you will find it helpful to tape your speech and listen to yourself later. When you do record it, give it everything you have. Try to give it the same intensity you would if an audience were present.

If you can, get someone else to listen to the recorded speech, and ask that person to evaluate it objectively in certain areas:

Are the words distinct, and can you understand everything that is being said? This is most important. You, as the speaker, can't always tell, because you are so familiar with the speech; you know every word. If it is reported that there were areas of confusion, work on them until what is being said is distinct and clear.

Is the speed of the speech appropriate? Is it too fast or too slow? A good speech has a certain pace to it. Hurrying through it as if you were a tape on fast forward gives the audience the feeling that you are rushing in order to "get it over with," whether that is true or not. To take a slow and laconic approach with the pace of your speech is to invite yawns and often an audience eager to go home. That presentation is sometimes referred to as "being one beat off."

Finally, is the speech dynamic? That means, simply, do you speak with feeling in your voice? A speech, any speech, delivered in a monotone is a golden pathway to speaker's oblivion. You don't have to be an actor or actress, emoting to the sky, but you should practice until you are speaking with good and proper expression.

How you appear before an audience also has a bearing on presentation. Where do you think the audience will be looking while you are speaking? The answer is that they will be looking at you.

Before you let that make you nervous, let us assure you that it doesn't matter whether you are thin or fat, tall or short, plain or fancy. What matters is how you appear before the audience. That needs a little explaining.

Decide what you will wear that day. Since you already know what type of function you will be attending, you won't be wearing some sort of leisure outfit to a black-tie dinner, but make an effort to select clothes in which you look and feel your best. If you feel good about your appearance, you cannot help but project that confidence to your audience. That will be how you appear before that group and how they perceive you.

If you are comfortable, then your audience will sense it and feel very well disposed toward you. If you are uncomfortable, that is what they will perceive. Remember that reality is nowhere near as important as the way in which we perceive that reality. Allow the audience to see you as comfortable, self-assured, and happy to be with them, and that appearance will elicit a very positive attitude in the people you address.

Such an appearance is difficult to fake, but confidence and a good and positive outlook on your part will set the process in motion. Smile and let your eyes twinkle. You can find reason to smile with any group—*any* group.

Project that appearance in your presentation, and your presentation will have them all but applauding befoe you speak your first word.

"A" Is for AUDIENCE—Establishing a Bond Between Your AUDIENCE and You

After all your preparation, you head to the place where you are to speak, and when you have arrived there, you will be able to take the next step in delivering that dynamic speech. At this point, you will analyze your *audience.* Your goal is to establish a bond with them, and to do that, you must analyze.

You will have time to study your audience before it is your turn to speak. Use that time to gain an assessment, albeit informal, of what they are like and what they want in a speaker.

Look at them; listen to them; and particularly pay attention to their reactions. What *are* they like? What *do* they like? How do they fit in with the speech you are going to give and the way in which you are going to give it? But let's break that down a bit further.

What is the atmosphere of the group? Is the atmosphere formal or informal? Are they being quietly civil, or do they truly like each other? Are they engaged in polite behavior, or are they having a great time? Is the atmosphere frosty or friendly? All of this plays a part in just how you will establish rapport with them, and in a while, we'll explain how. Right now, let's continue our analysis of the audience.

What is the tone of the group? A group, any group, can be quiet, or they can be noisy. They can be respectful, or they can be restless. Indeed, an audience may be "on your side" before you walk into the place, or you may be speaking before a downright hostile audience, which is not far-fetched in these days of budget and curriculum disagreements. A group may wear many faces.

Determine, if you can, the tone of the group. If, for instance, they talk through other speeches, then they are most likely going to talk through yours. If they are respectful of others, they will be respectful of you. If they are restless, how will they react to a forty-minute speech? If they are happy and content, will they appreciate a deadly serious speech, completely devoid of humor?

What is the reaction of the group? If you have a chance to do so, pay attention to the way in which they react to other speeches before yours. Of course, if you are the only speaker of the evening, this may have to be limited to how they respond to the host or hostess, or the person running the meeting or introducing you.

If you've had the chance to watch them react to other speeches, however, try to analyze what pleases them and what upsets them. For example, did one speaker display a gigantic vocabulary only to be greeted by polite applause, while another spoke plainly and "brought down the house"?

What does all this analysis and questioning and observation of your potential listeners have to do with bonding with an audience? Simply this: Your analysis of your audience will tell you what approach to take when your turn comes to speak, and that approach will determine the degree of bonding that takes place.

Certainly, you have a prepared text for your speech, but even a prepared speech may be delivered in several ways. It can be formal, conversational, or even intimate, as friend to friend. Again—your approach will be determined by your perception of your audience.

Let us give you an example:

The principal was asked to give a speech at a dinner given by a local chapter of a nationally known organization. This group was very active in township politics and did a great deal to support the schools of the community. Consequently, the principal agreed.

She even asked all the right questions, determining that she would speak on the topic, "Elementary Education in the Twenty-First Century." Her speech was to last about thirty minutes, and was to come directly after dinner. She was to be the major "event" of the evening. She was assured that the group were quite interested in the topic.

She researched and wrote and revised and wrote again. She honed and polished until she had a speech that was nothing short of magnificent. Intelligent and insightful, it detailed current trends in education and projected them into the next century with an erudite look at societal changes and the schools' response to them. It was a worthy address—one that could easily have been given at a convention of educators.

She practiced and practiced until she felt that the speech she would give and the way in which she would give it were the very best she could do. That evening, she dressed conservatively but very stylishly. She felt good.

Then she arrived at the affair. She was greeted by several cheers, some waving from across the room, and quite a few parents of children in her school, who literally ran to meet her. She had arrived halfway through the cocktail hour at the open bar. Laughter resounded everywhere, and a few couples had taken to the dance floor when one gentleman got a guitar from his car and began to play. They were having fun—of that there was no doubt.

The principal was seated at the head table with the officers of the organization. The president remarked that he knew their guest was going to continue the good time they were having. Three or four times during the dinner, various men and women visited the head table and remarked, "We are sure looking forward to your speech; you can really make us laugh!" or varying words to that effect.

The time came for the speech, and there she was. Before her was her prepared and rehearsed speech, an intelligent and serious look at the needs of elementary education in the next century. Before her, also, was a crowd of very mellow people, smiling and laughing and applauding and a few whistling. Before her lay a choice.

She could give the speech she had written and rehearsed, and—however accurate, intelligent, and well written it was—she could watch the audience lose interest and fade away. She had analyzed her audience, and this was the result of her analysis.

She stood up, turned over her speaker's notes, and began, "How many of you think you can remember the song 'Itsy Bitsy Spider'? That's a very good elementary school song, so let's see if we can sing it. Come on, get up; I'll lead." And the group sang "Itsy Bitsy Spider," finishing with a gigantic round of applause for themselves and the speaker. Thereafter, this speaker told anecdote after anecdote about the children in school, included a few stories about some of the parents who were present at the dinner, took a moment to remember a well-loved teacher who had died over the past year, and ended with a statement that whatever the new century brought, the schools and parents would handle it together.

The applause was deafening. People thronged to the dais. Within the next week, she received twenty-three letters of congratulations and support, and four more invitations to speak at various functions.

We should add that this woman has great discernment and sensitivity as well as a fantastic ability to "think on her feet." Nevertheless, here is an example of how analyzing the audience and adapting to that audience's needs helped to establish a bond with the audience that paid fantastic dividends.

Suit your speech to your audience, and you can't lose!

"R" Is for RELAXATION—How to RELAX and Enjoy Your Speech

Let's begin this section with a fact that most people do not realize, but a fact that often makes the difference between a successful speech and a difficult one. We suggest you memorize it.

IN MOST CASES, YOUR AUDIENCE *WANTS* YOU TO SUCCEED

That's right, in almost every case, the audience to which you are speaking is looking forward to hearing you and wants you to do well. Realizing that can be pivotal in learning to relax before your audience, and that RELAXATION is a significant factor in speaking success.

If you have done all in your power to make your speech entertaining, informative, clear, and concise, then you need do only one more thing to assure your speech's success—relax and enjoy yourself. If you are nervous, your audience will be nervous. If you are uncomfortable, your audience will be uncomfortable. If you are obviously enjoying yourself—so will your audience.

Let's look at that a little more closely. If a group has gone out of its way to invite you to speak, it is a fair assumption that they are having you because they expect that you will do a good job and that they will like you and listen to what you have to say. Be rational about it, and you will certainly come to the conclusion that no one ever obtained a speaker whom they expected to be boring or to antagonize their group. Of course not. They want you to be good; they want you to be accepted by their people; they want you to succeed.

The audience at a function wants to hear something interesting. Again, being rational, can you conceive of an audience that hopes the speaker will be boring or falter over words, or forget half the speech? Certainly not! That audience wants to be informed and entertained and taught in an interesting manner. In short, from the minute you enter the room, they *want* you to be a success.

It's a basic fact of life that we like people who like us. Think of the people who are your friends; they like you, and you like them in return. Now, keep thinking of those friends and consider how they act when they are around you or visiting in your home or out in some social situation with you. Do they chew their fingernails? Sit stiffly with their eyes on the floor? Speak in a voice so low that you have to strain to hear them? Talk about things that you clearly do not understand or have no interest in? Act as if the one and only thing they truly desire is to leave your presence? Is this what your friends do?

The answer is obvious. The behavior described above is not indicative of a friend; it reflects someone who is very ill at ease in your presence. You might tolerate such an individual, but you would not particularly like her or him. You and this person would not be friends.

Has this analysis been fair? Consider that these highly nervous traits do nothing to establish rapport in a social situation, and they certainly do not enhance a speech if you display them during the time you are addressing an audience. Indeed, that same audience that wants you to succeed can be very easily "turned off" by any perceived nervousness or disturbance on your part.

Here's exactly how it can happen. You get up to speak, and you are nervous and very tense. You hold on to that podium for dear life. You begin to clear your throat, and you keep doing it. Your eyes never leave the notes you have made. You begin talking to the podium, and fairly soon, even with a microphone, people begin leaning forward to try to hear what you are saying. You keep looking at your watch, wondering how much longer you have to go. What does all this mean to your audience?

First, you have taken an audience that was primarily on your side, and you have alienated them. Can you hear them think, "Why doesn't he look us in the eyes? What is he trying to hide? I can't hear what she's saying, why doesn't she speak up? Why does he keep looking at his watch so much? Is he in a hurry to get out of here?"

You can guess what the result of those questions in the minds of the members of the audience will mean. Instead of building that *bond* between yourself and your audience that we mentioned in the last section, you have succeeded in building a *wall* that will be all but impossible to scale.

An audience reacts in kind. The audience will take its lead from you, the speaker. If you get up on that stage and you exhibit all the signs of nervousness and being terribly uncomfortable, then that is the way the audience will react to you and your speech. Before very long, you will notice that your audience is becoming fidgety and restless.

If, however, you can get up there and smile and mean it; if you can look at these people and, with your facial expressions as well as your body language, tell them that you are very glad to be there; if you can make that audience aware of the fact that you are enjoying yourself, then your audience will smile back, your audience will feel happy that you showed up, your audience will truly enjoy you.

We like people who like us!

Speaking before people can be a truly enjoyable experience. If you really believe that and learn to enjoy speaking, then you *will* be a good speaker. If you don't believe it, if it is nothing more than a task, and an arduous one at that, then don't worry about it, because you won't be asked to do it very often.

If there are three rules for a relaxed presentation, they are these: Relax, Relax, and Relax. Face that audience expecting to have an enjoyable time; in your mind, realize that you are going to help them to understand something new or to deal with something different—or even just make them laugh; keep in mind that your speech will make a difference in their lives.

In short, be a friend. If you can think of an audience as a roomful of your friends, all eager to hear what you have to say in this totally nonthreatening atmosphere, then you will be relaxed. Look them in the eyes, enjoy being with them, and exhibit all the other relaxed and friendly attitudes and behaviors that will tell your audience that you are not only on their side, but that you *like* being with them and speaking to them.

If you are relaxed and at ease, and enjoy your audience, your audience will be relaxed and at ease, and enjoy you. And one thing more—you will be in demand.

"E" Is for ENTHUSIASM and EMPATHY—How to Win With ENTHUSI-
ASM and EMPATHY

Many things in this world are contagious. Of course, things like the common
cold and measles and chicken pox immediately come to mind, but there are other
things—we are certain you will agree—that are "caught" by others. There are
courage, and honesty, and dedication, and purpose, to mention just a few. Indeed,
whole civilizations have risen because people became infected by a contagious
idea.

In this section, we want to talk about another contagious idea or concept, only
this one helps to build fantastic speeches. That concept is:

ENTHUSIASM

Print that word in block letters on a large card and tack it to your wall. If you
want to be a topnotch speaker, be enthusiastic! Be enthusiastic—believe in what you
are saying. If you do, then even if your audience does not agree with what you are saying, they will respect you as a person of knowledge and conviction. Your enthusiasm
can build a lasting impression, and a very positive one, in the minds of your audience.
Enthusiasm can be your greatest ally.

Have you ever listened to someone who is really enthusiastic about a subject he
or she really knows about—really loves? When that person speaks, you cannot help
but listen, even if you have no interest in what he or she is saying. We once listened
to an individual talk about candlemaking (a very fine hobby, to be sure, but one that
we have never felt the need to pursue) and were enthralled because of the positive
and enthusiastic way in which that person described the elements of candlemaking
and the art needed and the great comfort that it produced in his life. He was enthusiastic, and his enthusiasm was contagious.

Get worked up about your topic; enjoy it; become convinced of its worth, and
become convinced that it is your absolute duty to make others see it just the way that
you do. With an attitude like that, you can't help but be enthusiastic!

A companion piece to enthusiasm is EMPATHY. Empathy involves sharing an
emotion or sense, often on a nonverbal level. Defining it far more simply than that,
empathy is placing yourself in the position of the other person.

Almost all of us have heard of the Golden Rule, which states, "Do unto others as
you would have them do unto you." If you wish to be treated with kindness, then treat
others with kindness. If you expect honesty from others, then be honest in return. You
can surely see the ramifications of this principle, and hundreds of volumes have been
written on it.

What does this have to do with preparing a speech and delivering it effectively?
The answer is, quite a bit. There are three steps in the process:

1. Put yourself in the place of the audience.

2. Determine what they want or need.

3. Try to fulfill that want or need.

That doesn't mean lying to your audience, but it does mean being understanding
in presenting the truth. That doesn't mean giving up your personal opinion, but it

does mean presenting that opinion in such a manner that your audience will respond positively. It means taking the time and the trouble to be caring and concerned.

Put yourself in the place of the members of that audience. What do they want to hear? Is anything bothering them about which they need to be reassured? What do they need to understand the topic? What do they expect of you as a speaker? Have they heard about you? How can you make them feel at ease?

Now that you have placed yourself in the position of the audience and have, as objectively as possibly, determined what they would like in a speech that you might deliver to them, try to be empathetic. As much as possible in the speech you develop, try to accommodate them. Do what you can to be what they expect you to be. Being empathetic applies not only to speaking, but to other related areas as well, such as the answering of questions from the floor.

When dealing with questions from your audience, empathy is your keynote. Put yourself in the position of the questioner. If you do this, you will never slough off a question or make light of it or the person who asked it. There will be no need to become defensive, and, because you have done your research, you can answer the question comprehensively and in a straightforward manner; empathy will see you through.

In Section Twelve, we will go into the answering of questions in far more detail, but you should understand that putting yourself in the place of the questioner goes a long way toward handling those questions with tact and dispatch.

Being ENTHUSIASTIC about your speech will inspire enthusiasm in your audience for the speech you are giving, and having EMPATHY for your audience allows you to fashion a tailor-made speech that is most certain to arouse the interest of the audience and place them on your side throughout.

Try being enthusiastic and empathetic, and enjoy the results.

IN CONCLUSION

It is within the power of most of us to create and deliver an effective and dynamic speech that will reach an audience and touch them deeply.

Just keep in mind the basic formula:

P—PINPOINT your topic.

R—RESEARCH your audience and your topic.

E—EXAMPLES should be appropriate and informative.

P—PRESENTATION should be refined to the best possible.

A—AUDIENCE should be analyzed and appreciated.

R—RELAXATION is the keynote to good delivery.

E—ENTHUSIASM and EMPATHY pay big dividends.

Keep these in mind and keep working at it, and you will write a speech worthy of the occasion and deliver it in a manner that will be long remembered.

$\mathcal{S}$ection 12

Inside Tips on Dynamic and Forceful Public Speaking

Everyone has problems, and the public speaker is certainly no exception. The speaker's problems, however, are unique, because they are shared, willingly or unwillingly, by the people he or she addresses. The old maxim, "If anything can go wrong, it will!" seems particularly appropriate when applied to speaking before an audience.

The siren that goes off in the middle of your speech, the member of the audience who asks you an obviously hostile question, the audience that is tired and restless before you rise to speak—all these and more prove a fantastic challenge for the speaker. It is, fortunately, a challenge that may be met and overcome.

On the following pages, you'll find some of the more common problems faced by public speakers, along with several very viable suggestions for their solution. They have served many speakers very well over the years.

We believe that they will work for you as well.

EFFECTIVE METHODS OF HANDLING SPEAKER'S NOTES

In the last section, one of the things we emphasized was not to trust to your memory when it comes to speaking before an audience, but to make notes for yourself. Now, we can almost hear you tell us that you have seen people give addresses on TV, and they don't appear to be reading anything. It really looks as if they have memorized their entire speech or that they are speaking *extempore;* off the top of their heads; right from the heart, as they feel it. That is the way it appears, but a great deal of work and preparation have gone into making it look that way. Then add to this the fact that these speakers are very good at what they do—very good indeed.

A person who speaks on television speaks from a prepared, written speech. This speech has been entered into a device called a teleprompter. What happens is that the speech, a line at a time, is projected onto a two-way screen that covers the lens of the TV camera. The TV camera can shoot right through that screen and see nothing of it or the words on it, while the speaker looks directly into the lens of the camera (and, by projection, at you) and actually sees his or her speech being slowly scrolled upward on the screen in lines short enough that the speaker can read them without any back-and-forth eye movement at all. The entire speech may be read in this manner while maintaining a steady gaze into the camera lens. The fact that the eyes stay steady negates the suggestion that there is any reading going on. Of course, it takes a real talent to read a speech and make it sound as if you are not, but, as we said, some are quite good at it.

Few of us are in the position to afford a teleprompter. If the truth be known, very, very few of us have need of such a device. If you ever get to the point where you are speaking on TV, the network will supply one for you, anyhow. For most of us whose speaking is more or less restricted to dinners and meetings and the like, it is, therefore, enough to know how to use our speaker's notes effectively and efficiently. Let's take a closer look at that.

If you stand up before an audience with a fistful of disorganized notes, you are headed for chaos, that is for certain. Few things give the impression of an ill-prepared speaker more than having to shuffle through notes or, even worse, muttering something like, "Now, let me see; I have it here somewhere. . ." That is something you wish to avoid, and something that you can avoid by a little careful work before you speak.

Begin with the preparation suggested in Section Eleven. Formulate what you want to say and tailor it to your audience and do all that is needed for a dynamite speech.

It is strongly suggested that you write or type out your speech in its entirety. Then, go about all the polishing and refining you think is necessary. When you have it just the way you want it, write or type it out in final form. Let this be the working copy for your speech, the copy from which you will deliver the speech. Take as much time as you can with this, since it will be the body of your speech and you want it to be as fine a piece of writing as it can be.

From this copy, begin practicing the delivery of your speech, and you now face two options for handling your notes during the speech. Each option has its values, and it is up to you to decide which one works better for you.

You can have your entire speech on the podium with you if you wish. Please do not misunderstand; you do not "read" the speech—we are not suggesting that—but the mere fact of having it there will allow you to refer to it now and then and keep you on task as well as supplying a sense of security.

If this is what you choose, highlight the topic sentence of each of your paragraphs. Then, if you glance down at your speech, the highlighted sentence will immediately bring your attention to the main idea you wish to convey, and, since you have spent much time on the preparation of this material, it will quickly bring to mind what needs to be said about that particular topic.

If you have gotten that far, you might want to try the second option. This will work just as well, and some people favor it for its "carry-anywhere" convenience.

You have highlighted the main idea or topic sentence in each of your paragraphs. If you now proceed to copy just those highlighted sentences, when you are finished, you should have a sentence outline of your entire speech. Now, if you copy each sentence onto a separate 3- x 5-inch index card and arrange those cards in the order in which the sentences appear in the speech, you will have a small packet of index cards (suitable for purse or pocket) with a total outline of what you are about to say.

This packet may be placed on the podium or even hand held if necessary, and each time you cover a topic or a section, you just flip the card over or move it to the bottom of the stack. In this way, you will have the speech at your fingertips.

Being able to carry around a packet of twenty or so index cards that can serve as your guide through a speech at a moment's call is something that many speakers prefer. Of course, that is up to you. Your notes are there to serve you and to keep you on track. Handled effectively, they are a great help to every speaker.

Use them well!

WHAT TO DO IF YOU FORGET

Come on now, be honest. Isn't it your greatest nightmare? There you are, standing before an audience that is waiting to hear and cherish your every word. You are introduced and you step forward to enthusiastic applause. Your speech begins and your opening anecdote draws great response. Things are going well—no, they are going perfectly. You are now ready to enter into the body of your speech—the "meat and potatoes"—the heart of the matter. You open your mouth to begin, and . . . and . . . and. . . And nothing! What do you say next? Where are you going from here? You *forgot*!

Relax, it's only a dream. Wipe that perspiration from your brow, and let's take a look at this consummate fear—that of getting to the middle of your speech and forgetting, totally forgetting, what comes next! This fear has kept more than one potential speaker from getting up and speaking, and that's sad, since the fear need not be the paralyzing demon that some are wont to make it.

Our answer to that problem came from a magician we know, an expert in that field—a performer who has considerable experience before people. He tells us that one of the principles of magic, or sleight of hand, is this:

NEVER TELL YOUR AUDIENCE WHAT YOU ARE GOING TO DO BEFORE YOU DO IT!

Never, for instance, would this magician say, "I'm going to show you an empty box, and then a pink rabbit will appear in it." If he did, the audience would know what to expect; they would be looking for that furry pink bunny, knowing that it was going to appear any moment, and if something went wrong, they would know it. If they didn't know what was to happen, however—if the performer never told them what was going to happen, and, let us say, the pink rabbit did not make an appearance—only the magician would know something was wrong. He or she could go right on and use the box for something else, to hold other props, for example; the audience would never be the wiser, and the magician would never be embarrassed.

How could this principle have application for you, as a public speaker? It will take some quick thinking on your part, but should you actually forget your speech (and that is very rare), you will be able to come out of it without embarrassment if you do two things:

1. Remember that your audience doesn't know you forgot.
2. Ad-lib within context until you get back to where you were.

If you forget, the audience doesn't know it; they have no idea of what you are about to say, anyway. If you don't stop dead and begin turning red or making it obvious that you are in dire trouble, or mumble something like, "Gosh! What comes next?"—if you don't do these things, no one will know that you forgot. Your ability to "fake it" here is all part of the relationship between you and your audience.

Here, then, is what your written speech or those note cards are for. You wrote the speech in the first place, so you should know the material. Take a quick look at the highlighted sentence or the top card (as previously described) and begin to ad-lib about the subject. Remember, you are the expert, so your ad libs should be right on target, and not wild ramblings. After only a few seconds of ad-libbing, your entire speech is virtually guaranteed to come right back to you.

There is also an old speaker's maxim that, if you have forgotten, you should repeat the last line you said just before you forgot. Supposedly, this will get you right back in line. You can try this if you like, preferably repeating the line silently, and it may work for you. There is no one thing that works best, and you should take the one that suits you.

If you can take it in stride and without panic—and if you merely begin to speak about the topic you were on when you forgot—it *will* come back to you, and when the speech is over, you may find that the only one who knows that you forgot—is *you*!

With these techniques on your side and the added fact that the only time you will have to use them is when you have forgotten your speech, you should approach every situation with confidence. If you have followed all the suggestions for the preparation of a speech, and if you have polished and rehearsed it, then the chances that you will forget are very, very slim indeed. Should it happen, however, you will be well prepared to handle it in such a way that your audience may not even know.

It has worked for others, and it will work for you!

WHAT TO DO IF SOMETHING GOES WRONG

"Murphy's Law," which states, "Whatever can go wrong, will go wrong," doesn't give much comfort to the public speaker, does it? Reason tells us that the longer we continue to speak before people, the greater the probability that something will go wrong during the speech.

That "something" may be anything from the electricity failing and the lights going off in the auditorium, to a loud noise such as a tray of dishes being dropped and shattered, to a heckler in the audience who will not stop. Whatever it is, it can be handled—and handled well—by any speaker who is aware of some factors that will, if used correctly, work in his or her favor.

Here's the first thing that you should remember in that regard. Get to know it, and it will serve you well:

WHEN SOMETHING GOES WRONG, THE AUDIENCE WILL NOT BE UPSET IF YOU ARE NOT UPSET!

Put another way, when something goes wrong, the audience will look to you and take its lead as to how to react from the way in which you react. If the "something" that goes awry causes you to be embarrassed, the audience will feel embarrassment; if it makes you flustered and uncomfortable, the audience will find themselves flustered and uncomfortable as well.

On the other hand, if what goes wrong causes you to smile, and you take it in stride, perhaps making some small humorous reference to it, then your audience will react in kind. You'll be able to continue your speech, virtually uninterrupted. Difficulties come and difficulties go—that's part of life, but how you handle them when they do come will determine how your audience perceives you. For example, if that waiter does drop a tray of dishes, just step to the edge of the platform, smile broadly, and say, "Look, if you disagree, just say so; you don't have to go throwing dishes!" You'll hear laughter, followed by a round of applause, and be able to continue with your speech.

In one incident, a speaker was interrupted by a sudden thunderstorm outside. Lightning flashed, and a thunderclap sounded that literally shook the building. The lights flickered tenuously before coming back. There were several audible gasps from members of the audience. They were all nervous and a bit worried. That's when the speaker walked slowly to the front of the stage, and—with a puzzled expression on his face—looked up at the ceiling. With hands outstretched, he intoned, "Did I say something You didn't like?"

Well, that most definitely broke the ice and warmed the chill in the air. The entire place erupted with laughter, there was tremendous applause, everyone relaxed, and the speech was very well received. A potentially difficult situation, one charged with emotion and even a bit of fear, was handled well because the speaker kept his wits about him and refused to be upset.

None of that is done consciously, of course. The audience does not say, "Oh, let's look to the speaker to see how we are going to respond!" Any speaker who has been around for a while, however, will attest to the fact that it does indeed happen. Your reaction—what you do and say, and the way in which you both physically and mentally handle the situation—will determine whether that audience is comfortable or uncomfortable. Your reaction will determine how the audience responds to the rest of your speech.

If you are aware of this reaction, you are ahead of the game when something does go wrong. If the interruption is only a minor one, such as a sneeze or a cough or a baby crying, you can just continue as if it did not exist, and the audience will most likely ignore it as well.

No one can teach you what to say or how to respond to the unforeseen, but if you prepare yourself mentally for those times, you will be ready to face them and keep your audience on your side.

It is really a matter of attitude, but it's an attitude that really matters!

A GUIDE TO THE USE OF VISUAL AIDS

Anyone who has been in education, even for just a few years, will understand what is meant by the term "visual aids." This term can cover such items as a VCR, an overhead projector, a CD or casette recorder/player, right on down to a poster board and a number of color markers. A "visual aid" is anything that allows your audience to see or hear something that illustrates or otherwise dramatically enhances their understanding of the content of your speech.

An audience's retention of the content of a speaker's address is far greater and longer lasting if visual aids are used. Therefore, if you are about to give a speech on some serious topic, and you want the material to be remembered, then you might want to consider using some visual aids to bring your point across in a dynamic and memorable way.

You'll want to use a little care and attention to detail in order to avoid some of the problems inherent in the use of visual aids. Remember these three things about the use of visual aids:

1. Use visual aids to augment your speech, not to give it.

2. Check it out beforehand to make sure it's crystal clear.

3. Always bring reinforcements.

Let's take a closer look.

Remember that a visual aid is used to *enhance* what you say. It *never* replaces your speech. When you are asked to speak, you are given a personal invitation, and the people you will be addressing are going to expect *you*. Therefore, if you show up with a 30-minute video that you introduce briefly, and play on a VCR—and then you take it and leave, those people are going to feel cheated at best and antagonized at worst. Moreover, you have placed yourself in a rather precarious position. If your entire speech consists of showing the video, what will you do if the tape breaks or if the VCR is inoperative? Let your visual aid be just that—an aid to understanding.

Second, check out the availability of the visual aid you want to use. You may have asked your contact person if a VCR would be available at the dinner where you are going to speak and been assured that it would be. You arrive with a five-minute tape that really exemplifies the entire point of your speech. There you are, but where is the VCR? There is none! With not a little panic starting to grow, you seek out the person who made the arrangements.

"But," you tell your contact, "when I spoke to you the other day, you said there would be a VCR here for me to use." "No, I didn't," the person replies. "I remember distinctly that you said, 'Do you have a VCR and is it working properly?' Well, I certainly do have a VCR at home, and it works just great. Oh, did you mean a VCR here? Well, no, there is no VCR here, but I just assumed that you knew that. You don't need one, do you?"

Always . . . always . . . always double- and triple-check your sources when dealing with the availability of visual aids. The time it will cost you to check it out thoroughly will be more than compensated by the absence of unwelcome surprises.

Finally, you would be well advised to bring reinforcements. If you are going to use a slide projector, bring an extra light bulb; if you have a VCR that's portable, you might want to consider putting it in the trunk of your car; maybe you should take your portable recorder and one extra copy of that tape you want them to hear. Several pieces of poster board and a set of highly visible color markers can also be extremely useful as a backup.

In one famous (or, rather, infamous) case, the speaker arrived to find herself addressing an audience of over 100 people, with *no* microphone. "Where's the microphone; I can't seem to find it," she commented to the host of the evening, thinking that it must be stored away somewhere. "Microphone?" came the reply. "You didn't say you wanted a microphone. Besides, aren't you speakers supposed to bring that sort of stuff?"

To put a tag on this story, a microphone was finally located, and it arrived and was successfully hooked up, but not until about three minutes before it was time for her to speak. She reports that she got through the speech, but her stomach kept reminding her of how frantic she was before the problem was resolved. It was not a situation she wanted to go through soon again.

Never assume that all the appropriate preparations have been made. Follow the U.S. Coast Guard motto—*semper paratus*—"always prepared."

Using visual aids can be an enriching experience for you as a speaker, as well as for your audience. They can ensure that your audience retains what you tell them, and they can add dynamic impact to any presentation. A little preplanning and anticipation in this area should go a long way toward making certain that all goes well for you and your audience.

That's something to strive for.

HOW TO HANDLE A QUESTION FROM THE FLOOR

Some speeches are given, and then they are over, and everyone goes home; however, this is not always the case. Very often, and particularly with speeches of an informational nature, it is expected that you will answer some questions from the floor. Often, this is the most exciting and rewarding part of the evening, as the interchange between speaker and audience makes for a dynamic flow of information and ideas.

The format can also fall flat, and become very boring, especially if the questioner from the floor does not speak up and half of the audience has no idea of what question has been asked. That leads only to confusion. Moreover, if the speaker answers in a long, disjointed rambling way, he or she appears unsure of the facts and causes doubt in the minds of the listeners, something that does not enhance a speaker's image. A speaker who stumbles over the answers to questions does not inspire confidence.

To avoid this and to handle questions from the floor in a fluid and dynamic manner, you should do two things:

1. Always repeat the question.

2. Use the A*R*E*A formula to answer the question.

Let's look at each one separately.

First, when a question is asked from the floor, always repeat the question. A typical repeated question might go like this:

The gentleman has asked if I believe that the middle school will have a more positive effect upon the lives of our children than did the Junior High School. Is that corrct, sir? It is. Thank you.

This repetition accomplishes three things. First, it assures that your audience, your entire audience, has heard the question. Second, it assures that the question is correctly stated before it is answered. Third, it gives you a moment to formulate your responses according to the following highly successful formula, the A*R*E*A formula:

A = ANSWER

R = REASON

E = EXAMPLE

A = ANSWER

Simply put, you give the answer to the question. Then you give a reason or reasons as to why you answered that way. Next, you give an example that either supports or proves your point. Finally, restate your answer. If you follow this formula, you have a very firm, relatively short and pithy, highly impressive way in which to make certain that your answer is both dynamic and effective, as well as memorable to your audience.

After only a very little practice, you should be able to completely formulate your answer with the A*R*E*A formula in the time you use to repeat the question from the floor. Yes, your mind can work on more than one thing at a time, and the result will be of great benefit to your audience and to you.

Here's a practical example. Let us suppose that the question dealt with is the one that was previously stated in this section, the one about the middle school and the junior high school. Here is the answer using the A*R*E*A formula.

Oh, yes, I believe that the middle school will have a far more positive effect in the lives of our children than the junior high school ever did. You see, I know that some of our elementaryschool children are not ready to step into the world of secondary education, merely because they have come to the end of the elementary school; they need that bridge where they can grow into the secondary school; something that the junior high school simply did not provide. I know of one student who left this township, was placed in a junior high school setup, and simply could not take the pressure; at the same time, I know of many ofour students who have gone to the middle school and learned to succeed before they truly had to face that "higher education." That's why I am positive that the middle school will be a farmore positive influence in our children's lives than the junior high school could ever be.

Did you see the four parts in operation? Did you see the ANSWER, followed by the REASON, followed by the EXAMPLE, with the ANSWER repeated at the end? It makes for a well-organized answer. Effective, isn't it?

Give it a try.

DEALING WITH THE HOSTILE QUESTION OR HOSTILE AUDIENCE

Does the term "hostile question" really need a definition? It is any question so stated as to put you on the spot. Please understand, we are not talking about a difficult or intricate question that is honestly asked. Rather, we mean the "When did you stop abusing your child?" variety that begs the question, and whose sole intent is to put you in an unfavorable light.

You can deal effectively with a hostile question if you make sure that you take two steps in the order given:

> *1. Remain calm and treat the questioner with the utmost respect and courtesy.*

> *2. Break the question into its simplest parts, both stated and unstated, and answer each part separately.*

Now, let's examine both steps.

First, it is essential that you remain calm. You can think more clearly, and you will gain the respect of your audience if you stay rational in the face of hostility. Treating the hostile questioner with courtesy and civility will further aid in swinging the support of the audience to your side.

Next, make sure that everybody knows exactly what is being asked. Let's assume that someone has asked the question, "What makes you feel so superior that you have all the answers?" (We think you will agree that this is a hostile question.)

Here is a response that will exemplify step 2: "I'd like to answer that question, but as I see it, you have asked several questions. I think you're really asking *if* I feel superior; if I do, then what makes me feel so; and *do* I have all the answers? My answers are 'no,' 'it doesn't follow,' and 'most definitely not.' Now. Let me explain each in turn . . ."

By handling the hostile question in this manner, you have turned a potentially embarrassing situation into one that will work to your advantage by gaining the respect of the audience and perhaps of the hostile questioner as well.

What happens, however, if you are faced with an entire audience that may be termed "hostile"? This is not a far-fetched assumption, particularly for the educator who may find himself or herself addressing groups of citizens suspicious of "new" programs and weary of tax increases. There may, indeed, come a time when you, as a speaker, must face an audience that is not willing and eager to accept what you have to say—that may, in fact, be hostile.

It will not be easy, but it can be made bearable, and antagonism can be kept to a minimum if you keep a few rules in mind:

> *1. Acknowledge, in the begining, that there are differences of opinion: "You may not agree with what I have to say tonight . . . "*

> *2. Do not apologize for yourself: " . . . but I believe in what I am about to tell you, and all I ask is that you hear me out . . . "*

> *3. Base what you say on hard, cold facts: " . . . As I see it, these are the facts of the matter . . . "*

4. Never get personal: Attacking their personal beliefs or opinions is your surest avenue to complete and total alienation. Let the weight of your argument win them to your side.

5. Be aware of the possibility of hostile questions: Handle these questions in the way we described above, with tact, and by stating provable facts, never opinions.

Under any circumstances, facing a hostile audience is a far from pleasant experience. Fortunately, 99 percent of your public speaking will be before receptive audiences, but it is well to be prepared for the unpleasant possibility. In such cases, you will survive if you follow the rules detailed above and make every effort to project an image of confidence, assuredness, and calm.

There is one other factor to consider under this topic. It doesn't happen often, but when it does, the speaker had better be prepared to handle it. A speaker is occasionally faced with an argumentative member of the audience. This particular individual may be defined as that person who *will not let you continue.* Not that you will have someone "heckle" you—you simply will not be addressing that type of audience; you are an educator and not a stand-up comedian—but you may have someone ask you a question, hostile or otherwise, and then refuse to let the matter drop. Perhaps your challenger will press a point that he or she particularly espouses, or argue with some point in your answer to the original question, but this person simply will not stop and, what's worse, will not allow you to continue.

The key to handling this problem effectively is to get the audience on your side while responding to the hostile member with tact and understanding. No attempt should ever be made to belittle, make fun of, or "put down" the person so involved, even if the audience is obviously unhappy with that individual. In fact, the calmer you are and the more annoyed the audience becomes with the hostile member, the better it is for you.

Begin by answering all of this person's questions in a civil manner. Make certain that you add, "Does that answer your question?" at the end of each answer. As long as the person continues to ask questions, you should answer them. When, however, he or she begins to make a speech, you should not play along with the game. Remember that you are there to answer questions, not engage in a debate. If, for instance, the individual has just made an impassioned statement that had no connection to anything you said, you shold say something like, "I'm sorry, but I seem to have missed your question. What exactly would you like me to answer?"

This will, generally, be enough to stop the tirade. If, however, it does not, then you will have to put an end to it by appealing to the audience. For example, you might say, "Well, I can certainly appreciate your point of view, but we are faced with a time problem, and I am certain that there are other members of the audience who have questions. If it's all right with the ladies and gentlemen, I'd like to continue with the question-and-answer period. But, let me give you my word that if you will see me after the program, I will be happy to discuss your point of view at length."

Then, with a smile and a nod to the hostile member, call for the next question from the general audience.

With this approach to the persistent hostile questioner, you have given the audience the feeling that you are concerned about them while still retaining your calmness and dignity.

You have emerged a winner.

THE FINAL SECRET OF "BRINGING IT HOME"

There is a saying, "Reality does not matter half as much as the way in which we perceive that reality." Put another way, what happens to us is important, but the way in which we interpret what happens to us is at least equally important.

Consider the example of two teachers, each of whom had to have a tooth pulled for various reasons. One person spoke of the appointment almost as a passing thought. This individual left school early on the day of the appointment, had the offending tooth removed, went home and took it easy for the evening, dining, we were told, on toast and tea. This teacher was back in the classroom the next morning—the extraction a quickly fading memory.

The second individual told us about the impending extraction a week in advance, and asked to check the number of sick leave days available, just in case something went wrong. This teacher told the class, the faculty, the custodians, the cafeteria workers, and anyone else who would listen about the highly traumatic event soon to take place. This person was absent on the day of the extraction in order to "mentally prepare" for the event. Two friends were cajoled into going with the individual in order to drive home and provide comfort, "just in case." The friends stayed most of the evening to make certain that "all was well." The teacher with the missing tooth took off the next day and the day after that in order to recover from the ordeal. Students and faculty heard about it for weeks afterwards.

The point of these stories is that for both, the "reality" was the same—a tooth had to be pulled. After that, the similarity ended, because of the way in which each individual saw or "perceived" that reality. One person interpreted the event as a minor inconvenience; something to be gotten through and gotten over. Consequently, the extraction was just one more incident, and after reasonable care (for it *was,* after all, a trauma to the body), the soreness faded, and it was relegated to the past.

The other individual saw the tooth-pulling as a horrendous and traumatic event that would undoubtedly cause much pain, possibly bring serious complications, and most certainly cause total incapacitation for several days. That is exctly what happened. Although there were no "complications," the person reported great pain, fantastic inconvenience, and continued incapacitation. Upon return to school, this person had to "take it easy" for a few more days.

Please, please understand that it is neither our purpose nor our right to judge either of these people, and we most certainly do not do so. We use these stories only to point out that while objective reality stays the same, our perception of it and our expectations and our interpretations of it really *do* affect both the way in which we approach that reality and the way in which that reality affects us.

What does all this philosophy have to do with being a good public speaker? Plenty! And, some of you undoubtedly see it already. *If we can't change the reality, perhaps we can change our perception of it.*

Here's the reality: You have been asked to speak somewhere. You must prepare a speech, practice it, and give it before an audience at a certain time, perhaps or perhaps not answering questions afterward. That is the reality.

Now, how will you interpret this reality? Think about this question carefully, since your answer to that question will largely determine the relationship that you will have to speaking in public both now and in the future.

If you perceive it as a frightening, threatening duty; something you must do; something that is vaguely unpleasant; and the best thing is to get it over quickly—then this is what you will live with throughout your speaking career. Your only comfort will be that, since your attitude will undoubtedly show through every speech you give, that career will not be long, and you won't have to speak very often.

On the other hand, if you see it as a marvelous opportunity to meet new people; a chance to make your views known; an enjoyable experience filled with humor and fellowship and personal growth, then, we promise you, that is what it will be, for that attitude will be conveyed and noticed by your audience. Since we cannot help but like people who like us, you will be asked to speak more and more as your well-deserved reputation grows.

Finally, let us leave you with a secret that has served us for decades, just as it will serve you, if you take it to heart. Since we first started to appear before people a number of years ago, we have always expected and anticipated that we were going to love the people to whom we would speak and that those people would love us. Yes, it is as simple and as complicated as that.

If you are speaking before people who love you, you cannot possibly be scared. Where there is love, there is no fear. Because you love them, you are going to give them the best you can, whether you are speaking to 20 or to 200 people. Because you love them, honesty, concern, and integrity are going to be the hallmarks of your speaking and of your answering of questions. Because they will love you, you are friends before you ever get there. Because they will love you, you will take particular care to make certain that they are informed, that they understand, and that they grow from the speeches you deliver to them.

When this happens, and we assure you that it can, you begin to grow as well; you begin to attain an ease with speaking, and an ease with being in front of people, and an ease with people themselves. In time, you forget yourself and all your worries.

Speaking before people is not a task any more; it is something you love!

IN CONCLUSION

This section has offered you some insights and some practical tips that will help you with that dynamic and forceful public speaking you really want to do. You will find that they will work for you if you work at them. May they be of benefit to you.

This last section has also tried to convey to you that the vast majority of your speaking engagements will be pleasant, and even enjoyable. We hope you have learned that even if problems arise, they may be dealt with effectively. We hope you now understand that the attitude you convey is the attitude that will be returned, and that your attitude toward your public speaking will determine your success or lack of it.

The love you give in terms of effort and approach will be returned to you in a hundred different ways; you will be both appreciated and in demand.

If you take only one thing from this book, let it be that!

Notes

Notes

Notes

Notes

Notes

Notes

Notes

Notes

Notes